Contents

Philosophy and Kabbalah

SUNY series in Contemporary Jewish Thought
_____
Richard A. Cohen, editor

PART III: STYLE AS WITNESS

Introduction

> The interview over, I accompanied Benamozegh through the streets of Livorno for a few minutes, then he asked me to leave him. I watched him go; he walked away with short steps, deep in thought, punctuating his ideas with a series of involuntary gestures. Some who passed him greeted him respectfully and others watched curiously, surprised by his strange demeanor.[1]

The testimony of his Christian disciple Aimé Pallière was remarkably consistent with that of the Livorno chronicler who described how the children from the working-class districts would hide around street corners looking out for this strange, exotically named character. He would stop, making mysterious signs on the ground with his feet before turning the corner to be confronted with the mockery of the little ruffians, who would then run away, thinking it highly amusing.[2]

This small man with the unkempt air and the faraway expression was the preacher at the synagogue and teacher of theology at the city's rabbinical college. He was also a publisher of Hebrew books and, above all, a prolific and original writer. The work that flowed from his pen in three languages—Hebrew, Italian, and French—was copious and varied. He was known far beyond the confines of the city or even of Italy itself, by Jews and non-Jews, but this fame also brought with it ironical and virulent criticism or—more painful by far—arrogance or marked indifference.

Samuel David Luzzatto, the great master of nineteenth-century Italian Judaism, treated him with an irony that was almost offensive; his pupil David Castelli, once appointed to a chair in Hebrew literature, spared no expense in attacking a method he considered lacking in any scientific basis. The Italian philosophical community was generally unresponsive, and for reasons that were quite the opposite, Jerusalem's very orthodox rabbis forbade the reading of one of his most important works.

1

Yet, he was revered by his disciples, and his fame was great. He was held in high esteem by Ernest Renan, Adolphe Franck, and Giuseppe Mazzini: he has been referred to as "the Plato of Italian Jewry," and an Italian paper recently described him as an unbridled intelligence forced to limp along in what constituted philosophical circles in Italy at that time.

His intellectual approach was too distinctive to be accepted unreservedly: his work combined elements of an ancient tradition which bore the print of the oral with the philological and philosophical consciousness of the nineteenth century.

On his death he was spoken of as a genius, albeit a little-known one. Perhaps this was a way of expressing embarrassment in the face of thinking in which a certain greatness could be discerned, but which remained for the most part difficult to grasp, through being impossible to reduce to the terms of the dominant culture.

The work of this largely self-taught scholar descended from Moroccan rabbis and born into Risorgimento Italy was destined for honorable marginality, at least during his lifetime. Indeed, did he not complain, with an ironic paraphrase of a Talmudic dictum, that his place was nowhere, that he felt as though suspended in midair?

The study that follows is an attempt to untangle the threads of this work, in which the apologist tendency that recurs several times probably did more harm than good. What follows is an intellectual portrait of a Kabbalist philosopher who, despite certain archaic characteristics, was nonetheless primarily a man of his times: a Kabbalist who followed Vico, a Jewish idealist not ashamed to acknowledge his debt to the Catholic thinker Vincenzo Gioberti.

Philosophy and Kabbalah

*Elijah Benamozegh and the Reconciliation of
Western Thought and Jewish Esotericism*

ALESSANDRO GUETTA

translated by
HELENA KAHAN

Originally published as *Philosophie et Cabbale: Essai sur la pensée d'Élie Benamozegh*
© 1998 Editions l'Harmattan

Published by
State University of New York Press, Albany

© 2009 State University of New York

For information, contact State University of New York Press, Albany, NY
www.sunypress.edu

Production by Kelli W. LeRoux
Marketing by Anne M. Valentine

Library of Congress Cataloging-in-Publication Data

Guetta, Alessandro, 1954–
   [Philosophie et Cabbale. English]
   Philosophy and kabbalah : Elijah Benamozegh and the reconciliation of
Western thought and Jewish esotericism / translated by Helena Kahan.
      p. cm. — (SUNY series in contemporary Jewish thought)
   Includes bibliographical references and index.
   ISBN 978-0-7914-7575-1 (hardcover : alk. paper)
   ISBN 978-0-7914-7576-8 (pbk. : alk. paper)
   1. Benamozegh, Elia, 1823–1900.   2. Mysticism—Judaism.   3. Cabala—History.
4. Philosophy, Jewish.   5. Judaism—Relations—Christianity.   6. Christianity and
other religions—Judaism.   7. Judaism—Apologetic works.   I. Kahan, Helena.
II. Title.

   BM755.B4G8413 2008
   296.1'6—dc22   2008003118

10 9 8 7 6 5 4 3 2 1

A Few Biographical Pointers

> The name Amozegh, a Judeo-Berber coinage, would appear to derive from the Hebrew root MZG (mixing, tempering), and the Berber word *Amazig*, which the Berbers use to refer to themselves, would also seem to come from the same root. In this instance the ethnic Amazig would have submitted to the mixing of diverse populations that occurred at a given moment to produce the Berber grouping. . . . In conclusion, the word *Amazig*, preceded by the Hebrew filiation indicator *ben*, could be translated as "Berber's son."[1]

It is at the very least curious that the destiny of a man whose every intellectual energy was devoted to the channels between two cultures should seem to be prefigured in his very name. He himself, as a good Kabbalist, allotted great importance to names, which, far from being conventional combinations of phonemes, in his opinion reflected some essential relationship with their actual referents.

While a biographical sketch of the events in Benamozegh's life is of scant interest, his intellectual course is, on the contrary, interesting, fraught—extraordinary, even.

Elijah's birth took place in a positively biblical atmosphere. When he was born in Livorno in 1823, his father Avraham was already seventy-one. He had remarried, with the consent of his first wife, in the hope of having a son. He had asked an emissary from the Holy Land who passed through Livorno to pray for this on his return to Jerusalem. A prayer that was answered.[2]

Avraham Benamozegh was from Fez, in Morocco. At the time Livorno exerted great influence on Jewish communities in the Maghreb and many economic migrants settled there.[3]

The Benamozegh family boasted a number of important figures who were illustrious members of Moroccan Jewish society in the seventeenth to nineteenth centuries, though it seems that Avraham was not himself one of the intellectual elite, for all that he had pursued serious studies and possessed significant biblical and talmudic learning.[4] Elijah's mother, Clara Coriat, was descended from a long line of famous rabbis that went back at least as far as the sixteenth century. Clara's own father, Avraham Refael, was born in Tetuan and was a rabbi first in Mogador and later in Livorno, where he died in 1808.[5]

There must have been a lot of to-ing and fro-ing between Tuscany and North Africa, since we can track Yehudah, one of Clara's brothers, from Mogador to Pisa, back to Mogador and finally to Livorno. This Yehudah, a worthy and reputed Kabbalist, became the teacher of little Elijah, whose father died when he was only three. In his short *Autobiography*, Benamozegh proffered a moving depiction of "long winter nights when [my] uncle would read the *Zohar* with me, from start to finish, sometimes twice together, by the dim light of a candle."[6]

Livorno was at that time still a trading center of international importance, after the depression that had succeeded the naval blockade of the Napoleonic Wars and before the irrevocable slide into decadence that followed the unification of the Italian state. The city's Jewish community, a real state within the state,[7] founded by Spanish and Portuguese *conversos* at the end of the sixteenth century, had altered radically. The Iberian Sephardic population around which its economic and cultural splendor had centered for five hundred years was gradually augmented and eventually supplanted by Italian (principally Roman) and North African Jews. The Sephardic bourgeoisie was unambiguous in its distaste for these socially inferior coreligionists and its desire to keep them at a remove from both political power and, if possible, the town itself.[8]

Despite its "Italianization," Livorno's Jewish Nation retained a certain exotic flavor compared to the rest of the town or, indeed, to Italy's other Jewish communities. The German Jewish scholar Avraham Berliner, visiting in 1874, described worship in the Great Synagogue in the following terms:

> The various forms of dress afforded an interesting spectacle to the observer. There were European Jews in overcoats, Berbers in their bright white burnous, Orientals in turbans, and many others besides. They had all come together to pray in our sacred tongue with all the usual devotion. Yet their lively and change-able character was clearly perceptible: conversations would frequently break out in somewhat raised voices, accompanied by extravagent gesturing.[9]

For a young man without means, the route was clear: Benamozegh had to look for a job. "Crying at having to abandon [his] beloved studies," he found one with the Tunisian merchant Avraham Enriques. He then went to work at the Cave-Bondi entrepot as a warehouseman.

> I felt as though I were under house-arrest. How many times I laid aside the ledgers to take up instead my Torah and science books. I am grateful in memory toward my master, who often entered unannounced, catching me in the very act of hiding my books. But never once did he reproach me: on the contrary, he took the opportunity to converse with me on these subjects.[10]

In other contexts he explained that his "science books" comprised the works of the liberal Catholic philosopher Vincenzo Gioberti and added that he used to read Spinoza, hidden among the bales of cotton in the warehouse.

In 1846 he was able to obtain a small grant which enabled him to give up work and study full-time. This he did in the Beth Yosef Franco Medras (Academy). By then he had already written a commentary on the Psalms and begun another on the Book of Isaiah.[11]

He was rapidly appointed preacher-rabbi and soon afterward, professor of theology at Livorno's Rabbinical College. He went on to serve as a judge on the rabbinical tribunal and founded a publishing house of some substance.[12] His life was, however, principally occupied in the writing of a series of works and in teaching, the former often being the fruit and extension of the latter.[13] He wrote biblical commentaries, philosophical essays and treatises, summaries in which the theological position is underpinned and justified by his erudition. While it is possible to classify his works into traditional categories, they are all connected by the same shared ideas and style of thought. His approach was essentially eclectic, reflecting his deep conviction that there existed a unitary truth behind its diverse manifestations.

Benamozegh never moved away from his native city. He left it only on two occasions: the first, in 1846, was a trip to Pisa (barely a dozen miles) to meet the eminent French philosopher Adolphe Franck, who had opened up new avenues in scientific investigation of Kabbalah. The second "journey" had the same destination. This time he was more than sixty years of age and his purpose was to attend—incognito—a philosophy of law lecture at the university.[14]

Yet, at the same time, he traveled the immense distance from North African Jewish culture—impregnated with traditional pietas and Kabbalah—to the most sophisticated philosophy then being advanced in Europe.

Without moving outside the Jewish religious framework, Benamozegh became increasingly open to the Italian and then the French scientific milieu, attempting to adapt his own Kabbalistic heritage to the post-Hegelian, evolutionist, and positivist thinking of the second half of the century. Such a delicate operation required both boldness and self-confidence and the result was a synthesis that even today is far from unanimously accepted: at the end of the day his insouciant yet passionate amalgamation of cultures and sensitivities a priori unable to communicate seemed to satisfy no one. This was due to his being at once deeply traditional and highly modern in spirit, something of a case apart even at a time when the "modernization" of religion was a live issue, for Jews and Christians alike.

Samuel Colombo, a pupil of his, expressed Benamozegh's program thus:

> Look at the past firmly and steadily and at the same time explore progress, which is making such rapid strides. Far from adoring only one or the other, look for a formula to understand them in real harmony.[15]

Toward the end of his life, a meeting with Aimé Pallière, a young Catholic theologian from Lyons, gave him an opportunity to develop the ecumenical side of his thinking. Pallière was a religious yet restless soul who had made moves first toward Protestantism and then toward Catholic modernism; personal contact with the Italian rabbi drew him so far toward Judaism that he even considered converting. Benamozegh dissuaded him, arguing that the religious future of mankind would be based on a multiplicity of monotheistic experiences. He did, however, invite Pallière to become an apostle of universal monotheism, without binding himself in obedience to the particular laws of Israel, nor espousing the Christian dogmas of the Incarnation or the Trinity.[16]

For a while Benamozegh really believed this new religion would be realized. This hope—like that of seeing his ideas and works accepted within Europe's wider scientific community—was by and large frustrated. It was not without bitterness that he embarked in 1897 on the publication of a journal, *Bibliothèque de l'hébraïsme*, entirely devoted to disseminating his work in various fields of Jewish studies which would otherwise be ignored. Benamozegh died on February 6, 1900. On his tomb, his son Emmanuel inscribed the following:

> The last representative, and prince, of a whole family of scholars.[17]

Of his teaching, based on Kabbalah—generally considered to be the most exclusionist and antirationalistic doctrine ever produced by Jewish culture—his pupils retained three central ideas: the rejection of blind faith, a tendency to harmonize science and religion, and confidence in mankind's progress toward universal brotherhood.[18]

PART ONE

Philosophy and Kabbalah

Kabbalah and Progress

The present is movement, and movement is progress.

—Elijah Benamozegh, *Teologia*

In the nineteenth century, the "century of progress," various philosophers in France and Italy attempted to reconcile religious dogma with an ideology so dominant in the *Zeitgeist* that it could be referred to as "the true faith of our times."[1]

They all faced the same problems, namely: how to reconcile truths that were deemed to be eternal with the continuous improvement in man, both intellectually and morally; how to justify the coexistence of unique, determining events—creation, revelation, and redemption—with the idea of an uninterrupted continuum; finally, at a more specifically philosophical level, the question of the origins, causes, and ends of progress itself was raised.

If they were marginal in comparison with the overwhelming mainstream majority, who saw religion as being at most a stage in human development to be overcome, such thinkers continue to be of particular interest, both at a historical and a theoretical level. Their temporizing, difficult balancing act and radical criticism can all help us develop our understanding of what lay at the center of this ideology of progress: an inherently secularizing ideology, destined—in a variety of forms—to enjoy rapid and almost universal success.

These intellectuals are generally grouped together under the term *neo-Catholics*. They included in their number a writer—Pierre-Simon Ballanche (1776–1847)—who started out with legitimist sympathies, and "dramatic" characters such as Hugues de Lamennais (1782–1854), whose path led from the extolling of the pope's absolute infallibility to a final position verging on the democratic. Another of them was the Piedmontese philosopher Vincenzo Gioberti (1801–1852), the man who inspired the "neo-Guelf" movement that saw the pope as the ideal person to initiate Italy's political—and liberal—

9

unification. Gioberti too, it should be pointed out, moved, in the aftermath of an unhappy foray into politics, toward the democratic, relinquishing the idea of a central institutional role for the Church.

These voices were joined some years later by another. In this case, the concept of progress contrasted not with the Christian but the Jewish tradition. This was not, however, the salient aspect of Elijah Benamozegh's work: after all, the Christian and Jewish thinkers of the time shared the same concern to defend the religious viewpoint against the attacks of all-conquering secularization. His singularity lay rather in the conceptual instrument he employed: Kabbalah, forged in the Jewish esoteric tradition. At first glance, nothing would seem less suitable to a "modernizing" discourse, all the more so as Kabbalah was in those years going through one of the most critical periods in its extremely controversial history, in which it was considered in "enlightened" Jewish circles as a tissue of superstition and falsehood unworthy of being called a doctrine.[2]

The most obvious difficulty lay with the theoretical issues involved: How could a secret, esoteric—not to say mystical—tradition be made to harmonize with a current of thought extensively based on progressive transparency and an inevitable use of reason?

What arose was a historically interesting phenomenon: the translation and reworking of ideas and terms formed no later than the thirteenth century into the philosophical context of nineteenth-century Europe. Given that Benamozegh's early training was in the Judeo-Moroccan tradition, we can see how arduous and risky such a cultural transferal must have been. It was a tortuous exercise, nonetheless original, even at times fascinating in its methods.[3]

Benamozegh's avowed, and ambitious intent was to reconstruct a comprehensive Jewish philosophical system that—according to him—would "reestablish with the most advanced human sciences the harmony that has been broken."[4] The task, he wrote, seemed so hard that he would have been happy to draft just the beginning, Maimonides himself having been unequal to the undertaking. The ambitious parallel was pushed to the extent of stating a series of credos, after the example of the Spanish philosopher's articles of faith.

In reality, the outcome was a philosophical system similar to that of some of the Catholic thinkers mentioned above.[5] In short, the Italian rabbi's theology seems to fit entirely into a certain European cultural setting, while his conceptual sources—including some of his definitions—are almost always identifiably from Kabbalistic texts. Some striking examples will be analyzed here.

Theology and the
Discovery of the Unconscious

I have long been at work on perfecting my theory of *concentric conscious-nesses* that culminate in God, the *consciousness of consciousnesses* . . . to place the *consciousness* as the first protological principle of the universe, in the place of intelligence, will, etc. . . .

Now that the Unconscious is playing an increasingly important role . . . we may allow that it is the sense or the awareness of the greater field of shared consciousness; it has at least been proved that we do not have total consciousness of ourselves, and that our consciousness has not unsurmountable boundaries.[1]

Benamozegh published these lines in 1897, three years before he died. The heralded theory was never finished but significant traces remain, strewn throughout his various works. It involved replacing the classical definitions of God as the Being of Beings or the Thought of Thoughts while circumventing the objection that attributing a consciousness to God would impose limitations on his absoluteness, since any act of consciousness implies an originating and external subject.

The universe, Benamozegh wrote, comprised a quantity of creatures with varying degrees of consciousness. One can imagine a hierarchy of species according to the consciousness each of them has of the universe in its entirety. At the top of this hierarchy would be God, the "consciousness of consciousnesses"; individual consciousnesses would be his ideas.[2]

In substance, there is nothing new in this formulation, a familiar mix of Platonic (or Neoplatonic) idealism and Aristotelian metaphysics. However, the use that is made of the idea of consciousness (to which Aristotle referred for instance in *Metaphysics*, Book Λ, ch. VII, and Maimonides in the *Guide of the Perplexed*, 1.68, and which is not exactly the same as the traditional knowledge or "intelligence") and its opposite—the unconscious—refers us to the idea, widespread in all currents of European thought in the nineteenth century and prefigured by Leibniz, whereby progress consisted of an increase in consciousness. This idea obviously expressed the optimism of the age, centered as it was on man's ability to assimilate everything, to unify and relate to himself the most diverse aspects of the human and natural world. By the end of the century the extension of psychological research to include the individual unconscious may be interpreted as the logical outcome of this trend.[3]

When Benamozegh spoke of "God as the supreme and comprehensive consciousness" he brought a fairly common idea back into the religious sphere, in a sense celebrating its apotheosis. Human consciousness, pushing its boundaries ever outward, approached ever vaster consciousnesses, and thus God himself: in this way a process of "divinification" was undertaken. He unreservedly shared the enthusiasm for this idea of earlier thinkers like Wilhelm von Humboldt or Gioberti, which formed the cornerstone of Ludwig Feuerbach's thinking and was to be found in Nietzsche[4] as well as in Ernest Renan, who for his part wrote,

> For us idealists a single doctrine is true: the transcendental doctrine according to which the goal of humanity is to constitute a higher consciousness, or, as it used to be expressed, "the greater glory of God."[5]

Likewise, when Benamozegh defined the unconscious as a "confused perception of the wider field of shared consciousness" requiring exploration and integration into a progressive movement,[6] he was adopting an idea that, after being stated by Schelling, had been developed by Eduard von Hartmann (1842–1906) in particular.

In *The Philosophy of the Unconscious*,[7] Hartmann set out a general theory of the will, understanding, freedom, and history, based on an idea with marked—and not superficial—resemblances to Freud's "Unconscious."

For Hartmann, the Unconscious was an unindividualized force that inclined to achieve its ends with infallible certainty, an indivisible principle that preceded multiple manifestations, a true One-and-all. Within this force, the will and the idea could not be separated as the will had no other aim than the realization of its content, that is, its associated idea. The action of the Unconscious could not be considered blind because lacking in thought; on the contrary—its progress, sure of its goals, was proof of a true clairvoyance which could reasonably be defined as a *supraconscious* intelligence. According to Hartmann, this "being" was possessed of a supremely wise and omniscient intelligence and was superior to any consciousness, since consciousness implied a separation between subject and object, and by extension limitations: refusing the consciousness of God in these circumstances was not to diminish him.

This was a key point, and one Benamozegh could not concede. He knew Hartmann's work well and was able to accept many of its core premises; but he also embarked on an in-depth, radical emendation.

If it was true that history was about progress toward consciousness, its starting point was not the *unconscious*, however intelligent, but *consciousness deployed to its full extent*. This was a typical conceptual framework for Benamozegh: movement and change were admitted, but with the assumption of a stable point before and outside the process. History was the march toward a level of perfection already glimpsed by mankind in the form of an initial revelation; and the increase of human consciousness was a gradual, infinite drawing closer to total consciousness, or God.

The differences between the two men's thinking were especially obvious in their definitions of intuition, whether prophetic or mystical. Where Hartmann saw the spontaneous manifestation of the Unconscious, to which can be ascribed the feelings, thoughts and desires that suffuse consciousness at certain moments, Benamozegh, in contrast, discerned the spontaneous manifestation of a perfect consciousness anticipatively revealed to an individual or a people.[8] As for the possible objection that ascribing a consciousness to God would imply an object of consciousness, limiting—by its inherent nature—his absoluteness, Benamozegh maintained that God was not to be separated from his object: his consciousness was in reality a monologue,[9] within which individual acts of consciousness were as parts of a whole. He thus believed himself to have got around the objection.

However, what is interesting here, from the perspective of the history of ideas, is the name Benamozegh gave his theory: he wrote of "concentric consciousnesses" and conceived God as the largest circle in which increasingly small circles were contained, representing decreasing degrees of consciousness. The image, if not the idea, is a Kabbalistic one. In one of the classic texts of philosophical Kabbalah, *Pardes rimmonim* (The Pomegranate Garden) by Moshe Cordovero (1522–1570), in the section devoted to the arrangement of the *sefirot*—divine emanations—alongside the images of the tree and the primordial man (used, as it happens, in other contexts by Benamozegh), the image of the concentric circles is employed. The ten *sefirot* are described (and drawn) by Cordovero as concentric circles where the relationship between the larger and smaller ones is that of cause and effect. Thus, for example, a large circle represents the *sefirah keter* ("the crown") and encompassed within it is the *sefirah hokhma* ("wisdom"), following from it as an effect, and shown as a smaller circle.[10]

This is a striking example of synthesis, at a morphological level, of a Kabbalistic frame of reference and a "modern" sensibility. But there was more. Benamozegh also drew inspiration from the Jewish esoteric tradition in matters of content. Georges Vajda's study of Ezra ben Solomon of Gerona's fourteenth-century commentaries on the Song of Songs[11] exposes a particularly interesting doctrine of creation. According to this theory, creation involved a movement from the unknown toward the known; a progressive manifestation of something that had always existed. The "nothingness" of *Yesh me-ain* (creation ex nihilo) was not, therefore, nonbeing but the fullness of being that is in essence the unfathomable depth of the hidden deity. The act of creation was dynamic and continuous and corresponded to a gradual, cosmic revelation of knowledge. The nineteenth-century philosopher's notion of progression of consciousness could be seen as a reworking of an old Kabbalistic idea.

It could also, however, be seen as a modern manifestation of a Gnostic mindset. Several scholars have pointed out the links between gnosis and Kabbalah. Gershom Scholem's theories on the influence of the Gnostic theology of the Cathars on Provençal Kabbalah are well-known.[12] Other authors go even farther than Scholem, unhesitatingly identifying a line of historical continuity running through the Gnostics of the early Christian period, the doctrine of the *Zohar*, and that of Yitzhaq Luria and the School of Safed.[13] Benamozegh in fact defined the Gnostics as "Christian Kabbalists."[14]

One of core elements of Gnosticism was its elevation of knowledge. Only knowledge of his deepest Self, manifested through revelation, allowed man to exist on a spiritual level. Self-consciousness freed man from matter, itself an error of creation: the cause of evil was not sin but unconsciousness. Valentinian Gnosticism (2nd century) contained the idea of a God with the primary attribute of self-consciousness. In opposition to Plotinus's indeterminate Being, the Gnostic God was identifiable with consciousness in action.[16]

Significant differences nonetheless exist between ancient Gnosticism and its modern counterpart as propounded by Benamozegh. For the latter, it was no longer the *individual* but *humanity* that must penetrate the unconscious. The *dynamic* aspect was certainly also accentuated: history, for Benamozegh, was the stage for the irresistible, gradual, yet infinite advance of humanity into the territory of the unconscious.[16]

The Universal Relationship

Benamozegh's philosophical writing contains many long digressions on the Hebrew letter *vav* (which acts as the conjunction *and*), the word *asher* (the relative pronoun *who*) and their esoteric meanings, which culminate in a statement of a profound relationship between all things and all levels of existence: the idea is reminiscent of the Renaissance concept of "universal sympathy," itself overtly Neoplatonic and Kabbalistic in inspiration.

For modern European readers, Benamozegh's argument could appear strange, yet—apart from the form in which it is couched—it, too, was one of the core ideas in nineteenth-century European philosophy. We shall be examining its characteristics, developments and possible sources in more detail.

In the *Zohar*[1] an explanation is offered for the Biblical formula wherein God, addressing Moses, defines himself as "I am that I am" ("*Ehiyeh asher ehiyeh*").[2] The *Zohar* gives a meaning to each of the three words in the process of the individualization of beings. *Asher*, grammatically speaking a relative pronoun, acquires the value of a noun: it is the second stage of the process, "used to indicate the mother pregnant with all things and about to give birth to them to reveal the supreme name."[3]

Benamozegh made use of this interpretation, altering it slightly, to justify an idea common in the scientific and philosophical thinking of his time: a deep, radical unity informed the whole universe and linked all beings together.[4] *Asher* was thus read both as one of the names of God, and as a word that retained its connotation as a relative pronoun, whose role was to unite the two terms.[5]

This is not far removed from Vincenzo Gioberti's perspective in *Protologia*, the "Science of First Things." According to Gioberti, the universe "in itself" was certainly one, whereas "to us" it appeared to be composed of distinct and heterogeneous substances. Progress therefore consisted in (infinite) reconstructing of this original and essential unity through human discovery of ever vaster and more comprehensive systems of relationships between things. Nature, at the end of the day, sprang from unity and tended toward unity: the aim of man was to accelerate and assist this process. This was what Gioberti termed man's "co-creation," a term Benamozegh fully accepted. The Zoharic expression was updated with all the optimism of the ideology of progress, in which the universe was perceived as the chosen theater for human action; in fact, as an object left at man's disposal, whose mysteries were bound to be unraveled with the ceaseless advancement of understanding.

As it was, even the French philosopher Auguste Comte, the founder of positivism, constructed his evolutionary system around the key concepts of unity and relationship. His perspective obviously differed from that of the religious philosophers, but the basic structure of the thought was, in this instance, fundamentally similar. For Comte, sociology, with its capacity for unifying all the sciences, took the place of theology and metaphysics; the existence of inherent relationships at all levels of reality was a prerequisite for such a project of unification.[6]

The profound unity of the created world was, for Benamozegh, suggested by a somewhat obscure *midrash* that glossed God's words to Moses, "and thou shalt see My back,"[7] as meaning, "He showed him the knot of the phylacteries." The knot was, according to Benamozegh's interpretation, the world on the point of being made, the universal law that dictated the relationships between beings. Possibly developing one of Yitzhaq Luria's[8] ideas, the Italian thinker went on to suggest that the image of the knot of the phylacteries allowed the authors of the *midrash* to express the notion of a "point of transit between God and His creatures," themselves represented by the two leather straps hanging down from the knot.[9]

The idea of relationship was also present at a gnoseological level: knowledge of things resided in their relationships, given that we understood not the things themselves but their ideal connection—God.[10]

A list of similar remarks could go on indefinitely, so I will restrict myself to a single interesting passage where the *midrash* is once again interpreted in a spirit in keeping both with Kabbalah and nineteenth-century natural philosophy. The *midrash* relates that when Moses ascended to heaven, the letters of the law did not wish to combine together to come down into this base world "until the Great Name made a pact with them: the Honorable Name would be united with them." For Benamozegh, the "Great Name" was none other than the *sefirah tiferet*, which he interpreted as the ideal of order and unity and the "Honorable Name" was the *sefirah malkhut*, or the divine in the world.[11] According to the *Sefer Yetzirah* (Book of Creation), which formed the basis for Kabbalistic speculation on the subject, the letters of the law were the archetype for the world and God was thus "the cement, the natural bond which holds them together."

Conditioned Progress

A Kabbalist trained in the Judeo-Moroccan tradition, Benamozegh as a philosopher belonged firmly within the nineteenth-century European philosophical mainstream and articulated a number of its central ideas. But these ideas are drawn throughout on a conceptual framework and terminology steeped in Talmudic and Kabbalistic thought.

His theology can, however, be envisioned without specific Jewish reference. In fact, what was of real importance to him—at least in his discourse with "the outside," which became the primary one over the years—was to resist skepticism and its ethical consequences on the one hand, and on the other to embrace wholeheartedly the perspective of indefinite human progress. These were exactly the same forces as those driving his neo-Catholic contemporaries.[1]

For Paul Bénichou, who devoted a chapter to these authors in his study on the "prophets" of progress, "since the eighteenth century, the real dividing line between orthodox or theosophical Christianity and lay humanism" was the rejection of the "dogma of the Fall and Redemption in favor of the doctrine of continuous progress."[2] The question was couched in the following terms: Was man a progressive being whose evolution—internal as well as external—had not ceased since his creation, or had he lived in a state of degeneration from the moment of original sin until his delivery by Christ?

Ballanche's answer, while accepting the primordial fact of the Fall, envisaged continuous progress since then. The importance attaching to the unique, dramatic moment of redemption was thus lessened: "Created to repair the sin of the rebellious angels, [man] collaborated, before his own fall, in the completion of creation; he will therefore assist in its regeneration and that of his own nature. He will make matter spiritual; restore the universe's primitive magism and exercise over things a power, the limitations of which we will be incapable of setting."[3]

Lamennais, for his part, in his "second period"—that of *Paroles d'un croyant*—abandoned the hypothesis of a state of original perfection which was in manifest opposition to the laws of progress. "Man has fallen from his primitive state" became "Man is not what he should be."[4]

For Gioberti, the central event of human history was the revelation that occurred with the death of Christ: at that instant, the veil covering his face was rent (here the word *revelation* is understood literally as meaning "disclosure"), the mysteries were made directly visible ("face to face") and became clear.[5] The accomplished totality of that special moment was not in contradiction to the necessity of historical progress:

> Christianity is thus a completed revelation, in its entirety, through-out its course, from its origins through to palingenesis. The veil was rent at the death of Christ because Christ, as palingenetic anticipation, epitomized and showed the entire Christian cycle. But the perfect transformation of the mysterious into the visible, of the supernatural into the logical, of faith into science and vision, the completed initiation . . . of perfect religion, will take place only during palingenesis, in heaven and not on earth.[6]

This accords at almost every point with what we could call Benamozegh's "cultural program," which might be characterized as elucidating and spreading the ideas of an initially secret science, Kabbalah. In fact, the very dynamic of development required the esoteric to be displaced by public knowledge that would reach completion only at the end of time.[7]

To express this idea, Benamozegh distorted somewhat the famous Hegelian metaphor of the fruit and the flower, highlighting the movement from the hidden to the visible—"the fruit was hidden in the flower"—rather than the dialectical moment of sublation—"the fruit is the negation and fulfillment of the flower."[8]

The revelation Benamozegh had in mind was that of Sinai:[9]

> I believe that religious Revelation as an expression of the spontaneity of the species, as revelation of the Species to the Individual, must contain elements that transcend the sphere of individual reflection, since everything mankind, or the species, can achieve in the course of its development should be already contained within this seed. . . . Through its progressive nature mankind possesses the means to elevate itself to the level of the revealed Word, because Revelation is an early manifestation of the intuition of the Species. . . . I believe that if Revelation constitutes the Spontaneity of the human species, on the one hand it should be unique, primordial and immutable and on the other, in the light of the fact that it develops, gradual.[10]

History was thus the history of mankind's gradual acquisition of the truths, which had been communicated to it at the favored moment of the Revelation.

Within Jewish theology, this was an original theory, but it is not without similarity to the medieval concept of the "two paths" to truth: the first—the philosophical one—was slow and hard, reserved for those with particularly well-developed mental faculties; the second—the path of revelation—was open to all and ignored the processes to furnish the results directly, *simul et semel*.[11] Benamozegh's concept diverges from this in two ways, both typical of nineteenth-century European thought: firstly, it is optimistic about the *collective* march of *all humanity*, and not merely the intellectual elite, toward a full acquisition of human and natural truths, dilating to attain a divine level; and secondly, it adds to the essentially *static* mediaeval vision a *dynamic* element, that of progress through history.

Despite its historical aspect, Benamozegh's theory of Revelation was neither relativistic nor subjectivistic. We should not be misled by the terms *intuition* and *reflection*. For all they belong to a psychological vocabulary, they are not subjective. They refer to knowledge that, for all it is potential and progressive, remains objective. Revelation and the ensuing process contain an absolute truth. With Benamozegh, we have not reached the point, arrived at with certain Catholic modernists, of envisaging Revelation as the *objectivization of the religious consciousness*; in so doing they effected a subtle yet decisive shift which placed religious content in the realm of the subjective. Benamozegh, as we shall see below, was conscious that such developments might occur. This was why he devoted so much energy to fighting relativism and subjectivism, both of which he viewed as dangerous deviations.[12]

The categories *intuition*, *species*, and *spontaneity* were widely used at the time Benamozegh wrote these lines. Gioberti made intuition a vital element in his system, opposing it to *reflection*. According to him, intuition was the psychological organ that made it possible to envisage progress: "Prophecy is the intuition of progress. To speak of progress is to speak of the future, to speak of realized futurity. Prophecy is the intuition of the act in all its power."[13] It was Benamozegh who applied these categories to ancient Jewish history: the age of the prophets was that of spontaneity; the age of the doctors and beyond, that of reflection.[14]

In the concept of "species" can be recognized the post-Darwinian biologizing of the Comtean notion of *humanity*: an eloquent demonstration, if one were needed, of how philosophical and pseudoscientific themes circulated in the nineteenth century among thinkers of widely varied backgrounds.[15]

Spontaneity was considered, at least from Friedrich Schiller onward, to have been the happy condition enjoyed in the Classical age, especially by the Greeks.[16] In a sort of Romantic origins myth, they were seen as having been in touch with nature without any mediations; artistic production and religious belief were straightforward, immediate, and devoid of tension and divisions: all in all, a happy condition lost to the moderns. On the other hand, the work produced out of such spontaneity were seen as naïve, less mature, precisely because they were strangers to suffering and heartbreak.[17]

It is therefore especially interesting to see this category being applied to the revelation of Sinai, perceived as being the "dawning" of the existence of the Jewish people; the moment in which—to borrow another phrase from Schiller—the image of the species was not yet dispersed and fragmented.[18]

For the progressivist mentality of the second half of the century, a sense of agony had generally given way to optimism. The acute perception of the declining "richness" of individualism and the predictable affirmation of a society of the masses could be interpreted as a positive evolutionary step. In *Il Gesuita moderno*, Gioberti identified with accuracy the middle class as the certain protagonist of the future; this, in his general theory of philosophy, corresponded to "human synthesis" as the point of equilibrium between the oppositions of phenomenological reality. For his part, Benamozegh referred to rabbinical sources in celebrating the decadence of the individual and the progress of the mass, equating it with a loss of spontaneity and natural instinct, counterbalanced by increased consciousness and freedom.[19]

History and Truth

The most formidable adversary to the theist thinkers who shared a notion of historical evolution was the German philosopher Hegel. He had constructed a system that incorporated individual manifestations of nature and history in an all-encompassing design, of which Becoming—conceived as being progress—was a basic, "ontological" law.

Within this system, the role of religion was unclear, sometimes equivocal. In places it is looked upon as a necessary stage in spiritual development, albeit later surpassed by philosophy, while at other times it is seen as being its equivalent in a different form. In the *Encyclopaedia of the Philosophical Sciences in Outline*, concerning philosophy, Hegel wrote that its aims were the same as those of religion, as, "For both the object is Truth, in that supreme sense in which God and God only is the Truth."[1]

Elsewhere, in the "Absolute Knowledge" section of *Phenomenology of Spirit*, Hegel wrote that "the Spirit manifested in revealed religion has not as yet surmounted its attitude of consciousness as such; . . . Spirit as a whole and the moments distinguished in it fall within the sphere of figurative thinking, and within the form of objectivity. The *content* of this figurative thought is Absolute Spirit. All that remains to be done now is to cancel and transcend this bare form."[2] Religion was thus seen as connected to philosophy, being surpassed by it at the point where philosophy became better equipped to express absolute knowledge in the most effective manner, being unencumbered with perceptible figurative thinking.

Their philosophical sensibility allowed Gioberti and Benamozegh to avoid any apologetic polemic on the historical role of religion, in contrast with what occurred in Germany after Hegel's death. However, both Italians, one Catholic and the other Jewish, did attack the underlying structure of the Hegelian discourse, sidestepping scholastic confrontation over details.[3] This point needs to be stressed: Benamozegh was not, at this stage, especially interested in Jewish religion and its legitimacy in the wake of the Hegelian "last word." The philosophical historian Emil Fackenheim has nonetheless pointed out that the theoretical position of Judaism was even more awkward

21

than that of Protestantism, the "last" religion, whose modes of thought had been transformed.[4]

Gioberti and Benamozegh's primary objections concerned two main areas: firstly, the relationship between history and truth and secondly, dialectics.

Regarding the first point, their criticism focused on Hegel's "historical absolutism," or his identification of history with truth. For to the German philosopher there was no such thing as a priori truth that could be resorted to outside of the historical process: truth was the totality of the manifestations of the becoming Spirit. It went without saying that Becoming must be liberated from any ephemeral contingencies and be, of necessity, rational. That necessity was in fact *immanent*. "The quality of spirit is to be derived from, become for, and made by itself. To truly exist, it must needs be produced of itself: its being is an absolute process," he wrote in *Lectures on the Philosophy of History*.[5]

It was to this immanent truth, this self-sufficiency of history, that Gioberti and Benamozegh were reacting: for them, truth preexisted, or, more accurately, coexisted with history, while maintaining a gap history strained infinitely to close. Becoming did not exhaust the possibilities of being, merely representing a path from its origins—creation—to its end—palingenesis or regeneration, an infinite approaching of the creator.

In defending their theist vision, both authors went beyond Hegel's real position, at times attempting to caricature a man they thought of as a believer in lawless immanence[6] or man's all-powerfulness:

> We will not behave like the titanic Hegel, who said to his disciples: in our next lesson we will create God. He thus sank to the level of the fetishists, his blasphemy denounced in advance by David when he wrote, *Kemohem ihyu 'oseyhem* [They that make them shall be like unto them, Ps. CXV, 8]. We will act more like Moses who, in the fleeting moment God passed before him, quickly lowered his head—and adored him.[7]

Both Gioberti and Benamozegh ignored the importance of Reason in the Hegelian approach to history and its correspondence with God's providential design: for Hegel, actually, universal history was true theodicy—the justification of God in history.[8] Moreover, the culmination of Spirit in philosophy as conceived in the Hegelian system, was, for them, a disappointing exaltation of subjective thought; such criticism wrongly ignored the line taken in *Phenomenology of Spirit*.[9]

We have to believe that for the theists, immanentism necessarily led to a void: Hegel's doctrine represented, if not the negation of the absolute, at least a step in that direction, to wit, the beginning of a decline of meaning in history and the opportunity for anarchy of values.

The stakes were high indeed, involving the possibility of diluting the truth in history, denying the need for solid moorings and absolute reference criteria outside the historical process itself. Religions such as Judaism and Christianity, which invested one key moment of history as being the fundamental source of all truths—metaphysical, ethical, and otherwise—could not contemplate a process "with neither head nor tail,"[10] entrusted only to itself and bearing within it the principles of its own development.

For Gioberti, it was the theory of palingenesis that made an understanding of progress possible; for Benamozegh, it was the Jewish doctrine of messianism, with certain nuances of his own.[11]

To their eyes, not only the beginning and end of historical process were mapped out, but also its course: it was not left to itself as though operating through immanent rules and spontaneity. In consequence, Gioberti—who employed the Platonic terms *mimesis* (imitation) and *metexis* (participation)—thought in terms of the nullification in God of the "mimetic" phases of Becoming (the apparent, the ephemeral, the perceptible) and the conservation of the "metexic," or participative element (the real, the progressive, the intellectual): "The annihilation of negation is creation. . . . God annihilates only in order to create; he nullifies the mimetic negation of the act to make this act of power occur."[12]

Likewise, when he compared human progress and the creative act:

> Progress . . . is almost the path along which the life of the world
> passes. But the course of the world is born in the creative act; there
> is, therefore, in the world, intrinsic progress and in the creative
> act, extrinsic progress, which manifests itself as effect.[13]

Benamozegh drew on Kabbalistic sources to support a similar idea. God, he wrote, reinterpreting a rabbinical *midrash*, was the origin, the development and the end of Becoming: the *alef*, the *mem*, and the *tav*, or the letters at the beginning, in the middle, and at the end of the alphabet which make up the word *emet* (truth).[14]

It should be noted that Gioberti's and Hegel's definitions concorded on some points, for both spoke of the "negation of negation" as the fundamental relationship in Becoming and of real (or metexic, participative) history built on the ruins of apparent (or mimetic) history. But here, again, the key detail that separated them was the assessment of the active principle of change, the deployment of immanent spirit—for Hegel—and God, through his will continually creating the universe—for Gioberti ("The nullification of participation is absolutely possible; but it will not happen because God, in creating an infinite and eternal power, shows that he does not wish to destroy it").[15]

Gioberti and Benamozegh were concerned not only with the possibility that Hegelian philosophy, pushed to its limits, would render movement directionless (while progress is *iter*, way, and religion *derekh*, path)[16] but also with the danger that it might determine an end to the process. Progress needed to be infinite, since its object was infinite: Benamozegh seems to have borrowed an expression from the *Sefer ha-Bahir* (*Book of Brightness*, one of the oldest Kabbalistic texts) when he wrote,

> Ordinary Jews say that the Messiah has not *come* but that he *will come*. Ordinary Christians, on the other hand, say not that he will come but that he *has come*. They are both wrong. The Messiah has not come and he will not come: he is *in the process of coming*.[17]

Hegel, in contrast, saw himself as the philosopher of perfected thought: for him, spirit had finally managed to free itself from symbolic representation and think itself, through philosophy. All mysteries had been made clear: the long journey of the spirit was at last over.

For Gioberti, as for Benamozegh, many mysteries still remained to be explained, even if progress was a movement toward rational understanding.[18] Hegel was seen as overconfident, with pretensions to revealing absolute science, not through symbols, but in a literal sense.[19] Benamozegh concurred: "How was it that Hegel was the first to reveal true science to man? Did mankind thus begin to become absolute with Hegel?"[20]

A religious mindset such as this was obviously unsympathetic to the notion of the end of history, in the sense of a full and final realization of human potential, because man—made in God's image—"recreates" divine creation through his historical progress but, at the same time, the gap that existed between man and God was an essential one, never to be closed.[21]

Yet, these writers definitely had the feeling of a deep division, the presentiment of a new age. As Ballanche wrote, "A new age is beginning. A new century is dawning. All minds are attentive. The people are troubled by a feeling of unease. . . . Thoughts are all confused; all beliefs are shaken; the world teeters; and yet, the reign of wonders is not over."[22] Ballanche also held to a "subjective" vision of progress: everything was already contained in dogma and man discovered it gradually.

Above and beyond specific formulations, we find ourselves, therefore, confronted with contrasting mentalities. Benamozegh's anti-Hegelian assertion—citing Gioberti in support—was peremptory:

Deriving more from less, *Being* from *Becoming, actus* from *potentia,*
is the height of absurdity. . . . Water does not rise an inch above
its source. The effect can include nothing that was not already
in the cause.[23]

The nub of the dispute is entirely contained in these few sentences.
The Hegelian sense of historical enrichment was dismissed, or at least made
conditional. The future was not to be considered as opening out on change
and novelty in their radical sense: history was fully conceived from the
outset, it remaining only to unfurl it gradually.[24]

"Pantheism: The Great Error
of Our Age"

The contrast between Hegel on the one hand and Gioberti and Benamozegh on the other is actually a new expression of a classic moment in the history of philosophy: the confrontation, struggle even, between pantheism and theism. The new elements brought to this traditional polarity were a dynamic vision of reality—historical sensibility, the idea of progress—and the consideration of "mankind" rather than "man" individually.[1]

For Benamozegh, Hegel was without doubt quite simply a pantheist, and he saw pantheism as "the great error of our age."[2] The mind of a Kabbalist would obviously have been sensitive to the apparently subtle yet decisive distinction forming a chasm between the transcendental and immanent viewpoints.

The definition of Hegelianism as a modern form of pantheism was, it must be stated, not new for the time and Benamozegh was doing no more than adding his voice to the many others who had already expressed themselves before him. The problem was, however, a particularly tricky one for a Kabbalist as the theology of the *Zohar* was itself many times considered—not least during Benamozegh's time, by Samuel David Luzzatto[3]—a pantheistic divergence from Hebraic doctrine.

Benamozegh had already written a fine essay that analyzed the system of Spinoza ("il grandissimo genio")[4] and very clearly identified the difference between Spinozist philosophy and the theology of the *Zohar*.[5] But, in the specific case of the refutation of Hegel, the new tone of the traditional confrontation was once again set by the idea of movement. To the old problem of the distinction/identity of thought and extension was added that of the relationship between cause and effect, power and action: in a word, between Being and Becoming.

The observations on the second key point of Hegelian philosophy—dialectics—once again propounded the basic idea, found in all Benamozegh's theoretical writings, of the impossibility of proceeding from the lesser to the greater in the absence of an initial idea in which successive developments

27

were contained. Movement itself, Benamozegh often repeated, was only possible on the condition that there was a prior, absolute starting point to "accompany" the historical process.[6]

The first triad of the Hegelian system, the one that marked the start of the entire system, was thus criticized from the beginning, as resulting in Becoming that would be a product of two abstract totalities, Being and Nothingness.

> [Hegel's] Becoming, which is composed of Being and Nothing-ness and which is pure potentiality, is empty, abstract: it is a first entity that is not one, since all abstracts are secondary; it is reflected rather than intuitive, a sterile assertion that stands the order of things on its head, while claiming to maintain it: because it starts with the abstract and ends with the concrete; it starts with Nothingness and ends with the Idea.[7]

But, in that case, we could argue that the whole Hegelian dialectic was inadmissible, since it understood movement to be gradual enrichment in a concrete direction: "moments" taken singularly give rise to their opposite precisely because they are set down "abstractly," and without context, as absolutes. For Hegel, "the truth is the whole": the idea followed its course, submerging itself in time and giving rise to Becoming that "is," in its totality, the truth. In Benamozegh's terms, this was a "God *in fieri*";[8] for the Jewish thinker, Becoming is subjective rather than objective, the first truths appeared only gradually to men but had been there all along.

Benamozegh's examination continued, concentrating on details, to the point where he proposed an alternative dialectic resulting from the juxtaposition of two triads—the human and the divine. He argued that, for man, it was true that thesis and antithesis were resolved at a higher level in the synthesis: this was man's return from a state of multiplicity to original unity, a movement that, ultimately, coincided with historical progress.[9] But, in God, actuality was already present, fully deployed at the inception of the creative process and in this case it is necessary to think in terms of a dialectical triad in which synthesis precedes thesis and antithesis. The creator and created together form the following combination:

divine synthesis

thesis   antithesis

human synthesis

Benamozegh found a reference to this new dialectic configuration in the *Zohar*,[10] where it alluded to the union of the *segol* [∴] (Hebrew vocalization mark equivalent to the phoneme "é") and *segolta* [∴] (traditional Biblical cantillation mark, acting as punctuation), giving rise to the figure [∴]. The seal of Solomon, the Christian cross, and the Hebrew letter *aleph*, in its original cruciform structure, were seen to evoke this philosophical "truth."[11]

For Benamozegh, human synthesis was not the result of dialectical opposition but the harmonizing—tempering—of two extremes: thus, certainty arose from the mediation of assertion and doubt, and beauty was constituted simply from the harmony of the different elements.[12] Naturally, the source of this notion was not Hegel, but Gioberti once again. One might say that it was through him that Benamozegh "read" the German philosopher.

Gioberti indeed asserted that the dialectic of opposites may be taken as referring to God rather than to man. Only with regard to God was it possible to speak of absolute opposites and infinite parts, which end in perfect unity, while in the finite world of men balance was the mode closest to unity: the dialectic reconciliation within Being was achieved through identity and, within the existent, we must speak in terms of harmony and tempering. Here "each opposite, without relinquishing its particular nature, limits itself and adapts to the other, to find a correct equilibrium."[13]

But, for the Catholic thinker, separation is an essential and permanent feature of the human world, because equilibrium is instable. This was a crucial distinction between Gioberti and the Kabbalist Benamozegh because, as we shall see, for the latter some separation was inevitably a feature of the divine being, and not only of the human world. This, in fact, was a characteristic moment in the doctrine of the *sefirot*, which sought to identify a dynamic multiplicity within the unity of God.

This was illustrated in the Jewish rite by many examples of duality, especially the one on the day of Yom Kippur when one goat—the scapegoat—is consecrated to "Azazel" and another to God. He explained this as a celebration of divine synthesis: the day of Yom Kippur is placed under the sign of the *sefirah binah*, beneath which are opposed the *sefirah gevurah* (to which the goat is consecrated), and the name of God expressed as the Tetragrammaton. Here again, the synthesis is placed above the dialectic elements, rather than below as in the Hegelian system: "At that sublime height"—wrote Benamozegh—"all distinctions disappear."

The dualism of this extraordinary rite thus demonstrated a recognition of a certain multiplicity within God at the same time as an ascension toward unity "up to the point, as Hegel would say, where the identity of contradictions resides."[14]

Moderate Idealism

A Tendency Toward Union

Progress was not peculiar to human history alone: it was also inherent in God. This led Benamozegh to his startling explanation of God's definition of himself given in Exodus III: 14, grammatically expressed in the future tense: "I will be who I will be," which according to him meant that God not only *is* but *also will become*. Movement is inscribed in God's essence, and this movement is progress. God is projected into the future, even if it is not God itself who moves, but the divine side of men. Progress consists of the tension between two poles, which Benamozegh generally called the "Ideal" and the "Real," in keeping with the idealistic terminology of the times, and which he identified with the *sefirot tiferet* and *malkhut*.

This terminological translation was not in fact unusual for Benamozegh, who very often interpreted basic Kabbalistic formulations idealistically. To give an example, the declaration that precedes the accomplishing of a religious act, the *mitzvah*, "To unite the Holy One, blessed be he, and his *Shekhinah*," provided in his interpretation a perfect expression of idealism, consisting in elevating of the divine presence in the world, bringing the finite back to the infinite, and the immanent God designated by the Tetragrammaton letters *vav* and *he* to the transcendent God designated by the letters *yod* and *he*.[1]

The separation of the divine world, and its reunification as an effect of human action; the question of the possibility of definitive fusion between the upper and lower worlds, or the dynamic relationship between the reconciliation and drawing apart of the two worlds; the need for a global vision of reality, and the risks associated with isolating one element from the whole: these were some of the basic problem areas Benamozegh inherited from Kabbalah.

He could certainly have given a dramatic reading to the first of these questions, highlighting, for instance, the notion of being torn away, or exiled from the divine presence—the *Shekhinah*—as viewed by the *Zohar* and by Yitzhaq Luria. It would not be hard to imagine such a concept in the Romantic context of the search for an Absolute no longer to be found in the world of men.

An example of this way of thinking is the work of the German philosopher Franz-Joseph Molitor (1779–1860), who had made Kabbalah the center of his theoretical interests. According to him, the Jewish esoteric tradition was the inspiration for Christianity, which had resulted in the German idealism of Hamann and Jacobi. The living seed of future regeneration (palingenesis) had been planted, now what was needed was a way to reunite and breathe new life into what had earlier been separated or left to die. Molitor rejected the Hegelian idea of perfect synthesis between Logic and Reality, believing rather in an ongoing, unifying human mission to replace his *real* relationship to the universe with an *ideal* one.[2]

These ideas corresponded perfectly with Benamozegh's.[3] However, to this idealistic vision accenting loss (of harmony, of union between earth and heaven), Benamozegh added a fin-de-siècle progressist optimism which led him not to stress the notion of fracture, preferring instead to define the purpose of every moral and intelligent creature, bringing the real closer to the ideal order: in short, idealizing nature.[4]

That nature already contained within itself the possibility of elevation, since *Shekhinah* was present in the dispersion of the phenomenon. Furthermore, God had impregnated the finite with the infinite: that was the meaning of the Midrashic and Kabbalistic formulations. "He cast down the truth (*emet*) to the ground,"[5] and, "He sent down from heaven unto the earth the beauty (*tiferet*) of Israel."[6]

This was the spirit in which Benamozegh offered an alternative interpretation of the Egyptian myth of Osiris perfumed in his coffin and the biblical verse (Gen. XLIX: 33) that states that Jacob, before dying, "gathered up his feet into the bed"; two mythical, allusive descriptions of the fall of the ideal (*tiferet*) and its contraction during its union with the real (*malkhut*).[7] This mention of Egyptian myth, as we will later see, was a genuine philosophical contribution by Benamozegh to Oriental studies, then enjoying a great explosion of interest even within the Italian Jewish milieu.[8]

Another Kabbalistic reading of the same issues was Abraham Yehoshua' Heschel's (1907–1970) dynamic, existentialist one a hundred years later, a reading that sees God as turning indefinitely toward man, straining to close the abyss that separates them.[9] On these lines, Heschel's thinking contrasted with the traditional philosophical view of God as the immobile Being par excellence and the reference point for all movement; it is far more inspired by the dynamic of the life of God as described in many passages of the *Zohar*.

This did not concord with Benamozegh's view. According to the nineteenth-century thinker's vison, if there was a tendency toward union, it was the fruit of activity from below, from the element of the divine within nature, within man. This was the only way in which it was possible to speak of God in terms of movement, given that his very stability was the necessary condition for all movement, just as his perfection was the condition for progress. The Livornese scholar's Kabbalah thus lay somewhere between Romanticism and existentialism: yet further proof of how these doctrines could be adapted to various different historical sensibilities.

Benamozegh's analysis pays particular attention to the question of total fusion between transcendence and immanence or, to put it another way, the reabsorption of one of the two into the other. But this question directed him to what was then a major debate in Italy, and even more so in France: the polemic surrounding Spinoza's philosophy and modern pantheism.

Distinctions Preserved

THE PHILOSOPHICAL CONTEXT

During the 1840s, Victor Cousin—then the most prestigious philosopher in France—endured virulent attacks by various Catholic thinkers who accused his philosophy of being "pantheism in disguise."

This polemic might seem outdated and of no more than scholarly interest; yet, the analyses of such religious philosophers, who were extremely sensitive to change—if only to condemn it—may help us understand certain dominant positions from a different perspective: in a sense, history seen from the margins.

In the single year of 1840, books were published by two priests, Henri Maret and Vincenzo Gioberti.

The former, in his *Essai sur le Panthéisme dans les sociétés modernes*,[1] saw Cousin's philosophy as a typical manifestation of a century that "no longer has the force to believe, nor yet the force to deny: it no longer dares affirm [anything]."[2] After close analysis of a number of the themes in Cousin's philosophy, Maret drew the conclusion that it was—in truth—disguised pantheism which, in spite of solemn declarations as to universal morality and respect for religion, contained within it the seeds of atheism. Cousin's "humanitarian" posture and concept of progressive truth were in his eyes confirmation of the fact. Maret's own statements were peremptory. He wrote, for example, that "French philosophy in the nineteenth century is forced to declare that it is pantheistic, or admit that it is nothing,"[3] and that pantheism was "the true heresy of the nineteenth century."[4]

Gioberti went less far. In his *Considérations sur les Doctrines Réligieuses de M. Victor Cousin*,[5] he limited himself to showing how, regardless of appearances and the author's protestations, Cousin's philosophy led to identifying God with the world and the assertion of a unique substance. Gioberti nonetheless acknowledged that pantheism was closer to theism than to naturalism and that Cousin had risen above the "savage materialism" that had characterized the eighteenth century, to arrive at a more refined system, "from doctrines of vulgar impiety to the seductive illusions of theological rationalism."[6]

35

Maret also recognized that pantheism was both a reaction to materialism and an improvement on it, as well as the almost ineluctable outcome of rationalism.[7] We may therefore assume that the philosophy attacked by these authors was that of a France desirous of being both secular and respectful of religion; that rejected the materialistic and sensualist doctrines of the Enlightenment without falling into transcendental absolutism; that wished to retain ethical certainties without tying them to any positive religious faith.

This somewhat toned-down version of Hegelianism, probably anxious to provide political legitimacy to an antiabsolutist and antirevolutionary State, was perceived by the theists as all the more dangerous for its saving of religious appearances.

In this polemic, the work of Spinoza played a role that was far from negligible, as had been the case in the dispute on pantheism that took place in Germany in the late eighteenth century, and which was at the origin of what was called "Romanticism." In an article on pantheism written in 1875, the historian of philosophy Emile Saisset described the Dutch philosopher's system as the most consummate statement of this type of thinking. Two things need to be borne in mind at this point: firstly, at the time the article was composed, in France the controversy was still raging ("If there is one word that is often heard these days in the controversy among schools and factions, it is *pantheism*"), and, secondly, Saisset wrote the article as a contribution to the *Dictionnaire des Sciences Philosophiques*,[8] edited by Adolphe Franck, himself profoundly knowledgeable about Kabbalah and a pupil of Victor Cousin.

Maret appeared to share Saisset's view;[9] he spoke of pantheism with great indulgence, considering it a noble, if mistaken, leaning toward the unity inherent in all forms of philosophy. His criticism was based on ethical arguments—the negation of free will—and on atheistic developments in Germany. A few years later, Franck was to come to precisely the same conclusions.[10]

Benamozegh's brilliant essay on Spinoza[11] must be read in this context. According to Berliner, this text holds a place of honor in the history of philosophy, and Renan apparently wrote to Benamozegh about it.[12] What immediately occasioned it was another article by Saisset in the *Revue des Deux Mondes*, on Maimonides and Spinoza.[13] At the very outset of his essay, Benamozegh admitted having discovered Spinoza primarily through Saisset "in my earliest youth,"[14] thus demonstrating how receptive he was to French literary production.

Benamozegh's article, like Saisset's, dealt with Spinoza's sources. We will see how a philosophical thought was grafted on at a philological level: the demarcation line between pantheism and Kabbalah was drawn through terminological discussion. Benamozegh's interest is purely theoretical and

takes him straight to several of the system's nerve centers. The consequences—ethical or political—seem to interest him little.

To complete the picture, we should bear in mind that Maret had previously identified Spinozism with Kabbalah and expressed the opinion that the
tendency still existed among his own Jewish contemporaries, constituting the
conclusion reached by Jews who wanted to escape "rabbinic immovability
without worshipping he whom they have rejected and whose blood has fallen
upon them,"[15] a statement that we will not comment upon.

SPINOZA'S ERROR: DOWNWARD UNION

Among a great number of philological as well as theoretical points made in
this essay, one essential idea stands out: the kernel of the Spinozist system
was to be found in Kabbalah, though it distorted a key detail which provided
the distinction between transcendentalist and pantheistic thinking.

Spinozist philosophy's debt to Kabbalah was illustrated in a set of
quotations, drawn mainly from the Dutchman's letters, but also through
strictly philosophical points.[16] Taking as his starting point the possibility of a
Maimonidean source, as suggested by Saisset, Benamozegh wondered whether
the Spinozist triad composed of *substance* and its two known attributes,
thinking substance and *extended substance*, should not be regarded as parallel
to the three kabbalistic terms, *sefer*, *sofer*, and *sippur*, mentioned in the *Sefer
Yetzirah* and themselves strictly related to the traditional gnoseological triad
of *knowledge*, *knowing subject*, and *known object*.[17]

Partially following Franck, but producing his own interpretation,
Benamozegh translates *sefer* (literally "book") as unique substance, *sofer*
("scribe") as "res cogitans," and *sippur* ("story") as "res extensa." These three
elements corresponded to the *sefirot keter* ("crown," also identified by Franck
with substance), *hokhmah* ("wisdom"), and *binah* ("intelligence"). The latter
three *sefirot* were represented respectively by Kabbalists using the dot, the
letter "yod," and the letter "he," their shape evoking the three dimensions
of extension.[18]

With the correspondence worked out, the argument could then be
advanced. For Benamozegh, *binah* (intelligence) represented not the *material* extension but the *idea* of extension: the logical thing, ideal matter. For
reasons that have yet to be explained—including, perhaps, the sheer number
of terms in the Kabbalistic lexicon—Spinoza appears to have taken *binah*
for *malkhut* ("kingdom"), actual material extension.[19] Taking the idea of
matter—an aspect of substance—for matter itself, Spinoza thus identified
God with Nature, and thereby took a step toward pantheism at precisely
the point where Kabbalah stopped short. "Spinoza resembled his precursors,

the Kabbalists, in almost every respect except one, and on that one point they were separated by a gulf."[20]

Substance and matter were *dodim*, "lovers," rather than *re'im*, "companions," or "equals" as substance and metaphysical matter were. So Benamozegh wrote in notes published in 1897. By this he meant that the tendency toward union between God and matter remained, in effect, a tendency, in which distinctions were preserved.

Spinoza's error—and it goes without saying that this was a deliberate choice rather than mere inattentiveness—lay in eliminating distinctions. In Benamozegh's words, this led him to draw the celestial world downward.

At the end of the day, the Livornese rabbi's scholarly arguments were intended to use Spinoza's prestige to boost that of Kabbalah. He admitted as much in a letter written to *Vessillo Israelitico* some sixteen years after the essay in question: since all the great contemporary philosophical systems, including Kantianism, were derived from Spinozism, demonstrating how it had drawn on Kabbalah was tantamount to recognizing the great relevance of the "philosophy of the Hebrews." This was the way Benamozegh took part in the Spinoza-centered debate just discussed—slotting pantheism, without denunciation, into place alongside Kabbalistic doctrines: a criticism devoid of any animosity toward the excommunicated Jew the Dutch philosopher was.

The Italian scholar Mino Chamla has demonstrated that the crux of the "Spinoza question" in Jewish circles concerned "Jewish modernity."[21] An increasing number of different positions regarding Spinoza's philosophy were in fact being reached among nineteenth-century Jewish intellectuals. Themes of tradition and "betrayal" arose alongside, and in addition to, the issues of doctrinal orthodoxy seen in Maret and Gioberti, and the ethical concerns found in authors such as Saisset and Franck.

In France, Salomon Munk's *Mélanges de philosophie juive et arabe* (1859) evoked the strict relationship between tradition and reason, where the former also needed to extend to include the esoteric tradition. Esotericism would enable the rights of reason to be maintained when the dogma of revealed truth began to be imposed in an authoritarian manner. In this sense, Spinoza's utter escape from tradition could be seen as an unsound rationalism that failed to take into account the previous conquests of reason.[22]

The clearest, and most virulent, rejection of Spinoza came, however, from the Italian grammarian, biblicist, and poet, Samuel David Luzzatto (1800–1865). On several occasions, in separate works, and two articles in particular, as well as in personal correspondence, Luzzatto dispatched Spinoza's position as deterministic and antifinalistic. Thus far, nothing very new. The attack is, however, taken farther, into the arena of the philosopher's private life. In the introduction to *Ha-Mishtaddel*,[23] his commentary on the Pentateuch, scathing remarks are made about a man who left his community and found himself alone, abandoned and betrayed by those he considered his friends. According to Luzzatto's reasoning, this proved the falseness and impiety of his position.

Luzzatto, it is true, was first and foremost antiphilosophical:[24] "My God is not that of Ka.n.t. but that of Ta.na.k. [Tanakh, the Hebrew Bible]," he wrote to Leopold Zunz with studied irony.[25] He can be defined principally as an antimodernist mind, despite some major traits of his intellectual personality running counter to this interpretation. For instance, when attempting to explain manifestations of evil in history, he has no hesitation in associating Robespierre "and his friends" with Nero and Attila, as examples of absolute negativity, and Napoleon, the inheritor of the French Revolution, is referred to as a tyrant whose fall was an act of providence.[26]

Living in a Jewish community within the Austro-Hungarian Empire which enjoyed early emancipation in the late eighteenth century, Luzzatto appears to be faithful to the concept of a multiethnic state within which the various national and religious communities enjoy comparative autonomy. Hence his emphasis on the importance of connections across the community and his severe condemnation of Spinoza the individualist, and traitor.

Benamozegh was, as we shall see, an enthusiastic follower of the Italian "Risorgimento," which was to lead to the creation of a unified state. From a historical perspective, such a nation-state was incontestably more "modern" than a multinational empire.

This is simply one paradox among many to surface when the two characters are compared;[27] on the one hand, the scholar who was a central reference point for Europe's "enlightened" Jewish intellectuals and on the other, the Kabbalist, of whom the German Avraham Berliner wrote:

> With his extraordinary abilities, and the rare gifts his mind possessed, he could have brought those who had wandered from it back to Judaism. But he was born under an unlucky star—geographically speaking—and spent his entire life trying to show the primordial and fundamental nature of Kabbalah, inhabiting a thoroughly Oriental mind.[28]

CHRISTIANITY'S ERROR: UPWARD UNION

The Metaphysical Flaws of Christian Morality

If Spinoza's crucial error was absorbing *sefirah binah*—ideal matter—into *sefirah malkhut*—actual matter—and thereby making physical extension an attribute of God, Christianity made the opposite mistake. If the former deified the world, the latter stripped it of any value at all. Both were guilty of extremism, unifying that which ought to remain separate and ossifying an idea that was originally founded on the tension that existed between two poles—the upper and the lower.

The "pillars of the modern age: Jesus, the father of the Church and Spinoza, the father of German nationalism"[29] both emerged out of Kabbalistic Judaism, which they betrayed through an oversimplification that stripped away its complexity and power of universal interpretation.

> While Spinoza sacrificed the Mother to the Daughter, the ideal to the physical object—and thereby abolished the supernatural and the divine—Christianity on the other hand, sacrificed the Daughter to the Mother, thus condemning sense, nature, and time to the benefit of the Spirit, the supernatural, and the eternal.[30]

In the passionate and analytical essay entitled *L'origine des dogmes chrétiens*, Benamozegh completely overturned current opinion, finding, point by point, origins for Christian dogma in Kabbalistic thinking. The analysis concentrates principally on the Christian Trinity, both generally and in terms of its individual persons, for whom he attempts to set down a genealogy based on some triads of *sefirot*.

The conclusion he reaches, through two hundred pages of richly argued text, is as follows. The Trinity of the Father, Son, and Holy Ghost was inspired by the triad of *hokhmah* (wisdom), *tiferet* (beauty or logos), and *malkhut* (kingdom). His proofs displayed a remarkable ease with—unsurprisingly—Talmudic and Kabbalistic texts, but also with evangelical ones, as well as much evidence from gnosis and Christian heresies.

This essay, intended as a riposte to the works of David Friedrich Strauss and Joseph Salvador,[31] appears both imposing and certainly original. I shall leave assessment of it to specialists in the subject, but would nonetheless point out that the tone is eminently philosophical and that here, as elsewhere, a highly theoretical sensitivity trained in the study of Kabbalah is placed in the service of criticism and philology.[32]

It is, however, impossible to move on before mentioning—though without going into detail—various forceful but cogently argued assertions made in the essay. For example, gnosis was looked on not as a mixture of Christianity and philosophy, but as the esoteric facet of Christianity—its "Kabbalah"—and as such, naturally, of Jewish origin.[33] If gnosis was unable to spread and was, indeed, decisively combated, this was because of its complexity and the entirely public character proclaimed by Christianity for its own doctrines.

To take another point, the extremely detailed analysis of various heretical Christian theologies[34] was similarly conducted in the light of Kabbalah. Benamozegh found Judeo-Kabbalistic roots in even the most recent heresies, basing himself on the (biologically inspired) presupposition that identical seeds—Kabbalah—would cause the same plant to develop in the same ways, whether planted in Jewish, or transplanted into Christian soil.[35] The oscillations and varying positions within Kabbalah had their equivalent in heterodox and schismatic Christian theologies.[36] This was, for instance, how he explained the fourth-century Greek schism which turned on differing interpretations of the relationship between the three persons of the Trinity, drawing on diverse triadic arrangements found in Kabbalistic treatises.[37]

Benamozegh's contention was therefore that Christianity's greatest error was to efface *malkhut*, this world, in favor of *binah*, the world to come.[38] The ensuing vacuum, the Christians filled with the "prince of this world," thought of as a demon, or the spirit of evil, while the same definition applied to the *malkhut* of Kabbalah has positive connotations. The *hokhmah—tiferet—malkhut* triad was mistaken, in Christian theology, for another, the most exalted in the sefirotic hierarchy—*keter* (crown)—*hokhmah* (wisdom)—*binah* (intelligence). Benamozegh's translation has the holy, the supernatural, and the eternal being confused with truth, nature, and time.[39] Triads that should have been kept separate were combined, a confusion with major consequences at a speculative as well as a practical level.

This study was laid out in *Morale juive et morale chrétienne*, the second part of a work of which *L'origine des dogmes chrétiens* was the first part. Published several times until very recently and primarily known for its apologetic content, *Morale juive et morale chrétienne* was intended to demonstrate that traditional Jewish morality was no less exalted than Christian morality; The most interesting aspect of the work, however, probably resides in the theoretical arguments used in the demonstration.[40] Here the Kabbalist engages in an analysis of the moral and material consequences of Christian theology, grounded in a tradition of radical thought (the names that spring to mind are those of Machiavelli and Nietzsche), whose conceptual details are, though, naturally drawn from the Jewish esoteric tradition.

Christianity is thus seen as doomed, by virtue of its theological roots, to disregard the world. At heart, its ideals are mysticism and mistrust of matter. Benamozegh saw in it a dangerous trend, too clearly separating body from mind, interested only in elevating the latter at the expense of the former. The proclaimed freedom of the spirit could easily become the very opposite:

There is a materialism that ensues from the refinement of spiritualism . . . .
History shows that mysticism, when given free range, inevitably leads to the most unbridled license, now through the impetuous

ardor of the body delivered to itself, now through a sensuality sanctioned in advance by the very spiritualism that formerly scorned to impose order and temperance upon the body.[41]

Political consequences no less important were suggested. Christianity, if the doctrine is taken to heart, is not political, its sublime morality ignores the worldly realities of social action, and the issue of power more particularly. Confrontation with this reality has been—after the age of the martyrs—the religion's hardest test. In the same way as *malkhut* is subsumed into *binah*, the throne is absorbed by the altar, creating a vacuum that makes Christianity's presence in the world "embarrassed" and "embarrassing."[42] The consequence of such exquisite and sophisticated ethics was to superimpose the spiritual on the political, giving rise to the cruel contradiction of State religion.

> What, then, is State religion? It is consciousness treated as a citizen, the mind governed as the body, faith backed up with executioners; it is violence employed in the service of a religion of pure charity. A morality that preached only love and never respect (an inferior but infinitely more necessary virtue), by dint of wishing to be more just, was condemned to be violent.[43]

Benamozegh wrote that while Paul of Tarsus saw all who refused to accept the new message as *enemies*, the Jewish sages had the more moderate—"relative" rather than "absolute"—alternative of seeing them as *political opponents*.[44]

It was a theme Benamozegh stressed. Christian morality gave the illusion of being more noble than Judaism in taking everything away from restricted groups and bestowing it on humanity in general, but this gain in breadth meant a corresponding loss in intensity.[45]

The key error of this morality was its abstraction, which stopped it taking into account not only real facts, but also the positive qualities that went hand in hand with the political: the sense of family and, above all, of nationhood. The shared origins of all peoples as taught in the Bible ought to inspire tolerance and respect for others, something that could perfectly well coexist with national feeling, whereas Christian cosmopolitanism sought to eradicate demands that were noble in themselves, and in any case inherent to the human condition.

To the classic Christian argument according to which Judaism was *exhausted*, he opposed the notion of Christianity as *incomplete*.

This idea provided the metaphysical basis for a theory of progress in which the players were national personalities.

The same liberal-type ideology also resulted from a definition of Christianity as a doctrine that suppressed the political level only to find itself inevitably forced to fill the void arising from that initial act with another act weighty in its consequences: the replacement of the ordinary political dialectic—in which the concepts of power and adversariness were entirely natural (provided they remained at the level of the material)—with religion. What follows is the absurd and cruel idea of the domination of consciousness. Religion and politics need to be kept separate and the wrong done to Jewish morality, according to Benamozegh, was to contrast Christian morality not with the wider Jewish tradition but Mosaic law, thereby confusing different levels and as a result necessarily condemning Judaism as a purely exterior doctrine.

Beyond the religious polemic, if we strip the wording of its contingent references, we find a typically liberal scheme of thought: a demand for the separation of Church and State. It is also possible to understand the political scope of an affirmation such as that made in *Morale juive et morale chrétienne* whereby Judaism was compared to Semi-Pelagianism, an ancient doctrine condemned by the Church, that extolled the freedom of the individual by reducing the importance of the intercession of Divine Grace.[46]

In fact, when the occasion presented itself, Benamozegh was vigorous in expressing his patriotic and liberal sentiments. His "Italianness" was sincere, as was his pride in belonging to the Jewish "nation." The author who made the Kabbalistic source of Jewish dogma the center of his intellectual activity was the same man who expressed the political and national—not just the religious and moral—character of Judaism. The warm correspondence he exchanged with the republican patriot Giuseppe Mazzini (reproduced at the beginning of *Teologia*), not exactly a given for a Kabbalist rabbi, was significant in this regard.

It may not be necessary to point out that here again Benamozegh's liberal sympathies (expressed also in Italian historical contingency, as we shall see) found their justification in theological distinctions and that his political stance had its raison d'être in the complex hierarchies of the *sefirot*. It was more than simply the artifice of a preacher, representing in fact the coherent development of a thinking that, nourished by Kabbalah, nonetheless spoke the language of the nineteenth century.

As Benamozegh interpreted it, Christianity had drawn the lower realm toward the higher, confusing two levels that should have been kept apart. But this was not its only error. It did not restrict itself to conflating the *sefirot malkhut* and *binah* in the hypostasis of the Holy Ghost, it also associated the *sefirot tiferet* and *malkhut* materially and definitively in the person of Christ. Benamozegh contended that, with the dogma of the Incarnation,[47] Christianity invalidated one of the basic tenets of Kabbalah—namely, the perpetual tension between the real and the ideal, symbolized precisely by *malkhut* and *tiferet*. Jesus combined in himself God and man, thus realizing the coupling (the *zivug* of Kabbalah) of the wife (*malkhut*, the feminine side) and the husband (*tiferet*, the masculine side).[48]

This coupling, Benamozegh points out, must perpetually take place between two beings who remain separate, like the first man and his rib, which was part of him but had been detached from him. The union operated by Christ echoes the primordial union of the androgyne, the *du-partzufin* (a being with two faces) mentioned in the Creation story and accorded a cosmic value by the Kabbalists.

This ideal union is destined to remain unaccomplished: Christianity blocks the *tension*, which is transformed into an *event* that has happened once and for all.

The Incarnation fixed the tension between the world and the ideal, in a sense neutralizing history, and human efforts toward elevation; in addition it reduced the perpetual movement of humanity and the universe to the figure of a single man. The result, in Benamozegh's eyes, was "prodigious shrinking" and "petty imitation":

> With the union worked by Christ, the broad horizons, vast
> thoughts, and lofty conceptions of the Kabbalists were shrunk
> to the miserable proportions of an individual whom people have
> wanted at all cost to make divine.[49]

His critique of the other basic Christian dogma, that of the Trinity, was in very much the same spirit. The *partzufin*, or faces, of Kabbalah have been transformed into *persons*, turning what should have remained attributes into substances. This semantic slide upsets the delicate balance of Jewish esoteric theology in which definitions are—and are meant to stay—elusive and evocative, as their subject is essentially ungraspable. Indistinct half-light is more evocative, and more fecund, than the full light of day.

At several points in his essay on the origins of the Christian dogmas, Benamozegh stated his desire to restrict himself to a purely critical work. Yet, with hindsight we can see that this criticism takes its place in the much larger project that came to fruition in *Israel and Humanity*.

The discovering of Judeo-Kabbalistic origins for Christianity demonstrated its real monotheistic roots, something that came to the surface in a number of anti-Trinitarian Christian heresies. In this sense, Benamozegh allows himself to make the extraordinary assertion that these heretics can be considered as children and martyrs of Israel and offered as such for the veneration of the faithful.[50] Consequently, the real obstacle to religious progress was the doctrine of the Incarnation, about which Benamozegh wrote in the harshest terms, defining it as an "impiety" that had prevented the advancement of monotheism for centuries. Nothing short of the disappearance of this dogma would enable the religious problems of the age to be solved and "Israel and Humanity to clasp one another and meet in a embrace of peace, joy, and love."[51]

The Historical Jesus

Joseph Salvador, in *Jésus Christ et sa doctrine*,[52] sketched a historical and cultural portrait of the historical Jesus that set him within a Jewish context. This was obviously not the first such attempt, but what was notable about it was the way Judaism was depicted, not as a religion that lost its historical relevance with the birth of Christianity but very much as a civilization with the right to a place in the modern world alongside Christianity, which it complemented. This was reconstruction from a Jewish viewpoint, for all that it showed great sympathy with the evangelical message, but it was limited by the fact that Salvador had no real mastery of Hebrew, his knowledge being, therefore, essentially biblical and historical. This meant that Judaism struck him as politico-nationalistic and juridical in character. The importance of the Law was thus reassessed, and it was perceived in other ways than as the obsolete premise of the Age of Grace, but the terms of the traditional distinction between Law and Spirit were retained.

The great merit of *Morale juive et morale chrétienne* was the way it presented a comparison between the two religions that took account of Judaism in a general sense, as a civilization with written laws, and a living tradition of values, beliefs, and behavior. According to Benamozegh, true Jewish morality found its expression in the thousands of pages of the Talmud, the *Midrash*, and the *Zohar*, which latter extended the continuum in another register. Jesus's preaching, however sublime, not only echoed, but was entirely inspired by rabbinical teachings that were older and often superior, including in the specifically ethical domain. If Judaism corresponded to a sense of the worldly and the real, it was also a set of principles and practices, on which Christian morality was not only dependent but to which it was also subordinate.

Morale juive et Morale chrétienne was an apologia, and thus, by definition partisan. It is therefore opportune to place in parentheses the hierarchy of values it expressed. However, the method used—the contextualizing of early Christianity in Jewish culture as it appeared in early sources—should be considered on its own merits. This methodology required a Talmudist with a critical intellectual approach: someone like Benamozegh, in other words. His philosophical sensitivity enabled him to bring out unimagined connections, and his Kabbalistic training possibly led him both toward a

vision of historical continuity that might not have been open to a rationalist, and also to consider seriously myths, not only concepts. A "Kabbalistic"
reading of Jesus' discourse leads to surprising results. Benamozegh emphasizes
the notion of proximity between Jesus' doctrines and those of the Essenes,
implicitly crawling toward the eighteenth-century—Christian—Romanesque
reconstructions dominated by a fascination with esotericism.[53]

In *Morale juive*, as in *l'Histoire des Esséniens*, the theme is well developed.
Drawing on the rare contemporary sources, principally Philo of Alexandria
and Flavius Josephus, Benamozegh reconstructed a set of associations that
have been largely borne out by recent historiography, following the discovery
of the Dead Sea Scrolls. Contemporary Jewish historians of the origins of
Christianity such as David Flusser have, with documentary backing, taken up
ideas that were for Benamozegh intuitions nourished by passion, and made
possible by the synthesizing abilities of an eclectic mind.[54]

The viewpoint of a philosopher who did not neglect history proved
in this case to be a fecund one, perhaps more so than a philological rigor-
ousness that aspired to the role of an exclusive criterion of interpretation.
The irony of Luzzatto, the "scientific" historian who wrote to Benamozegh,
inviting him to be serious and set aside the idea of a "Kabbalistic Jesus,"
proved, itself, paradoxically lacking in historical perspective.

Reconciliaton

Immanentist Monotheism

Morale juive et morale chrétienne and *L'origine des dogmes chrétiens* respectively belong to the genres of apologia and of history of religion. In fact, both are works of philosophy, a field that was obviously of real interest to Benamozegh who, whether drawing on ethics or dogmatics, goes right to the theoretical heart of both. His examination of Spinozism, Christianity—in its orthodox, heterodox, and schismatic manifestations—and Islam has the negative function of preparing the way for his own theological project. Up to that point, Kabbalah is considered merely as the criterion for the evaluation of doctrines that seemed to him manifestly unbalanced: henceforth it will become the kernel of a positive proposition. It is presented as a justification of the role of Judaism in a Western world at its cultural and economic zenith, fashioning for itself a conquering identity founded more on a scientific—or pseudo-scientific—discourse than on religious values. This presented a dual problem for a thinker who came from a minority religion and was personally rooted in an "Oriental" tradition. To gain a clearer understanding of Benamozegh's position, it is therefore necessary to look first at the general context, and more specifically at a series of responses to this hegemonistic ideology: it, like them, found expression notably—and understandably—in the Orientalist milieu.

THE TRIUMPH OF THE OCCIDENT AND THOUGHTS ON DIFFERENCE

Hegel's historical philosophy had portrayed a kind of philosophical canonization of European self-representation. Western civilization was depicted as the culmination of a long Odyssey of the Spirit, which rediscovered itself in Protestant Germany and in the pen of Hegel himself. This journey—and its conclusion—were held up as being absolute in nature, part of some sort of divine plan. What reaction was possible for a contemporary from a cultural and religious minority who, having witnessed the triumphs of a Europe that had been the inheritor of Christian civilization, had no wish to retreat into particularist and purely reactionist pride?

Two historians of linguistic phenomena, Tzvetan Todorov[1] and Maurice Olender[2] have clearly shown how the ground in which this ideology grew was primarily linguistic. The author who expounded this view most clearly, and the most influential, was Ernest Renan. Alongside the attempt to "Europeanize" Jesus in his historical work, Renan also turned his attention to the field of linguistics. Through the notion of "interdependence" between the "genius of the language" and the "genius of the people" he allowed himself to make value judgments about entire civilizations. With his *Histoire générale et système comparé des langues sémitiques*,[3] Renan decisively crossed the dividing line between science and ideology. A linguistic treatise, it was also a program that postulated the superiority of European—or Indo-European—over Semitic civilization.

> In every order, progress for the Indo-European peoples consists in removing themselves as far as possible from the Semitic spirit. . . . The great Indo-European race is obviously destined to assimilate all others.[4]

Later deviations in the terminology of "race" should not mislead: at the time, the same vocabulary was used by "Semitic" scholars, notably by Benamozegh himself. This was not yet racism. Todorov proposes the terms *racialism*[5] and *ethnocentrism*, in which the cultural plays a more important role than the biological, though that is not ignored.

Renan indicates what this superiority comprised:

> Infinity, diversity, the seeds of development and progress seem to have been denied to the peoples of whom we are going to speak. We see that in all areas the Semitic race appears incomplete by dint of its very simpleness. It is, dare I say it, to the Indo-European family what grisaille is to painting; what plainchant is to modern music: it lacks that variety, that breadth, and that overabundance of life that is the condition of perfectibility. Like the infertile mind that after a graceful childhood attains only mediocre manhood, the Semitic nations came to their full flowering in earliest youth and have no role in their maturity.[6]

A Europe seeking an identity for itself sought it through comparison, so another civilization was attributed all the opposite characteristics, giving it the function of defining the European identity *a contrario*, like a sort of mirror. To extol the (Indo-) European talents for science and art, the religious instincts of the Semite needed to be brought to the fore, and the creative complexity of the one were contrasted with the simpleness of the other. The Semitic peoples were essentially static, and in the dynamic evolutionary design of mankind they were destined to be displaced by the Indo-Europeans, who were receptive to the future.

Even before Renan, Johann Gottfried Herder had described Hebrew as the language of poetry par excellence, though maintaining it had expressed itself fully from the very outset: its simplicity sheltered it from the complexity of historical languages.[7] For the German philosopher, the language of the "poor shepherd folk" had nothing in common with the miserable, muddled Hebrew of the Diaspora, when the "poor yet comely and pure village girl . . . [had] borrowed the finery of her neighbors."[8]

This approach was severely criticized by a younger Orientalist, James Darmesteter (1849–1894).[9] Born into a German Jewish family that had emigrated to France, raised and educated in a secular tradition, Darmesteter devoted himself to Oriental studies with dazzling success. On Friedrich Max Müller's invitation, he translated the key Mazdeist text *Zend-Avesta* into first English, then French. The author of such instantly authoritative works as *Haurvatât et Ameretât* (1875) and *Ormuzd et Ahriman* (1877), Darmesteter taught Iranian, initially at the École des Hautes Études, later being appointed to a chair at the Collège de France. He also found time to write several essays on English literature, including a book on Shakespeare, as well as critical editions of *Macbeth* and Byron's *Childe Harold's Pilgrimage*.

Alongside his scientific work, Darmesteter was an active participant in the late nineteenth-century debate of ideas that focused on the crisis in values triggered by the rapid decline of religion and the resounding triumphs of science. *La légende divine* (1890) was a lyrical expression of the hopes of the "believing atheist" ("You suffer, because you are the future . . .")[10] who undergoes a religious crisis and attempts to overcome it. *Les prophètes d'Israël* (1892) offers a positive proposal for finding a way out of the crisis.[11]

This proposal was based on what he called "Hebraism," and which amounts to the same thing as prophetism, which does not mean Judaism, nor a positive religion or additional priesthood. He saw Judaism as a religion founded on ritual and destined to perish or ossify and on the other hand dismissed the idea of a new religion, as the world did not need yet another dogmatic system to add to the graveyard of its predecessors. "Pure" prophetism, through its questing after truth, was allied to science, and in its ideal of justice, inspired what was best in Christianity. It invigorated both and enabled them to coexist peacefully. This was a universalist project that would eventually result in what we would now call pluralism, and it was fed by the "fieldwork" of a scholar who approached other cultures with great openness of mind. Darmesteter was as much at home with wandering Afghan poets or the last few Mazdeist sages as he was in Romanticist European circles. He was highly critical of, and denied any legitimcy to the racism that was developing so threateningly in Germany in the guise of nationalism and anti-Semitism.

Darmesteter's criticism of Renan concerned not the details of his analysis so much as the very concept of race. Renan had recognized that the term was impossible to apply to the Jews by reason of the sheer amount of mixing that had occurred in their long history, and Darmesteter stated that the same was true of all peoples: race was nothing but a scientifically sterile myth that should be replaced with the idea of *tradition*.

> In this century the historical sciences lived off one idea—that of race. When one lives off a single idea, one ends up dying of it. This idea of race, having renewed, or to put it better, created modern history, long ago began to sterilize and falsify it. Its day is done: now it should give way to a new idea, that of *tradition*. In historical epochs the word on the lips no longer bespeaks the blood that runs in the veins.[12]

In no civilization, Darmesteter went on, and in the Aryan-Semitic civilizations least of all, did history achieve the work of race. What it achieved was the fruit of mixings, blendings, and influences. Of *tradition*, in other words.[13]

Darmesteter thus moved beyond the racialist perspective and laid the foundations of cultural anthropology.[14] At the same time, this Jewish scholar, born in France but into a German family, who wished to transcend Jewish particularism and embrace a rational faith in the universal, traced out for the West not a conqueror's destiny in accordance with biological—or spiritual—imperatives, but a temporary mission as a guide. On Europe in general, and France in particular, fell the heavy responsibility of bringing just fulfillment to humanity. Paris was the new Jerusalem, and the center of a secular messianism that upheld the values of Reason and Justice.

Another, more indirect reaction to Renan came from the French Jewish philosopher Adolphe Franck (1809–1893), one the major figures in nineteenth-century French university circles. Franck has often been seen as a sort of authorized representative of Victor Cousin's eclectic philosophy. He was, among other things, the author of *La Kabbale, ou la philosophie religieuse des Hébreux* (1843) and the editor of the important *Dictionnaire des sciences philosophiques* (1885). The power of nineteenth-century France is perceptible in Franck's philosophical writings, as is the sense of responsibility it inspired. While Gioberti tapped the reservoir of historical and literary rhetoric to justify the particularity of Italy,[15] and Hegel elaborated a complex conceptual architecture to deduce a Germanic "destiny," Franck felt no compulsion to justify or uncover the might and greatness of his nation as they were so evidently visible. It was more necessary to channel them, and stop them going awry.

Hence the great care he paid to the linkages between the theoretical, the ethical, and the political; the need for philosophy to be socially committed; the rejection of authoritarianism; and above all the vision of the relationships between civilizations. Franck was a firm believer in the absolute quality of ideas—in the *good*, the *beautiful*, and the *true*—but this did not interfere with his dynamic, pluralistic vision of relationships between civilizations. Steadfastly opposed to the cultural violence of colonialism, he saw the mixing of civilizations—*races*, as he persisted in calling them—not just as an incontestable fact but the real driving force behind humanity's advancement.

> The diversity of the races, which is a fact impossible to deny, and to which is connected one of the great strengths of civilization, one of the greatest charms of society, the diversity of talents and genius, in no way undermines the moral and intellectual oneness of the human species, or—and it is the same thing—the universality of the laws of reason and conscience. . . . Is what we call Christian civilization (I do not say Christianity) therefore so simple that the trained eye cannot discern [in it] the ancient elements that came from the Jews, Greeks, Persians, Indians, Chaldeans, and all the peoples of Asia?[16]

The task was harder for Jewish intellectuals who kept to the religious tradition. They could neither accept Renan's Eurocentric vision nor, for obvious lack of opportunity, could they simply turn it on its head and replace "Aryan" superiority with "Semitic" superiority. They did, however, stress the importance and permanency of a Jewish religious particularity that they looked upon as necessary to the harmonious development of humanity.

Samuel David Luzzatto sketched out a "system" of civilizations that, while fairly simplistic, nonetheless offered an interesting alternative to the Eurocentric perspective.

Luzzatto was a conservative but not a reactionary. He was convinced that in his day and age the most dangerous intolerance was to be found in a certain idea of progress; as a good conservative he was sensitive to some features of modernity, in particular the imperative of movement and a totalitizing tendency. He called this attitude "Atticism" because he saw it as having sprung from Greek civilization, and he described it in various of his writings, including a long Hebrew poem called *Morality or Atticism*, where he describes it as a jealous God that will tolerate no other gods beside itself.[17]

The alternative to Atticism was Judaism, but a Judaism almost shorn of its historical characteristics: at root, ethics as opposed to utility; sentiment as opposed to reason. Indeed, this last opposition was the basis of his violent hostility to Spinoza.

Luzzatto did not stop there, however. As a thinker from a minority, he was not in a position to set one faction up against another (in this instance tradition against innovation), his thinking could not be monolithic at a time when Jews like himself were struggling to preserve their right to be different. His thinking therefore centered on the idea of alternation:

> Civilization is . . . necessarily periodic rather than progressive; it does not have a point at which to stop. Repose may only be envisaged in the perfect reconciliation of two elements, something that cannot take place without great sacrifice on the part of the progressive element, which must, notably, and uselessly, set a brake on its own expansion. The stationary element, which is essentially immutable, is incapable of sacrifice.[18]

For Luzzatto, there was a pendulum movement to humanity: at times it would seek beauty, utility, and efficiency, immerse itself in progress, but just as this "Hellenizing" tendency seemed to reach its peak, a need would be felt for the opposite—for goodness, justice, impartiality, and stability: in a word, for the Hebrew spirit. But this authority was in turn rejected, and the other principle was sought again. Both trends are as necessary as they are inevitable, being part of the human heart. Though perhaps reductive, the idea is nonetheless remarkable. Luzzatto's dialectic is not that of *transcendence*, the result of which is a unit that absorbs the elements that went before it, but rather of *oscillation*, where no element is eliminated. The particular, in Luzzatto's model, keeps its identity and is not subsumed in the whole.[19]

PLURALITY WITHIN UNITY

Seeking plurality within unity and making this delicate balance the center of a positive religious proposition was the theoretical framework for Benamozegh's *Israel and Humanity*. This work was intended to be the culmination of Benamozegh's philosophical and theological efforts, but it was not actually published until fourteen years after his death, sensitively edited and touched up by Aimé Pallière.[20] *Israel and Humanity* also represented a reaction to Renan's "unique" thinking.

The work enjoyed a degree of popularity, being reprinted and translated as well as attracting a number of studies, including recent ones. It has probably been seen as an instrument for justifying and stressing the importance of Judaism's place in European culture, which allowed a relationship with Christianity—or any other religious manifestation—to be envisaged from a tolerant, ecumenical perspective. The element of apologia has perhaps been given more weight than the theoretical one, though that aspect of the work is actually the more original and interesting.

Within his lifetime the author did publish a lucid *Introduction*[21] to this ambitious book, which anticipated the main questions he would try to answer. It was—he wrote—a matter of confronting the religious crisis of the century, starting from an acknowledgment that Christianity and Islam had both been tried and tested, and no longer satisfied contemporary religious needs.

The theme of the religious void was then at the very heart of European philosophical debate, as was the idea of the "exhaustion" of Christianity. The most sensitive intellectuals, from Rimbaud to Nietzsche, reacted to the deepening void with a mixture of anguish and relief. Eduard von Hartmann was able to write in 1874 that,

> Christianity has run its course. . . . The ordinate of the Christian curve has finally become equal to zero again, as it was at the beginning, but the abscissa now no longer suffers comparison with what it then was.[22]

The image of Judaism as having had its day before Christianity was also a commonly accepted one: only Renan among contemporary scholars suggested that it continued to be vital and fertile despite appearances. But Benamozegh denied that Judaism had played all its cards. For him, its best side remained largely unexplored, its universal potential untapped.

> We were examining earlier just now if Judaism is a universal religion. . . . But here in fact is the way the question should have been posed: *Does Judaism contain a universal religion?* . . . It indeed contains at its heart, as the flower conceals the fruit, the religion intended for the entire human race, of which the Mosaic Law—which seems on the surface so incompatible with that high destiny, is but the husk or outer cover.[23]

In *Israel and Humanity* he sketched a theological system directly inspired by some Kabbalistic doctrines that dealt with God, the world, mankind, and the relationships between them. He was aware of how difficult such a task was at the end of the nineteenth century, the very word *Kabbalah* inspiring horror in enlightened circles, and the first flush of German idealism—which would probably have been more receptive—having given way, as in France and Italy, to a more positivist atmosphere. The somewhat perilous undertaking nevertheless threw up fairly clear ideas. The theory even had a name: "immanentist monotheism."

Benamozegh's discourse encompassed history, anthropology, and theology. It outlined a theory of the religious development of humanity founded on the alleged "genius" of peoples, or even of races with predetermined characteristics (the Aryan genius, the Semitic genius). If we discount the pseudoscientific style of the time, the aspect of the work most worthy of consideration is probably the use in this context of Kabbalistic ideas.[24]

Benamozegh's basic idea was this: the Semites were naturally inclined to unity, they had been and continued to be monotheistic, whereas the Aryans tended more toward multiplicity, as demonstrated by ancient polytheism and some salient aspects of the modern world. Neither can be said to be wrong as truth and error are always mixed rather than clearly opposed. In every lie there is a grain of truth, as in every idol there is a spark of the divine.[25]

The commonest idea of the religion of the Jews, wrote Benamozegh, was that of a transcendent monotheism in which God is detached from men and the world. This he calls "Karaite Mosaism,"[26] and rejects it as unsuited to the intellectual and religious needs of Western man.

Kabbalah, with its conception of God as both transcendent and immanent, was better placed to act as a link between West and East, and occupy the middle ground between the ancient and modern worlds. This immanent God is the *sefirah malkhut*, also referred to as *shekhinah* (literally, presence or immanence), or in other words, the God "who is in the world or, rather, through and in whom the world exists":

> [T]he transcendent God is expressed in the Tetragrammaton. The doctrine of immanentism reconciles these two beliefs, permitting equally the cult of the love of nature and faith in absolute truth, which is the necessary condition for believing in science.[27]

This immanentist monotheism was not only the most suitable religion for the West, it was also chronologically the first, pantheism and transcendentalism (of which Christianity was the most popular form) being later, and partial, forms.[28] The earliest religious thinking, according to Benamozegh, forged an immanentist idea of the relationship between God and the world, and creation—this is another trait typical of kabbalistic theology, the *Zohar* in particular—was in reality the act whereby the world was drawn out of chaos rather than constructed ex nihilo.[29]

> Popular monotheism . . . was more complete and absolute in Christianity than in Judaism itself, for it is principally to Christianity that we owe the dogma of ex nihilo creation, which, when taken literally, is the most rigid form of monotheism.[30]

The pairings Occident = transcendence and Orient = pantheism may be called ethnopsychological. Hartmann uses almost precisely the same terms and reaches the same conclusion, writing of the religion of the future as a synthesis of Oriental pantheism and Occidental monotheism;[31] he criticizes the transcendency of the Judeo-Christian tradition as ill-equipped to slake the thirst of the religious soul. He even coined a definition Benamozegh would take up years later, talking of "pantheist monism" and "immanent monotheism."[32] The German's philosophy, however, was close to an impersonal pantheism from which the Italian was quick to distance himself.

Viewing the world as in a sense participating in the divinity naturally raised the problem of plurality within unity.[33] It should be remembered that from as early as the thirteenth century many Jewish thinkers believed one of the main reasons Kabbalah was mistrusted was its multiplicity of *sefirot*, which could easily be taken for deities.[34] Like the other Kabbalists, Benamozegh addressed this central question. His thinking on the subject ensued almost entirely from his interpretation of the word *Elohim*—God—expressed in the plural in the Bible and the phrase *Elohei ha-Elohim*, God of gods.

Having explained the first of these forms (*Elohim*) in the traditional way, as attributes of God that act without impinging on his unitary nature,[35] he went on to focus on the second form (*Elohei ha-Elohim*), which he understood thus:

> It is a matter of a superior unity, and plurality within that unity, which in no way diversifies it; a unique God and his attributes, which are to a greater or lesser extent realized in the universe, beings compared one to another, ideas in relation to God who is the Being of beings, the Consciousness of consciousnesses who, when he speaks to them, does not leave His own self.[36]

This theological commentary was based, among other things, on juridical considerations in the wider sense: the prohibition on blaspheming any divinity is explained by the presence of truth—and thus of God—that is found alongside error in every object of worship.[37]

In support of this idea, Benamozegh cited Yosef Gikatilla's *Sha'arei orah* (*Gates of Light*), a key text of late-twelfth-century Castilian Kabbalah, though he was forced to stretch his interpretation a little. The names of the pagan gods harbored within them a spark of holiness, and their truth—while relative—was confirmed by the power contained in the words *elohim aherim*, the other gods.[38] "For Israel," wrote Benamozegh, "the gods of the nations, while not properly speaking false gods or vain idols, since each represents in their eyes an aspect or attribute of the true god, were nonetheless false insofar as they were incomplete." True monotheism consists in the conjunction of these elements into a single, supreme divinity.[39]

Benamozegh's unity-multiplicity principle allowed him to justify his central idea of the coexistence of immutability and progress. He applied it to science in the following, remarkable terms: science can have meaning only if we accept the stability of its principles, which are pure, absolute, and thus distinct from the multiform and variable matter to which they apply. Yet, matter is not lowly and contemptible, verging on nonbeing as held to be the case by the most extreme Platonic doctrine, but it has dignity; nature deserves the love due to realities from which God has not divided himself. Idealism and empiricism are both true and are reconciled in the Kabbalistic emanationist doctrine Benamozegh considered "complete Judaism."[40]

The core exposition of this emanationist monotheism is of a social order. It concerns the relationship of Israel to the nations, and the nations among themselves; it is also the feature of Benamozegh's work that had the greatest success, removed from its theological context.[41]

The concept of the "genius" or "spirit of the people"—*Volksgeist* in German—so widespread in the historical and philosophical discourse of the nineteenth century[42] is here treated from a Kabbalistic perspective, and expanded upon. The genius of the people is seen as corresponding to the *sar*, the angel or minister responsible—according to the *Midrash* and the *Zohar*[43]—for the government of each nation. These *sarim* are, in the original interpretation, nothing more than different aspects of the idea of God. Benamozegh does not hesitate to understand the "soul of a given people" as meaning "the idea each people has of God" and more: its God.[44] The conclusion to be drawn is fairly simple: the gathering—not, note, the union—of the various peoples leads to the reunification of God, the idea of whom had been fragmented. This was a modern interpration of a key Kabbalistic idea.[45]

The multiplicty of nations was no obstacle to humanity's unity—quite the opposite. Benamozegh extolled multiplicity and plurality, contending that with regard to the immaterial, unlike the workings of matter, unity is all the more perfect the greater the number of its elements, for then it links that many more details together. The various nations are only the "scattered members of the first man" in the same way as the various religions are the "fragmentation of the idea of God."[46] The original light is lacking movement; the white light of "pure monotheism," though blinding, is lacking life:

> Rays fall on the various ethnographic states which are like a prism, refracting and splitting up colors, which are the divine attributes; without the prism all the different shades would not be visible and there would only be the white light of pure monotheism.[47]

The rays in question are those of the God of Israel, who is at once national and universal. Judaism is a national religion at the same time as a universal one: Israel is the firstborn in the family of peoples, all of whom are necessary to reconstitute the original unit, it is the priest of nations, as specifically stated in the Bible: its function is to disseminate the religion that will enable all the peoples to rediscover their unity without losing their individuality.

Israel is thus figured as the *primus inter pares*, and its primacy resides solely in religious genius. Other peoples, other races, have different, but not lesser, tasks in the harmonious coexistence of humanity. Benamozegh distances himself as much from Jewish exclusivism—expressed, amongst other places, in large sections of the Kabbalistic literature, where Israel was seen as inherently superior to all other people because it was closer to God—as he did from the "Aryan" European triumphalism voiced by Renan. This position he rebuts not with Luzzatto's idea of *alternation*, but with his own concept of *articulation*.

The Semitic and Indo-European (he called it "Japhetide," after Japheth, the brother of Shem) spirits were complementary rather than antithetical: true progress would come about through their harmony in the same way that theoretically all movement—the prerogative of the Japhetides—requires a stable anchoring point. The Semites, as the "people of axioms,"[48] were able to provide this support.

The idea of the divinity of the people had already been made central in the thinking of the philosopher Nahman Krochmal (1785–1840) in his major work *Moreh nevukhei ha-zeman* (*The Guide of the Perplexed of Our Time*). In a theoretical system that borrowed from Hegel's philosophy of history, Krochmal introduced to Jewish thought the notion of *Volksgeist* or "the spirit of the people," literally rendered as *ruah ha-umah*. The picture he paints of the historicity of "the spirit of the people" applied to all nations except Israel: while they were subject to growth, achievement, and decline, Israel perdured without being profoundly affected by historical process. The reason for this was that the "spirits" of other nations were but a partial reflection of the Spirit while Israel had been bequeathed the Absolute Spirit that could never be invalidated.

It is interesting to note that Krochmal, taking justification from Hegel, made—as Benamozegh would also do later—an immediate shift from "the spirit of a people" to "the God of a people,"[49] whom he identifies with the *sar*, the prince or guardian angel. Krochmal's Hegelianism is as clearly, though less overtly, inspired by the conceptual world of Kabbalah as Benamozegh's thinking was. He wrote, for instance, that the partial divinities were "inscribed in God";[50] he gave a Hegelian-Kabbalistic reading to the word *shekhinah*, taking it to mean "living God" (*El hai*) and also, it should be noted in passing, understood the *sod* or deep meaning of the Kabbalistic tradition as the true, rational meaning. Even the expression "God of gods" (*El Elohim*), so crucial to Benamozegh, is explained by Krochmal as a description of an absolute rationality that unites within it all the various partial rationalities.[51]

Despite their points of similarity, the forty or fifty years separating the new *Guide of the Perplexed* and *Israel and Humanity* are plainly visible. Krochmal's eternal people (*'am 'olam*)—historic people arrangement applied to the whole of Jewish history (biblical and postbiblical)—and Hegelian categories of becoming were obviously part of it.[52] His providential view of history is obvious; in his thinking modern philosophy serves the purposes of apologia. In the fast secularizing western Europe of the late nineteenth century, Benamozegh could not allow himself to affirm such clear certainties or to support such marked particularism, and his terms and aims were of necessity more nuanced.

It must be added that Hegel's influence on Benamozegh was also fairly strong, but in his case it was combined with that of evolutionism, which at the time set the tone for scholarly research in fields far beyond the scientific. It was, obviously, evolutionism extracted from its original context and applied to an idealistic philosophy: Benamozegh was, and would always remain, antipositivist.[53] Thus, he took the Kabbalistic concept of *berur* (choice, selection) as neither more nor less than the gradual selection and assimilation by Israel of the sparks of truth to be found in other civilizations.[54] He stated this explicitly: "*Berur* is natural selection."

As for *'ilui*, elevation, this is translated as "movement and evolution":[55] "Evolution, being natural, organic growth, is orthodox and right."[56]

There is thus a fundamental unity between pantheism, polytheism, and monotheism: whoever expresses the harmony between them is simply translating an ancient principle of Hebraic theology into philosophical terms.[57] It is therefore clear that the task undertaken by Benamozegh—the philosophical adaptation of Kabbalistic doctrine—had a religious as well as a critical or scholarly purpose.[58]

This is the key to understanding the astounding, out-of-context dec-laration in another of Benamozegh's books, *Ta'am le-Shad*[59] (intended as a refutation of Luzzatto's arguments concerning Kabbalah), which draws a parallel between the material progress of modern civilization and the dis-semination among the Jews of the most intimate secrets of the Torah.

It is an idea that comes up time and again in *Israel and Humanity*, in a context that extends beyond the Jews. For the Kabbalists, Benamozegh reminds us, the secret doctrines will be revealed fully, and to all, in the era of the Messiah, when it will be time to teach the religion to all nations and reconcile the religious spirit of Jews and Aryans. The very notion of progress, articulated and nuanced, is thus at work, even in that most appar-ently refractory of fields, the esoteric.

Hidden Anthropomorphism

Feuerbach's Reasons

One of Benamozegh's greatest contributions to religious criticism was probably his identification of two levels within Judaism, which had different characteristics. The first—public—level presented itself as absolute monotheism and purest unity. The second—esoteric, hidden, and reserved for the deepest minds—allowed a certain degree of pluralism. In the Holy of Holies, the most hidden part of the Temple, were the two cherubs whose wings topped the holy Ark: the most secret part of the place where all images were strictly forbidden thus harbored anthropomorphic figures.

This was but one indication, though perhaps the most eloquent, of the existence of representation, of a veritable mythology even, within Judaism, wherein the biblical personification of the divine was a "prelude," and the "vast, bold" symbology of Kabbalah a logical development.[1]

On this matter, Benamozegh noted that Jewish doctrines were very definitely the opposite of pagan ones. The latter destined unity to the deeper level, and heterogeneous developments of mythology to the outer face, to serve as a sort of popular religion. The Jews on the other hand presented themselves as the champions of absolute monotheism while retaining anthropomorphism and pluralism (though, naturally, within a context of unity) as an esoteric doctrine, a secrecy explained by the extreme complexity and sensitivity of certain ideas.[2]

In fact, there is no contradiction between the highest degree of abstractness and figurative language. Benamozegh wrote in his youthful work *Eimat mafgia*[3] that the more abstract the idea, the more down-to-earth the description of it must necessarily be. Words thus displaced from their original meaning evoke the realities of another level, but this should not be confused with the allegorical, unambiguous, artificial explanations of philosophical exegesis. The point is to discover how far the material quality of the reference affects the true meaning, which is intended to be devoid of all materiality. In this regard, it may be profitable to examine the thinking of Ludwig Feuerbach.

Benamozegh's Kabbalistic training, with its legacy of an anthropomorphism not rejected outright as it was in the philosophical tradition, naturally drew him to explore the German philosopher's work. The ensuing encounter of materialist philosopher and Kabbalistic rabbi threw up interesting, and occasionally surprising, results.

Benamozegh identified two of Feuerbach's central statements regarding religion, and summarized them thus: (1) "God is man himself as deified by man; the typical man, interior, perfect, ideal, . . . the shadow of earthly man seen in heaven through the effects of a psychological illusion"; (2) This illusion disappears and yields to reality "as progress reveals man more fully to himself."[4]

It was not hard to examine—and invert—Feuerbach's intent. It involved using his acknowledgment of the real, universal presence of the religious phenomenon as ulterior confirmation of a historical-positivist argument. The facts are there, runs the classic argument: the idea of the divine is universally borne witness to, and that in itself can be seen as a proof, albeit not definitive, of the reality of the divine. The question of how and why the idea of the divine occurred is a secondary one, being a matter for a posteriori explanation with no incidence on the value of the argument.

How he goes on to analyze the first assertion is, in contrast, fairly astounding. The very core of Feuerbach's criticism, the anthropomorphic nature of this idea of the divinity, does not bother Benamozegh at all. On the contrary. He himself unhesitatingly confirms that man cannot fail to have a human image of God, whether arrived at through rational thought or spontaneous intuition. Benamozegh obviously derived his daring notion from the anthropomorphic symbolism of Kabbalah, with its quasi-paradoxical images that seem at first glance to run directly counter to the horror of images expressed in the philosophico-theological tradition.

Having admitted this much, it is hardly surprising that he should take the apparent paradox still farther in examining the second part of Feuerbach's thesis, which concerns the gradual disappearance of the objectified illusion we call God, and its "reabsorption" into a purely human context. The man of the future will no longer need God, according to Feuerbach, because he will have located within himself what he had formerly projected outward as an ideal image.

But, asks Benamozegh, who is this man of the future posited by Feuerbach? Is he not the fully "realized" individual whose potentialities have been enacted? In Benamozegh's terminology this is man-species, the ideal everyman as opposed to the individual, precisely because "[t]he *idea* of God is the revelation of the species to the individual."[5]

It is an extremely strong statement. It makes the individual who has fulfilled his every potential, and lost all individuality, coincide with the *idea* of God. The theoretical justification lies in the fact that for this person "not only his model, but also his beginning and his end"[6] is found in God. The audaciousness of this extended anthropomorphism or, if one prefers, this divinification of humankind, is confirmed by his definition of revelation: "in a literal sense, revelation of the man-species—potential and 'metexic'—to the individual, the 'mimetic.' "[7] Man sees his human destiny in divine revelation: put another way, the realized man is the *image* of God.

Yet, despite appearances, the meaning and intentions of Benamozegh and Feuerbach remained diametrically opposed.[8] Feuerbach's entire position is turned upside-down in its turn: the "illusion of theology" is not refuted as fact but reinterpreted as the essential, insurmountable frontier of the human perception of God. Moreover, God revealed himself in human guise ("In Biblical theophany, God has a predilection for the human form").[9]

The reduction of theology to anthropology was in Benamozegh transformed into the deduction of theology through anthropology: the ideal man was the highest testimony to God; immanence—once again—was not the end point so much as the route to transcendence. This is what Benamozegh called a kind of "divergent" or "inverted symmetry" between the reduction of God to his human truth, and the necessarily anthropomorphic nature of revelation. On one hand the relative terms are unified downward, on the other, upward.

Furthermore, from another angle the alterity of man/God is maintained, since divine revelation in human form is nothing more than a manifestation that refers back to an unknown and unknowable essence: similarly, realized man is not God but his image. Feuerbach's position, in contrast, could be entirely summed up in the movement toward unity he called "authentic identity":

> We will not obtain true, autarkic unity of the divine and human essences unless . . . we recognize anthropology itself as theology. At the root of any identity that is not an authentic identity, unity with oneself, there remains divorce and separation into two, insofar as at the same time the identity is, or rather, ought to be suppressed.[10]

Feuerbach's point of view may be interpreted as a new formulation, on a different level, of the classic pantheism/theism duality as, respectively, the spirits of identity and alterity.

Benamozegh's idea of divine revelation does not simply offer a vision of absolute alterity. In the traditional duality, for example, between *appearance* (for man) and *essence* (in itself) the first term retains a degree of positiveness. The human nature of divine appearances depends not only on the intrinsic limitations to human understanding, but is also a deliberate choice operated by God himself, who thus reveals an aspect of himself. Just as plurality is not the antithesis of divine unity properly understood, so sensory understanding is an instrument, albeit an infinitely inadequate one, of man's understanding of God.

From Lamentations of Exile
to a Sense of Mission

In 1889 Adolphe Franck gave a lecture to the *Societé des Etudes Juives* in which he clearly delineated the issues involved in the polemic surrounding pantheism. The French philosopher primarily stressed the moral consequences of such thinking, employing the traditional argument that good and evil are meaningless if the unique God-world substance is dominated by necessity. Franck was thinking principally of the moral, and hence political, indifferentism that would stem from modern pantheism. The pessimism of such an illustrious example as Schopenhauer, for instance, resulted in passivity with respect to crucial choices such as that between freedom and "vile Caesarism."[1]

It followed that Judaism's contribution to world civilization resided mainly in the metaphysical basis it offered for freedom, responsibility, and—ultimately—human dignity—through its proclamation of monotheism, of faith in one free God who created man in his own image.[2]

The conclusion of his great work on Kabbalah—as well as his justification for the choice of what was not at the time a particularly prestigious subject, in Jewish or non-Jewish scholarship—was the same. Through its doctrines and its support of rational research when the dogmatism of faith was becoming increasingly prevalent, Kabbalah deserved a place of honor in the history of universal thought.[3]

Franck's Judaism was thus fairly close to the ideals of the 1789 French Revolution, the centennial of which was then being celebrated, in a more moderate version suited to the style of the Third Republic. A doctrine based on reason and progress, it was not to be confused with the political or "*événementielle*" history of the Hebrews, even in their better times.

In the course of a quick comparison between Christianity and Judaism, he added one interesting detail: the former, he wrote, had a marked tendency toward mysticism and outpourings of the soul that were not always in balance with the requirements of life, society, or the family.

These convictions were certainly shared by Benamozegh, his contemporary, who was also a liberal. When the opportunity presented itself,

Benamozegh did not skimp on similar declarations, whether issued from the lectern or in occasional writings. He welcomed the formation in 1847 of a civil guard recruited from the citizenry, which represented a major step toward liberal reform.[4] His funeral oration on the death of Victor Emmanuel II, the first king of a unified Italy, was warmer than rhetorical convention required, extolling the man and the establishment of a state born of a struggle against oppression.[5] We have already commented on similar a position taken up in *Morale juive et morale chrétienne*; we should, in addition, remark the notion that Judaism was synonymous with tolerance, and that the few intolerant ideas found in Maimonides came from Islam instead.

The similarity ends there, however. Faced with the same problems as Franck, Benamozegh tends to subject them to immediate philosophical analysis, dissecting them to find their theoretical basis. Political polemic is rare in his writing, a fact that probably owes more to his distance from lively political debate than to his position as a rabbi.

Benamozegh can be seen—at least from the 1860s onward—as having belonged by choice to the French intellectual world. It was through learned French journals that he kept abreast of the cultural scene, and most of his allusions were to French philosophers. Moreover, it was French institutions—both Jewish and non-Jewish—such as the *Alliance Israélite Universelle* and the *Ligue de la Paix*, that gave public recognition to his work.[6]

We have seen that, as he applied himself to a seriously ambitious project, he gradually abandoned first Hebrew, then Italian, as a written language: all his last works were in French. Yet, he did not live in France. The isolation he had felt in his youth could not fail to become more intense. It is therefore unsurprising that themes that readily lent themselves to ethical or political discussion became, in Benamozegh's hands, primarily theoretical. In a sense, isolation made abstraction easier. The relativism that worried him was, as we have seen, more that of ideas than of morals or politics. A few crucial aspects of Spinozism or Hegelianism are examined in a theoretical way, while the political applications are almost entirely ignored. The same is true of his comparative study of Judaism and Christianity, which should—in principle—have dealt with ethical concerns but where, a number of apologetical considerations aside, the core of the work, and the part that was obviously of greatest interest to the author, was metaphysical. It should also be noted that his program of a "Religion of Humanity" centered around theological definitions and distinctions of the greatest subtlety.

Ethical and political references are therefore rare in Benamozegh's work, though this was not apparent from his literary beginnings.

At the age of sixteen, and already demonstrating an admirable mastery of Hebrew and Aramaic, Benamozegh wrote an introduction to *Maor va-*

shemesh, a book by his uncle and teacher, Yehudah Coriat. Drawing, naturally, on a reservoir of stereotypical expressions, he chose—significantly—to end on an invocation to God, imploring him to turn his face toward the people of Israel suffering in exile.[7]

Nir le-David, his commentary on the Psalms, which was probably composed before he was twenty, abounds in ardent moral declarations. In typical moralist rhetoric, he warns against thinking excessively about forbidden things, which can lead to a degree of familiarity with them, and hence to moral barriers being breached in practice.[8] He also describes sin as insinuating itself into men's hearts, and pushing them to deny the existence of God, of whom all men have an instinctive idea.

The young Benamozegh's political statements are even more astonishing. Livorno, despite its relative decadence, was still a front-ranking port city and commercial center;[9] and, above all, he was a member of a community that had, from its foundation two hundred and fifty years earlier, enjoyed a level of freedom and privilege almost unique in Christian Europe.[10] Yet, on several occasions[11] he describes the condition of the Jews as that of a community living in exile, and subject to external authority. His descriptions could even be somewhat dramatic.

> During the Babylonian exile, the Jews were not the target of mockery as they are now, when shame follows all those who bear the name.[12]

The Gentiles, he wrote in introduction to another psalm, do not allow us to organize our arguments to prove the existence of God.

Such extreme positions were undoubtedly the result of the author's youth and "foreign" origins. Indeed, to study his development is to do no more than delineate the transformation of a North African Jewish mentality into that of European "modernity." He was not surrounded by any particular animosity toward Jews (certainly less than had existed in previous eras), and religious oppression was no more than a faint, if nightmarish, memory.

This young, largely self-taught scholar then threw himself passionately into the intellectual world that was opening to him, though from his background he always retained the Kabbalistic heritage, and a "political" notion of Israel that set him apart from most of his contemporaries.

Livorno was his home, rather than being a staging post on the road to Jerusalem, as it was for so many other Moroccan scholars, of whom the most famous was Hayyim Ben Attar;[13] Italy was always his country, and cultured Europe his chosen land. Yet, his attitude to the Holy Land was a far cry from the scarcely marked indifference of those Jews who were increasingly becoming "Israelites" who wanted to be seen as professing a faith—occasionally reduced to a specific set of moral values or simple monotheism—and who set all nationalistic ideas aside.

In *Ta'am le-Shad*—published in 1863—Benamozegh stressed the profoundly political, national idea of Israel. It was what, in his view, explained the relative lack of theological development in Jewish civilization, concentrating as it did on laws intended to regulate normal political life, even in exile. This inevitably appears perfectly commonplace to the modern reader, but at the time it was something of an exception: the political characteristics of Judaism were seen at most as vestiges of the past, and Israel's survival relied on its contribution to Western culture. Franck's famous remarks expressed a fairly widespread view.

Benamozegh's position in the 1860s was devoid of any polemical spirit: the lamentations of exile lay far behind him. Indeed, in the commentary to the Torah *Em la-Miqra* he came around to the more general view that held the dispersal of the Jews to have been providential for all mankind. The peoples who came into contact with the Jews would, he wrote, glossing Genesis XXIV: 14, get an opportunity to encounter the authentic religious spirit they represented.[14]

In *Israel and Humanity* he emphasized the "internationalism" of the Jewish people,[15] who through their exile incorporate the fragments of truth disseminated among the nations.[16] In a remarkable passage, he clarifies this notion of internationalism—or cosmopolitanism—and gives a common idea a religious connotation.

> The commercial cosmopolitanism with which Israel is often reproached, and the internationalism in the worst sense of the word, for which, in the persons of the two leaders of that doctrine, Marx and Lassalle, both of whom were born Jews, it has proved the inspiration, and with which it has been reproached as a crime, are no other than a misapplication, in one case incomplete and materialistic, and in the other, misinterpreted and monstrous, of its true universal mission. The former is merely the image of a higher, more fecund cosmopolitanism of ideas, and the latter—international socialism—is simply a crude counterfeit of the international [religious] alliance which it is called upon to realize.[17]

It is true that in his commentary on Deut. XXVIII: 65, where the text speaks of the daily terror that will assail the Jews during their exile, Benamozegh quotes and agrees with the interpretation offered by the Italian Jewish scholar Isaac Samuel Reggio (1784–1855). This is somewhat unusual, as he is generally harsh in his criticism of Reggio: the difficulties and hardships are sent to stop the Jews from forgetting their task and assimilating with the other peoples. This is perhaps because the tone of his Hebrew writing differs greatly from that of his Italian and French works, since there he allows himself to place far greater emphasis on the superiority as well as the specificity of Jewish doctrines, if not the Jewish people.

In any case, even—or possibly all the more for—keeping this distinction in mind, there is a clear change from the writing of his youth. For all that he retained his own specific character, and his "dual language" (one for the "exterior," the other for within the group)—though the gap between them gradually narrowed—Benamozegh's trajectory was one of cultural adaptation. As an adolescent he wrote, "The nations feed on the spiritual treasures of Israel as bees suck flowers to make their honey."[18]

Nearly forty years later, his conception was universalist, one of peoples marching together toward a gradually revealing truth. In this vision, Israel held a prestigious, though not an exclusive, role in a family of peoples of equal dignity.

Philology and Philosophy

HEBREW: A PERFECT LANGUAGE?

For a Jewish thinker, and a Kabbalist moreover, issues of language were strictly related to the subject of Hebrew in particular. Linguists and philosophers of Christian languages had long admitted—with a few subtle variations—that Hebrew was the language of creation. Adam, who gave things their names, spoke Hebrew;[1] all languages could therefore be seen as corruption of, or moving away from, the *ydioma hebraicum*, beginning with the events of the Tower of Babel.[2]

In the sixteenth century, the Mantuan rabbi David Provenzali wrote a book (now lost) entitled *Dor ha-pelagah* (The Generation of Dispersion), in which he listed two thousand Hebrew words he claimed formed the basis for an equal number of Latin, Greek, and Italian words. It was still possible to present a thesis on *Hebrea est Linguarum Mater*[3] at Harvard of 1642. Gradually however, in the eighteenth, and above all the nineteenth centuries, linguistic nationalism and the study of a large number of languages with no possible resemblance to Hebrew contributed to dispatching the Hebrocentric theory to the purgatory of mythological belief.

Yet, in the middle of the nineteenth century, and in spite of the advances in comparative linguistics of which he was perfectly aware, a Jewish scholar such as Isaac Samuel Reggio continued to support the primacy of Hebrew.[4]

Reggio, who lived in Gorizia (Friuli), was a protagonist of the Jewish European Enlightenment movement, the *Haskalah*.[5] Like many Italian Jews, he was extremely well versed in the fields of linguistics and philosophy (his work includes an Italian translation of the Torah accompanied by a literal commentary in Hebrew).[6] He was known—and criticized—in scholarly Orthodox Jewish circles for the positions he took on the validity of the oral tradition: by emphasizing its historical, contingent character, he lodged a challenge to what he took to be an immovable dogmatism that endangered the future of Judaism.[7]

71

Reggio did, however, take a traditionalist approach to the matter of linguistics.

> The destiny of Hebrew is unlike that of any other language, which latter have been produced by men, and forged according to the need to communicate their intentions. To begin with, these languages lacked order, and had small vocabularies, but they grew richer over time, lexically as well as syntactically and pragmatically, and have now reached the stage of perfection in which we know them today. One only has to think of the original forms of Greek and Latin to see how poor they were and how many shortcomings they had.
>
> The fate of our holy language is the opposite: it had no infancy with [the attendant] shortcomings, but from its birth was fully formed and perfected. The first book written in the language was by far the most accomplished, and from it the grammatical rules were drawn that we still use today. Hebrew's destiny was the opposite of other languages': while they became perfected, it gradually slipped from excellence. Each generation lost many words, and even the meanings of a number of roots.
>
> Any sensible person must be surprised and wonder, "What is the reason for this difference?" Since this is an exception to the natural order of things, we can only answer by saying that the sacred language is not of human manufacture, but preceded the creation of the world: God spoke it from the beginning and taught it miraculously to the first man. . . .
>
> From all these examples we may conclude that Hebrew words do not resemble those of any other language, for they are alive, and God is in them.[8]

Even Moses Mendelssohn, who was the perfect authorial reference for Reggio, did not go so far in the characterization of the uniqueness of Hebrew. In the introduction to his 1873 Torah commentary, while he affirmed the superiority of Hebrew over the other languages, the German philosopher attributed it not to its *essence*, but rather to the fact that God had chosen it to speak to Adam, the Patriarchs, and Moses, at the promulgation of the Law.[9] It was thus its sacred usage that had made it special. This argument, by redefining the privileged status of Hebrew as one of the unfathomable choices of God, was an acknowledgment that languages were all equal from a human point of view. Science therefore could, and should, make no distinction.

The position of the rationalist—and in some ways "modernist"—Reggio on this subject was thus more traditional than his model's, as well as surprisingly extreme. To understand it, one must surely bear in mind the traditional veneration for Hebrew on the one hand, and an awareness that the language was one of the most distinctive, significant, and fragile elements of a minority culture on the other: in Reggio's day, Hebrew was rapidly disappearing as a basic part of the Italian Jewish community's repertoire of knowledge. This is nonetheless—certainly on a first reading—not enough to dissipate the impression that Reggio's remarks were resolutely naïve, out of their time, and dictated by primarily apologetic considerations. His discourse mixed empirical observation and theological explanation, which negated any scientific credibility he might have had. However, if the linguistic developments of the period are taken into consideration, this opinion must be mitigated.

The publication by Friedrich Schlegel (1772–1829) in 1808 of *Über die Sprache und Weisheit der Indier* confirmed and accelerated the "discovery of Sanskrit" that had so fascinated cultured Europeans at the end of the previous century. This work, rich in occasional linguistic observations, followed a pattern typical of a certain current of Romantic thought: it harked back to a past—often poorly understood, and virtually fabulous—against the grandeur of which the modern age could be measured, and which could serve as the inspiration for renewed progress. In this conceptual framework, Sanskrit as the oldest language appeared the most regular, effective, and poetic. According to Tzvetan Todorov, "the historian of languages could only relate their decline."[10]

As early as 1761 Adam Smith had distinguished between two kinds of primitive languages: "inflected" ones, in which the work order was free; and simpler, clearer, "uninflected" ones, where the meaning of the sentence came from the word order, which followed well-established rules. The evolution of languages, like that of machines, moved from complexity toward simplicity, but while machines became more perfect, languages became esthetically impoverished.[11]

From a purely conceptual point of view, Reggio's position resembled that of many a Romantically inspired linguist, though for him Hebrew took the place of Sanskrit in a schema of linguistic decadence. But the parallel ends when one examines the general project underlying that schema.

While for Schlegel and the other Romantic linguists alluding to the past was associated with the broadening of horizons necessary to forging a new Western cultural identity,[12] for the Jewish scholar this was *absolute* rather than functional: the past conferred confirmation and legitimacy on the traditional values of a minority. In other words, the formal reasoning of Schlegel and Reggio operated in the same way, but had different content.

The former used the idea of a great, perfect past to formulate a project: rediscovery was intended to lay the foundations for a new future. The latter saw the schema as the confirmation of a medieval, rabbinic philosophy of history that focused on lost perfection, to which he saw no remedy. In the context of linguistic theory is well visible the difference that separated the quest for identity of a European culture in a crisis of growing from the conservatism of a minority incapable of forming a project.

Some years later the grammarian, biblical scholar, and poet Samuel David Luzzatto eliminated discussion of the particular character of Hebrew from his field of study as being superfluous, or even injurious.

While overtly giving himself the task of defending and illuminating the Jewish tradition, Luzzatto had no prejudices in the scientific sphere. He did not accept the hypothesis of the particularity of Hebrew, and still less its status as the original language.[13] In the introduction to his *Prolegomeni ad una grammatica*,[14] Luzzatto restricted himself to expressing a theory of a unique original idiom, probably unwritten, and close to onomatopoeia: a sort of shared mother-language, largely biliteral and monosyllabic, that evolved slowly from a natural to an artificial character expressed in triliteral forms.[15]

This monogenetic linguistic theory did not stop him reacting skeptically to the work of his disciple Graziadio Isaia Ascoli (1829–1907), the founder of scientific comparative linguistics in Italy, which sought to prove strong, close links between "Aryan" and "Semitic" languages. Luzzatto remained hostile to this attempt at harmonization, which struck him as somewhat ideological and lacking in scientific basis.[16] Nor did he see the usefulness of the exercise, since the differences between the two main linguistic groups, as between the civilizations that expressed them, was a fact to be accepted and studied. His views, especially on history, were considerably affected by this idea.[17] According to Luzzatto, if connections existed, they were no more than a faint trace of the theoretical primordial unity of humankind: a shared root idea might produce similar words, as in the case of the Chaldean *'ith*, Hebrew *yesh*, Latin *est*, German *ist*, Greek *esti*, and Sanskrit *as*.[18]

Luzzatto also accepted the notion of a correspondence between phonemes and graphemes on the one hand, and elementary meanings on the other hand. This idea—within a totally different cultural frame of reference—was to be developed by Benamozegh.

HEBREW: A DEAD LANGUAGE?
THE POSSIBILITY OF MODERN HEBRAIC POETRY

In reality, no picture of Jewish intellectual production in Italy can fail to include an examination of the linguistic question. Alongside abundant poetic production, thinking about the language was continual, whether in the realms of poetics or philosophy of language, linguistics or grammar.

The direct heirs of the Spanish Jewish literature of the tenth to the fifteenth centuries, the Italian Jewish poets had in fact forged their Hebrew, and adapted it to the dictates of style and the reigning sensibility of the age, over a period of around six hundred years. This creative effort was always strictly coherent with the current movements in Italian poetry, from the sonnets of Immanuel of Rome, who "Hebraized" the *dolce stil novo*, to a eulogium to the art of Petrarch composed in the mid-nineteenth century.[19]

In the nineteenth century, poetry was still a preferred medium of expression for rabbis. There were a fair number of authors of unparalleled depth and sensitivity, who were also all capable of a remarkably rich style. It is not, therefore, surprising that in a time of crisis and questioning, the language was a major focus for concern.

In the introduction to his book of poems *Kinnor na'im*, Luzzatto stated that his work was set "in a far-off, and timeless land."[20] He defended himself in advance against any charge of literary ambition, since "what ambition might one harbor in a desert land?" A sort of cultural impotence can be discerned among Italian rabbis: their talent, and the subtlety of the devices they used, continued to be employed in a social terrain that had become unsuited to them.

For Luzzatto, language was not one manifestation of culture among many, but its very substance. In the case of Hebrew, the connection to the culture it expresses is so strong that the two ideas that for him characterized the Jewish religion, namely, compassion for one's neighbor and faith in divine reward, are *inherent* to the language. Luzzatto does not explain this statement, but draws a surprising conclusion from it. If you speak Hebrew, you end up absorbing these ideas. It was indeed Spinoza's good grasp of Hebrew that meant he was—although Luzzatto criticized his philosophy severely—not altogether a bad person.[21]

He noted very clearly the contrast between the rise of an increasingly avid European reading public, and the rapid desertion of Hebrew literature. It was obvious, he wrote, that a lack of understanding led to ignorance and alienation; many highly literate Jews were abandoning their traditional heritage not through choice, but through ignorance. This gave rise to the task (fraught with religious and national connotations) that he took upon himself: not limited to studying the language, he wanted to provide concrete examples: "What I propose to do is to wake my lyre and pour out my melodies, so that the beauty of the language of the Patriarchs may be recognized."

As he put it in a deeply sincere letter to Avraham Geiger, "Hebrew is my passion, and the resurrection of its literature the dream of my entire life."

Lelio Della Torre (1805–1871), a teaching colleague of Luzzatto at the Rabbinical College in Padua, and, like him, also a poet and scholar, did not share his voluntarism: he aimed above all to be a purist, and struggled to preserve "correct" language, which he also refused to admit should or might develop. For him, Hebrew was a dead language.

Oddly enough, Della Torre combined utmost conservatism with a certain creative daring. To begin with, he believed that the only true Hebrew was Biblical Hebrew. He was thus, in effect, following Judah ha-Levi when he affirmed that the meter being imposed on Hebrew poetry was entirely alien to the "genius" of the language, and a yoke that was destroying its beauty.[22] His later positions were more nuanced, as he came to accept the use of the meter of the Spanish classical age (Italian, and especially Ashkenazi, Hebrew poetry always struck him as irredeemably flawed); he himself composed in classical meters, and invariably used biblical vocabulary and forms. That did not prevent him from writing—ostensibly to demonstrate the enormous possibilities of that classical biblical language—modern, almost experimental poems, such as an amusing sonnet on the behavior of fashionable young things with reserved seats at clubs, theater-going ways, and novel-reading habits.[23] These snobs sported canes and yellow gloves, and mustaches that they were continually smoothing. The poem is a light example of linguistic adaptation that strictly adheres to tradition:[24] to give but a single illustration, the expression used to describe the mustache-smoothing gesture comes from a verse in the prophet Amos. The author himself draws attention to it in a note, and—in a gesture as funny as it is expressive of an attitude—adds an interpretation by the medieval commentator David Kimhi.

Despite these occasional outbursts, Della Torre did not believe in the dynamism of Hebrew. His purist vision was of a language that was now only literary: a magnificent, dead language like Latin. He seems to have been utterly ignorant of the pioneering experiments going on at the same time in eastern Europe, which would lead to a renaissance in Hebrew literature long before the achievement of the Zionist project. For a Western Jewish intellectual such as Della Torre, there was no future for Hebrew as a living language.[25]

Benamozegh did take a position on such crucial questions as the "particular" status of Hebrew and the theory of its exhaustion as a living language. In the first case he exposed, once again, his biculturalism. The second question allowed him to develop a theory of language consistent with the inspiration behind his thinking: it was a position that brought him close not only to Gioberti but also to another major figure in Italian philosophy, Giambattista Vico.

VICO AND THE ZOHAR

By the nineteenth century it was no longer possible to subscribe to an entirely "mimological" theory of language,[26] in which the relationship between words and things was *essential* rather than one of *convention*, though it was possible to discern an *organic* relationship between a people and a language. If every civilization left the trace of its worldview in its language, forgotten or corrupted cultures could be reconstructed from linguistic traces analyzed down to the smallest meaningful components—words. Giambattista Vico (1688–1744) had deduced a specific Italic metaphysics based on a few Latin keywords: the celebrated reciprocity, or "convertibility," of *verum* (the true) and *factum* (the made) led him to conclude that God was the primal truth, as he was the Prime Mover; from the indiscriminate use of *causa* and *negotium* (activity) he produced an equivalence between "proving through things" and "carrying out" from which he derived a metaphysics of equivalence between doing and knowing that stood in antagonism to Cartesian rationalism.[27]

Thus, Benamozegh followed in the steps of Vico, the *hoqer gadol*, the great scholar,[28] in the hard but necessary task of rediscovering an ancient theology by analyzing language. What Vico had done for the *antiquissima sapientia* of the Italic people, Benamozegh would attempt to do for the philosophy of the Hebrews—in other words, Kabbalah.[29]

It was, he wrote, a field that had been unexplored, or virtually so,[30] and could hold big surprises for scholars who dared to venture there: it was time the method was applied to the Science of Judaism. In a line of descent from Vico, and to a lesser extent Humboldt, Benamozegh was a philologist and linguist only insofar as those disciplines could offer a contribution to philosophy: the worldviews formed by populations were tucked away in the meaning of a verb; in the half-closed calyx of a word's etymology.

Language was the faithful reflection of metaphysics,[31] words are the result of sedimentation of ideas.[32] Benamozegh felt accordingly close to the likes of August Schleicher, Friedrich Max Müller, and all those Romantically inspired linguists who accepted the idea of language as a repository of culture: the definition of a term, to be true, needed to harmonize with the history of the concept of the thing being defined.[33] The list of words he considered liable to contain a metaphysical meaning was fairly long: for instance, the meanings of the Hebrew root '*ad* included beatitude ('*eden*), eternity ('*ad*), and adornment ('*ady*) and manifested the Jews' tendency toward metaphysics, whereas the Greeks associated adornment and the world (*kosmos*).[34] *Horef* meant at once "winter" and "youth"—opposites, the conjunction of which might suggest that true youth is the end of life, and thus raise the possibility of life after death.[35]

The proximity between the speech act and the sex act could be deduced from the dual meaning of *milah* (word and circumcision), and the phrase used by Moses—*'aral sefatayim* (with uncircumcised lips)—to describe difficulty in speaking. The relationship is confirmed by the juxtaposition in the *Sefer Yetzirah* between the fertilizing speech organ and the fertilizing biological organ.[36] Furthermore, Benamozegh called attention to the fact that real religious knowledge consisted in knowing the names of God, a formula that evoked the Talmudic "handing down of names,"[37] as well as the idea—familiar enough in Kabbalistic writing—that the text of the Torah was nothing other than a "theosophical novel," the real content of which was the enumeration of the names of God.[38]

The well-known passage from Exodus XXIV: 7, "All that the Lord hath spoken will we do, and hear," was read in the light of Vico's parallel between doing and understanding. Even the graphemes suggest a metaphysical interpretation: the *yod*, which in form suggests a period, and in esoteric terms corresponds to *sefirah malkhut* (a kind of *Natura naturans*), recalls the theory of "metaphysical points" and "metaphysical nature" devised by Vico.[39]

The eighteenth-century thinker's perspective, developed by the Romantics, constituted a perfectly adequate model for the linguistic sensibilities of a man whose thinking was shaped by the esoteric framework of Kabbalah. It essentially offered only the vaguest of inspiration, but the way Benamozegh combined modern linguistic and Kabbalistic examples went farther again, extending beyond words to individual letters. The example above is a highly "philosophical" one, but in other contexts he concentrated on a strictly grammatical level.

This hermeneutic daring—which harbored ambitions to truth, and was intended to be far more than preachery with pretensions to edification—can be defined by comparison with Samuel David Luzzatto's work of interpretation. Luzzatto had no hesitation about offering textual corrections even of the Bible, wherever he felt there were insurmountable linguistic contradictions, which was another kind of daring. Benamozegh respected the biblical text as inviolable down to the last detail,[40] and he used it as a basis for his flights of philosophy; Luzzatto the cultivator of plain meaning was willing to sacrifice that inviolability in the name of science.

For Kabbalistic exegesis in all its various forms, from the *Sefer Yetzirah* to the *Sefer ha-Bahir*, and from the writings of Avraham Abulafia to the *Zohar*,[41] not only words—the basic units of meaning—lent themselves to theological analysis, but their constituent phonemes and graphemes as well.[42] Benamozegh had immediately, spontaneously, found a modern way of presenting an ancient sensibility.

This later adaptation was developed in a dense response—in effect an essay—to the criticism of his former pupil, the positivist Orientalist David Castelli.[43] Castelli accused Benamozegh of making up fantastical etymologies with the sole intention of a posteriori justification of preformed philosophical ideas. According to him, the rabbi's approach was more like preacherly exegesis than it was scientific linguistic scholarship. Substituting and inverting root letters were techniques an elementary school pupil would mock in the light of lexicons and grammatical rules: in short, the need for "sublime metaphysics" was taking precedence over grammatical rules and factual analysis, which he ironically referred to as "trifles for the small-minded." Castelli was not alone to express such a judgment about Benamozegh's intellectual position. Other scholars, with a philological perspective, spoke privately in similar terms.[44]

Benamozegh's brilliant, scathing response was emblematic of his historicist mentality. It was based on the idea that normative lexicons and grammar were in fact designed for children, or those big children—positivists—who were happy to settle for results without knowing anything about the processes that led to them.[45] What use was it, he wrote, to pile up erudite details if the wider picture is lost from view? The goal and the means were not to be confused: in the history of philosophy, as in that of religion, philological work was necessary, but in the service of interpretation. What sense was there in meticulous research on the concept of God among ancient peoples if it did not help to answer the question, "What is God?"

At best, positivism produced sophisticated analysis; at worst, it made an exclusive cult of detail, and was above all hostile to synthesis: "It refuses to jump into a burning issue, but pokes around the edges, as though with tiny scissors."[46] It was an extremely convenient attitude: a sort of "philosophical chaise longue."[47]

Drawing on August Schleicher's classification of the stages in the development of all languages—monosyllabic, agglutinate, inflected—and occasional comments on Semitic languages by Ascoli, Benamozegh came to the conclusion that each element of a verbal root represented a very general idea. Primitive *sha*, which meant "put down in a stable way," had given rise to *shath* (to put), *sam* (idem, with the *shin* mutated into *sin*), *sham* (there), *shathol* (to plant, to install), *sheth* (behind, buttocks), *shath* (base, foundation), etc.[48] He thus found a justification for certain biblical etymologies: *Bavel* (Babylon) and *balal* (to confuse, to mix) were genuinely close, rather than naively, clumsily stuck together by the author of the biblical story about the confusion of languages. Likewise, Benamozegh suggested that the name of God, *Shadday*, had been inspired by *shadayim*, breasts, as the archetype of all the female, maternal divinities of antiquity. The grammarian theologian came up with numerous similar examples.

He attributed a general idea of relationship to the letter *vav*, which functioned grammatically as a conjunction, and according to the *Sefer ha-Bahir* served as an operator of metaphysical union between worlds (Guillaume Postel called this *copula universi* in his translation).[49]

It was a new form of concordism, where the terms were not modern science and biblical literal text but rabbinical theology (Kabbalah being seen as the true dogmatic content of traditional Judaism) and modern linguistics. This was hardly surprising, given that the underlying schema involved an original truth that well conducted research could not refute.

Certainly, this last manifestation of Kabbalistic language was not only the result of disinterested empirical research, but also represented a response to the need to accord language a weight of which it had been relieved by conventionalist doctrines. In this respect, Kabbalah offered a kind of privileged refuge, which was how—later—a poet such as Max Jacob could claim to be "a Kabbalist."[50] In Benamozegh we are witness to a would-be scientific approach that is completely at odds with any mystical attitude, and which demonstrates the persistence across time—as well as the plasticity—of certain conceptual frameworks, which manifested themselves in unexpected places.

It is nonetheless possible to formulate a theory of a partially "esoteric" attitude on Benamozegh's part. There is a short but astonishing note—in Hebrew, naturally—in his Biblical commentary *Em la-Miqra*:

> It is unnecessary to state that I will not claim that the origins of
> all languages lie in Hebrew, since modern linguists would deny
> the thesis. But we believers [*kat ha-maaminim*] do not need to
> hasten the end [*lidhoq eth ha-qetz*]. In any case time will show
> on which side the truth lies.[51]

The passage reveals a very different Benamozegh from the open, almost "ecumenical" character he shows himself to be in other works. His links with Italian and French philosophy seem to have been forgotten, ceding to a particularist faith that lacks only the objective conditions for displaying itself openly.

Yet, in the same text, and on the same subject (language), a number of small details—lapses, almost—offer a glimpse of a completely different orientation. *Em la-Miqra* was primarily intended for a Jewish readership, which allowed the author to use a tone he did not permit himself in his French and Italian writings. Despite that, in passages that are only a few lines apart, he writes of "our language" meaning Italian and "our alphabet" in reference to Hebrew.[52] This was no supporting reference in the manner of the Jewish exegetes who used phrases in the vernacular to aid their readers' understanding: it is an example of a genuinely dual sense of belonging. It explains the attempts—the validity of which does not concern us here—to show the similarities between Hebrew and Italian. He felt that the language of Moses, more than any other, had points in common with that of Dante, a theory that shows the extent to which the son of Moroccan immigrants, whose career had begun with a lament on the sufferings of exile, had been assimilated.

The Inevitable Choices of Nineteenth-Century Biblical Commentary

In view of the continuing progress in the moral and historical sciences, we do not despair of seeing criticism gradually leading theology to open up its texts to the primary conclusions it has drawn, thanks to those selfsame methods of free interpretation. So the empire of the supernatural, still further reduced by the progress of human reason, will see pass into the hands of science the remaining provinces so firmly and fiercely guarded by theology.

—Etienne Vacherot, *Revue des Deux Mondes*, 1868

We must no longer isolate ourselves from the great scientific movement that stirs souls in so many ways; Jewish Livorno can remain orthodox only by becoming scientific.

—Elijah Benamozegh, excerpt from the
Livorno rabbinical college study program

The nineteenth century produced a true revolution in respect for the reading of the Bible.[1] Darwinism on the one hand, and increasingly self-assured critical and philological sciences on the other, dealt severe blows to the unity and credibility of the Biblical account: the issue at stake was *inerrancy*, the revealed nature of the book that in Europe was still the ultimate point of reference for moral values, and theological as well as scientific ideas.[2]

The work of the Tübingen School and of Ernest Renan suggested a mythical reading of the biography of Jesus. In 1886 the transformation of the Sorbonne's faculty of theology into section V of the Ecole Pratique des Hautes Etudes marked the entrance of secular, scientific attitudes into the universities.[3]

In the Catholic and Protestant worlds, efforts were made to limit the "breaches in the walls of the citadel"[4] by partially opening up to new experience and relinquishing the requirement for absolute, incontestable, literal validity of texts. For the Catholic Church this primarily meant accepting that history and its instruments (linguistics, archaeology, etc.) offered substantial assistance in understanding the Scriptures, but it continued to stress the crucial division between sacred and secular hermeneutics: open scrutiny had limits that were inherent to the Bible itself. The Church's attitude toward critical-historical exegesis has been defined as "loving hatred."[5]

It is well known that Jews have no central religious authority to make decisions for the group. Responses to the challenge of "open scrutiny" were, therefore, individual ones. Here we will examine Benamozegh's position in its own right and in relation to various important Jewish exegetists of the time, S. D. Luzzatto in particular. Benamozegh's hermeneutics come through in several of his works, but by far the most important in that respect is the Torah commentary, *Em la-Miqra*.[6] Here we see again the mixture of modernity and hypertraditionalism that typifies Benamozegh's work, something that should not be a surprise coming from a man who was both one of Italy's last Kabbalists and the author of one of the first national projects for university (i.e., scientific) teaching in the history of religion.

In fact, it was more than a mixture: it was a harmony that had been studiously pursued. In an 1881 Hebrew text,[7] Benamozegh explored the position of Russian Jewry, and warned the community's spiritual and cultural leaders about apparent, purely external, harmony between traditional and modern knowledge. The Jews of Russia, he wrote, should take careful heed of the German experience that had resulted in widespread abandonment of religious practice, and themselves look for a deep harmony between Torah and the sciences.

The aims were obviously apologetic, since philological, archeological, and historical studies could only confirm the basic truths of the Torah and successfully repulse destructive critical attacks. However, the language used by Benamozegh affords a glimpse of a deeper, almost essential, level: science would provide a way of grasping the deepest, most hidden content of the Torah.

> Scholars need to hasten to reach the bottom of things. I was going to say, to get beneath the skin and draw out the sparks of the light of truth and holiness, by bringing back to the source of running water all the fragments of truth that have fallen into the well of the abyss.[8]

These Kabbalistic phrases probably express more than simple rhetoric: they allude, in effect, to the need to use modern scientific instruments to grasp the deeper, esoteric meaning of the Torah. Kabbalah and science thus came together in unprecedented concordism.

The argument was developed on unconsciously paradoxical lines: Benamozegh recommended Russia's rabbis, spiritual authorities, and Yeshiva directors, who had the responsibility for the cultural future of the world's largest Jewish community, to make unreserved use of the numerous contributions of non-Jewish (primarily Christian) scholars. The latter in particular shared many of the Jews' basic beliefs.

Once again Benamozegh gave the impression that despite his acute sense of history, his enthusiastic convictions outweighed his clear perception of reality.

The sustained comparative technique that demonstrated the truth of Kabbalistic doctrines, as well as the use of Christian authors, were salient characteristics of *Em la-Miqra*, a work unique in its genre.

AN ELOQUENT INCIPIT

The beginning of the Torah commentary is both astounding and instructive.[9] It is astounding because it begins with a quotation of a supposed Canaanite text and only starts interpreting the biblical verse half a page later. It is instructive because it contains within it almost all the elements to be found in the work. A closely argued whirl of ideas and quotations follow one another, on subjects such as mythology, linguistics, the *midrash*, the Talmudic glosses of Rashi and the Tosafists, Philo of Alexandria, the Greek versions of the Septuagint and the Gospels, ending with a reference to Gioberti.

The aim of the whole argument was none other than to demonstrate that the Kabbalistic interpretation of the opening verses of Genesis was not merely valid, but also rooted in deepest antiquity. It is worth summarizing: a very ancient Canaanite text mentioned by Azariah de' Rossi (sixteenth century) describes the coupling of a man called *Elohim* and a woman called *Bereshit* which results in the birth of a son, *Shamayim*, and a daughter, *Aretz*.

This, according to Benamozegh, was a deformation of the well-known Kabbalistic doctrine whereby *Reshit*—identified with *sefirah hokhmah*—and *Elohim*—*sefirah binah*—came together and gave birth to *Shamayim* and *Aretz*, the *sefirot tiferet* and *malkhut*. He went on to comment that the word *bara*, meaning to create, had its origins in *bar*, son, just as *banah*, to build, came from *ben*, also meaning son. In the Talmud, tractate *Megillah*, reference is made to a change in the order of the words in the Septuagint, to "God created in the beginning" from the "In the beginning God created" found in the original text. Rashi glosses this *in loco* as being because the translators wanted to avoid any danger of *Bereshit* ("in the beginning") being mistaken for a name, and that it is possible to interpret the passage as referring to the existence of two divinities. The Tosafists objected, saying such a phrase could never be taken for a name, and argued otherwise. Yet, the abundant testimony of Philo, the *Targum* of the Pseudo-Jonathan, and the *Midrash* confirm that primordial wisdom—*Hokhmah*—was called *Reshit*. This was what lay behind the prudence of the Septuagint in wanting to simplify the text to avoid delivering up to all and sundry such dangerous, profound doctrines, if it was for them to be misunderstood. The Canaanite author's mistake, in splitting the divinity in two, was repeated by Jesus, who defined himself in the Gospel of St John as *Reshit*. Gioberti confirmed the definition in his *Della Filosofia della Rivelazione*, to which he added an explanation worthy of his profound thinking.

In the page and a half long *incipit*, Benamozegh implicitly sets forth a series of basic ideas that can be listed as follows:

1. Kabbalah is an ancient doctrine from which numerous myths have—though deforming or "diminishing" it—been inspired;

2. linguistic research shows that the Kabbalah's ideas are contained in words: key philosophical concepts can be brought to light with judicious digging;

3. the translators of the Greek Bible were prudent, as were modern Kabbalists who avoided revealing the treasures of wisdom to "Christianizers" (*mithnatzrim*); hence Benamozegh's awareness of the proximity of Christianity to Kabbalah, and the dangers inherent in it. Luzzatto's jarring, ironic accusation—"*misticisti* (mystic Jews) = *gesucristi* (jesuschrists)"[10]—was addressed, and avoided;

4. Rashi, who knew nothing about Hellenic Judaism, nonetheless hit the target, despite the apparent "paradoxicalness" of his explanation and the "reasonable" objections of the Tosafists. The inevitable conclusion was that "he had the spirit of the Kabbalah in him."

This is well illustrated from the start, the frontispiece announcing a commentary based as much on philological and critical research as on the most recent studies of the dogmas of ancient peoples, and—naturally—on the rabbinic tradition.

Beyond the large number of elements brought together in a rather original manner, it must be noted that Benamozegh wanted to say some very old things in a modern tone. He explains the *incipit* to Genesis in the purest Kabbalistic tradition, but indirectly: rather than spelling out his ideas overtly, he prefers to show that such and such a doctrine or tradition attested to by scholarly research supports the plausibility and antiquity of Jewish esoterism.

It is as though the Biblical text is set at a distance, more surrounded by ideas than explained. The times encouraged restraint: indirect apologia—explanation through contextualization—replaced outright, upfront positive statements.

Six centuries earlier, Nahmanides had interpreted the first verse of Genesis in the same way, based on the dynamic of the *sefirot*. But he had been satisfied with relying on no support aside from the *midrash*, other biblical verses, and—above all—the oral tradition, thus remaining totally within the Jewish cultural space. He also hedged his argument around with innumerable precautions, "because it is dangerous to elaborate on this subject in writing." This approach was the opposite of the one taken by Benamozegh, who saw publicizing esoteric ideas as the only way of ensuring tradition survived.

Em la-Miqra is an extraordinary work. It is completely different from any of the other biblical commentary to come out of nineteenth-century Italy, which included Reggio's *Torath Elohim*, Luzzatto's *Ha-Mishtaddel*, and Moshe Yitzhaq Tedeschi (Ashkenazy)'s *Hoyil Moshe*, all of which drew on *peshat*, or literal meaning.[11]

Of the three, *Ha-Mishtaddel* is by far the most important. Benamozegh had neither the grammatical competency nor the literary sensibility, nor the enormous philological gift that enabled Luzzatto to address the Masoretic text by comparing the various manuscripts he owned.[12] It is also worth considering the two authors' work on Onkelos's Aramaic translation: compared to Luzzatto's *Oheb Ger*,[13] a methodical work of exemplary clarity, Benamozegh's *Ger Tzedek*[14] shows up poorly, even allowing for the fact that it is a juvenile work.

However, the latter's hermeneutic contribution should be sought in his philosophical and scientific interests, and in an openmindedness that Luzzatto in many respects lacked. The only *gematria*, or calculation of the numerical values of letters, to be found in Luzzatto's writing attacks "the Greek spirit," presented in his scheme as the great adversary to "the Jewish spirit." For him, *Yawan* (Greece) equaled *ruach ha-tummah* (spirit of impurity).[15]

As for the works by Reggio and Tedeschi, they are interesting (especially the former, a full Pentateuch commentary with an Italian translation), but at the end of the day have no ambition beyond helping the nonspecialist to read the Bible.

Despite the dimensions and the ambitiousness of the guiding project, *Em la-Miqra* failed to reach an audience, and elicited only a poor response. This was doubtless due to the miscellany of styles, which was also its originality.

The Kabbalists of the time were obviously not interested in Assyriology or Egyptology: names such as those of Vico or Renan—especially coupled with epithets such as "great philosopher" and "brilliant scholar"—were either unknown or downright suspect. The violent reaction of the rabbis of Aleppo and the more moderate one of their colleagues from Jerusalem (that will be analyzed below) are proof.

At the same time, what modern scholar was likely fully to appreciate this work? Even scholars favorable to the Livorno rabbi—Adolphe Franck, for example, or Avraham Berliner—could not fail to recoil from some of the affirmations scattered throughout *Em la-Miqra*: the superiority of Kabbalah, the uncompromising criticism of Christianity, etc. stood apart from his other French and Italian philosophical writings above all for a peremptory tone that contrasted with their more nuanced style of argument.

The commentary's typography should also be borne in mind. While in the Christian and independent arenas there was a trend toward general or partial introductions to the Bible (creating critical distance from the text and treating it as a subject for analysis), Benamozegh offered a specimen of classical commentary, following the text page by page, and—moreover—accompanying it with all the technical apparatus for synagogue reading.[16]

Economic reasons surely underlay this choice: Reggio and S. D. Luzzatto had already acknowledged how difficult they had found it to sell enough copies of their commentaries to cover printing costs.[17] Let us, then, imagine an ordinarily cultured western European Jew looking at one of the five volumes of *Em la-Miqra*. He would probably be looking for accessible explanations of difficult or controversial passages, sufficient to address the questions of the age. He would have found an erudite mixture of Kabbalah and comparative linguistics, combined with a knowledge of modern science and the history of ancient rites, all coherently organized and argued in a scholarly way. Too scholarly a way, as a matter of fact.[18]

CONDEMNATION FROM THE ORIENTAL RABBIS

The combination of an old form and modern content was also at the root of the categorical, adamant rejection by the rabbis of Aleppo and Jerusalem.[19] These representatives of an ultraconservative Judaism did not simply ignore the work; instead they condemned it with every stereotype the language of censure afforded them.[20] To these illustrious rabbis (including the incumbent Chief Rabbi of the Holy Land and his successor, as well as the head of the Beth-El group of Kabbalists in Jerusalem), the author of *Em la-Miqra* was a madman, a halfwit, a mixed-up atheist, a destructive spirit, and an insolent heretic, whose work needed to be burned. Whoever had a copy was to be looked upon as transgressing the biblical commandment, "Thou shalt not bring an abomination into thy house."

The reasons for this condemnation, contained in two letters dated 1865, can be summarized as follows.

To begin with, the author had found precedent for the laws of the Torah in the rites of the Egyptians and Canaanites, something that placed divine law on a footing with those of idolaters and reduced God to the level of a human legislator.

Secondly, he combined Kabbalah and mythology, thus culpably confusing the sacred and the profane, the holy and the impure.

Another grievance was the way the author gave the impression of taking Christian texts seriously, "which has never been seen in Israel! For him Kabbalists, Christians, and Egyptians are all one and the same thing, which deserves the reader's opprobrium."

Samuel David Luzzatto, who is mentioned—incidentally—in the letters, and thus associated with the condemnation, would not have had much time for this kind of remark, as he showed in similar circumstances. Benamozegh himself found the condemnation of the Holy City rabbis too painful, and wrote a long apology that extended over several supplements to the newspaper *Ha-Levanon*.[21] This "open letter" was a—failed—attempt to establish a rapport, though it was obviously a dialogue of the deaf. His tone is respectful; it is worth noting that a number of Jewish authors cited here as part of Benamozegh's self-defense are mentioned nowhere else in his work, a fact that demonstrates both his desire for orthodoxy and the size of his library.

Benamozegh claimed a place for himself among the champions of orthodoxy, but his arguments were far from standard. They drew on the respective value of sacred and secular studies. He responded to the Aleppo and Jerusalem rabbis who reproached him for using secular subjects to demonstrate religious truths by suggesting that this was a matter of tactics. He wrote that, ideally, a man would concentrate fully on studying Torah, but in view of the age being lived through, it was urgent to become informed on secular subjects, to be ready with a defense against the "vain doctrines" of the West. He defined this approach as pedagogical: a young man who studied Torah and science separately, without looking for harmony between them, would expose himself to the torments of doubt, on recognizing the contradictions between the two cultures, inevitably rejecting the one that was weaker from the standpoint of underlying "social discourse": in other words, the Torah.

At the same time as he called the rabbis of Jerusalem "[a]ngels and priests, all holy, etc.," Benamozegh alluded to their lack of experience: they were unaware of the cultural risks inherent in a clash between the traditional world and the West, as Eastern culture was holy, but weak in objective terms. He therefore took upon himself the task of raising the alarm and suggesting the cure that was needed. There is no lack of ambiguity in the terms Benamozegh uses here: they even show a certain irony with regard to his colleagues in the Holy Land.

> The old adage has it that nothing is worse than the slave who is suddenly set free. For light blinds those who have never seen it, if they are not accustomed to it gradually. Thus they [Bena-mozegh is referring to Algerian Jews] were abandoned by the Torah because they failed to study it in a state of purity. And if they had previously been educated in the paths of the Torah, with reliable texts and teachers, they would not have turned to charmers and sorcerers.[22]

Science is thus compared to light, and *Torah* study without its harmonious accompaniment is defined as "impure." Benamozegh goes on indirectly to suggest that the Oriental rabbis are like children, mistaking the vaccine for the illness, and rejecting it violently.

The belief in a strict, indissociable union between science and Torah was also subscribed to by others of Benamozegh's contemporaries, who like him were of Sephardic origin, and in particular by one fascinating character, Rabbi Israel Moshe Hazan.

Israel Moshe Hazan: Fundamentalism and Moderation

Israel Moshe Hazan (Smyrna 1808—Beirut 1863)[23] personified a kind of Sephardic rabbi who was both open to science and deeply convinced that it was no more than an instrument for understanding the works of God better. At the top of his hierarchy of values, without a doubt, stood the Torah, to which everything else was subservient, and of value only so long as it enhanced religious practice and values. This open, pluralistic attitude meant he was not an aggressive fundamentalist. Like Benamozegh, who knew and respected him,[24] Hazan championed strict union between science and religion: he wrote that separating them was a Western characteristic, and a mortal sickness.[25]

For him, what the Orientals unified, the Occidentals divided. This separation rendered science sterile, and religion weak, ultimately resulting in a materialistic culture without fundamental values.[26]

Another interesting trait of Hazan's intellectual personality is his great openness toward Christianity, which he sees as an ally of Judaism in the common battle against the enemy of skepticism. Hazan is probably the only rabbi ever to have asked the Catholic authorities for their approval of a legal decision;[27] during his time as a rabbi in Rome he always viewed the relationship with the ecclesiastical hierarchy as extremely important, not only tactically, but from deep personal conviction. For in his opinion, the real battle of modern times was that between the faithful and the atheists, and in this the upholders of "the old faith, daughter of the great God" and the "messianists" were brothers who shared a single text.[28]

Israel Moshe Hazan helps us better to understand Elijah Benamozegh. The latter's thinking may have its roots in the religious humanism of the Sephardic rabbis, which aimed to be respectful of other religions that shared the same horror of infidels, and which was open to science on condition that it did not lay claim to being an absolute doctrine.[29] The very style itself—rhymed prose, the argument richly interspersed with quotations (melytzah)—linked Benamozegh to Hazan. Comparison also obviously reveals differences. At the end of the day, Hazan saw the rabbi's role as the most prestigious in society, since politics should be modeled on, and bow to religion. Benamozegh, in contrast, espoused European liberalism, and preached the separation of the State from any Church. The former was a sort of external observer of modernity while the latter was fully immersed in it, and sought a profound understanding between it and the traditional authorities.

"As though hanging in air"

Benamozegh certainly belonged to two different worlds that were not always easily reconciled. He could have experienced this, in Romantic spirit (including that of Jewish Romanticism, as expressed in Israel Zangwill's short stories, for instance), as a tearing apart.

As it was, Benamozegh constantly strove for reconciliation. In his *Letter* to the Eastern rabbis, he found it in the use of irony: a deliberate distancing from reality as a way of making it less alarming. After many harsh, erudite pages of defensive argument, he ends on a light note: the translation fails to do justice to the brio of a passage constructed entirely around a series of antitheses, in rhyming verse that used *shibbutz*, the technique of Biblical cento:

> Alas, gentlemen! I will tell you what this situation resembles: an old man who had two wives, one young and one old, who hated each other like Hannah and Peninah.[30] With the passage of time his hair began to whiten; the young wife pulled out his gray hairs, and the old wife pulled out the dark, each so that he would be more like herself. And he, poor man, ended up bald.[31]

It is the same for me: science and faith are closely connected. They proceed together, but there are many people who see my fear of God as imbecility, or see my science as mere vanity, and my books as stinking carrion. And my petty self among them, neither impious nor a scholar, belong half to the devil, and half to the good Lord.[32]

To one man, I am a pious fool, to the next a heretic; I am called a scholar, but not a sage, and sometimes a plain herds-man, and a dresser of sycamore-trees;[33] here they don't believe Europe suits me, and advise me to go to Jerusalem and Mount Zion, but there they refuse to let me enter the sanctuary, and send me back outside among the scholars of the nations.

And I, for my part, remain as though hanging in air; neither rebel nor recognized writer, heretic nor believer, infidel nor Kabbalist, philosopher nor rabbi, blasphemer nor orator, I am not assimilated or awaiting the Messiah, neither Shammai nor Hillel, nor day nor night.[34]

This passage, worthy of a Chagall painting, contains numerous biblical and Talmudic quotations. The story of the two wives comes from the Babylonian Talmud, but its primary source is one of Aesop's fables,[35] where it concerns not two wives but two lovers. If Benamozegh knew this source, he wanted to send the reader a message by mixing yet again—this time through irony—the sacred and the profane.

THE OMISSIONS OF *EM LA-MIQRA:* THE CONJUNCTION OF KABBALAH AND MODERNITY

We have already looked at several different facets of Benamozegh's commentary. Here we will concentrate on the characteristics of his hermeneutics, the guiding principles that underlay it, and his deliberate omissions.

To begin with them, the negative approach will help us get a clearer grasp of the subject. It must be said at the outset that *Em la-Miqra* takes virtually no interest in *halakhah*—law. The Livorno rabbi could nonetheless be considered an expert, since he fulfilled the role of *dayyan* (judge) within that city's Jewish community, alongside those of preacher and educator.

We know of at least four of his responsa: it is striking that in the three most important, the ritual decision is dictated by underlying theological notions incontestably related to his thinking as a whole.[36]

In *Em la-Miqra*, when precepts are mentioned, it is to attribute an esoteric meaning to them, often in explicit antithesis to the moral and historical justifications offered by Luzzatto. It is true regarding *kashrut* (the rules on forbidden and permitted foods),[37] sacrifices,[38] and the Jubilee.[39] For Luzzatto, the aim of many of the Torah's commandments was to inculcate high moral ideals, while others were a concession to the spirit of the time during which they were promulgated. To Benamozegh this was not only wrong, but dangerous: the former idea led to ethics being invested with autonomy, and the latter limited the value of the Torah in time. *Mitzvot* had their effect on God and on the cosmic order; the Bible was not a work of ethics.

The ethical remarks are the second major area of omission. One has only to read the long digressions by Luzzatto or Reggio on sons being punished for the sins of the fathers, and to compare that with Benamozegh's silence on the subject, to realize the significance of such an omission. Another telling example is the passage on the rape of Dinah (Genesis XXXIV), which lends itself to ethical consideration, but elicits from Benamozegh only a few marginal philosophical comments.

There are two apparently diametrically contradictory sides to this denial of the Bible as an ethical treatise: the first derives from Kabbalistic teachings, the second from the notion—mentioned earlier—that the text, in the age of the triumph of science, *can no longer* be read as a source of authority.

Nor can it be read as a novel. In the refusal to accept the narrative level as fundamental and inescapable, we may note once again the combination of the Kabbalistic influence and a modern mind. We should recall the *Zohar's* peremptory assertion: if it were merely a matter of stories, men would write infinitely more beautiful ones. Moreover, the transformation of what had been the "great tale" and the "great code" par excellence into a "frail branch in the midst of a powerful, universal culture"[40] had already taken place.

The scene in Genesis in which an aged Jacob, close to death, sees the children of his adventurous, beloved son Joseph for the first time, is of no dramatic value to Benamozegh. What draws his attention is this moving passage is a verbal root that allows him to make a theoretical extension. The only drama that seems to interest Benamozegh is a metaphysical one in which "a mellow, mystical genius—he wrote in another context—opened its wings over a grandiose symbolism."[41] This is the metaphysics of Kabbalah presented in narrative form.

Let us examine Benamozegh's exegesis of this passage in detail, beginning with the Biblical text itself (Genesis XLVIII: 8–11):

And Israel beheld Joseph's sons, and said: "Who are these?"
  And Joseph said unto his father: "They are my sons, whom God hath given me here." And he said: "Bring them, I pray thee, unto me, and I will bless them."

Now the eyes of Israel were dim for age, so that he could not see. And he brought them near unto him; and he kissed them, and embraced them.

And Israel said unto Joseph: "I had not thought to see thy face; and, lo, God hath let me see thy seed also."

Benamozegh only makes a linguistic comment, concentrating on the verb *pilalti*, "I thought," "I calculated," and noting that in Hebrew "judgment" is *pilul* or *tefillah*; he deduces that *tefillah*, which also means "prayer," truly equals an "intellectual judgment," a "chosen thought."[42] The use of a Kantian category such as "judgment" to describe prayer might seem strange if the Kabbalistic background to the statement is not taken into account. For instance, Yosef Gikatilla—one of the most prestigious Kabbalist authors—claimed in the fourteenth century that prayer consisted in effective intellectual concentration on the aspect of God one wished to address.[43] It therefore relied upon a good understanding of that aspect, as expressed by one of the names of God. In Benamozegh's exegesis everything serves the same purpose: to show the value of Kabbalistic ideas, which for him were the underlying theoretical heart of the Scriptures.

Psychological remarks are therefore entirely absent. The story of Joseph, especially the seductive advances of Potiphar's wife—so rich in narrative potential it continues to be explored even today—merits no more than a passing comment on the Egyptians and the Hyksos.

Luzzatto, in contrast, enlisted his immense grammatical and linguistic erudition in the service of the "dramatization of text,"[44] and pledged himself fully—citing the opinions of his students alongside his own—to understanding the factual and psychological aspects of the various episodes in the life of Joseph. His closeness to the text is both naïve and moving: the Bible needed a narrative continuity which the exegete undertook to explain. We can easily measure the distance that separates this position from the hypothesis—postulated by contemporary Protestant scholars—of a "novel of Joseph" as a work apart, inserted in the Bible at a time when it was important to recognize the considerable influence of the Jewish diaspora in Egypt.[45]

THE POSITIVE HERMENEUTICS

We have seen what *Em la-Miqra* was not, which has nonetheless given us valuable information about it. Let us now examine the primary elements that constituted the work's originality and importance.

Comparativism

If there is one aspect of *Em la-Miqra* that is perfectly in keeping with the demands of its day, it is its comparativism, or contextualization. Nothing can be understood outside of a historical context; biblical tales are read in a new light when they are compared—in terms of both content and style—with the rites and myths of the ancient civilizations of the Middle East. Benamozegh was an enthusiastic follower of this program of enlarging knowledge.

In his hermeneutics, comparativism is a key criterion in explanation: he defines it as the possibility of clarifying difficult passages through the use of temporally and spatially related elements.[46]

He made no claims that this was innovative. Far from it. For the Benamozegh of the mature period, openness to science and curiosity about related civilizations were traits associated with the doctors of the Talmud. The broad-minded attitude of the scholars of the past was all the more laudable in that it represented the free training of the mind's desire for knowledge upon cultures and countries that oppressed—or had oppressed—the Jews.[47] That, actually, was the true essence of the Torah, a science among sciences,[48] regardless of what the "*mithasdim aharonim*," pious-seeming contemporaries, might think, Benamozegh fails to identify these orthodox obscurantists.

The start of Benamozegh's exegesis appears in a wholly different light. His first exegetic work, the Psalm commentary *Nir le-David* (1858) was a very thorough attempt to apply the principle *Bibliam biblice exponere.* In it, all the Psalms are interpreted using biblical tales about David, and are given a specific place in the Hebrew king's biography.

This approach probably represented a response to critical theories that supported the existence of external sources: a Benamozegh who was master of his intellectual means would not have needed to resort to strategies as naïve as they were extreme.

In his maturity he asserted that similarities did not detract from the originality of the Scriptures so much as enhance it. At root, comparativism was the tool he used to push home his dominant idea about the antiquity of Kabbalah. He reasoned thus: foreign—primarily Egyptian—borrowings are evident in the Bible. If the Scriptures are not to be stripped of their originality, it must be carried onto an esoteric plane. Only Kabbalah presents both (clearly acknowledged) similarities to and considerable differences from Egyptian rites: it is at once a mark of antiquity and uniqueness.[49]

The comparativist perspective both expands and takes the edge off the biblical text. In the course of his commentary Benamozegh gradually builds up a historical picture of the rites and beliefs of the Middle East during biblical times, an impressive treatise in which the Scriptures end up as no more than the guiding thread, and an opportunity for a broader discussion. The Bible is all but a pretext, a sort of "theosophical novel."[50] Commentary imposes itself on the text being commented upon, becoming almost independently readable. It is yet further confirmation of Benamozegh's dual inspiration of Kabbalistic tradition and philological modernity, each of which tends to reduce the importance of the authority of the transmitted text considered on its own.

The most striking example of this method—and at the same time a not insignificant individual contribution to Jewish exegesis—occurs in the commentary on Numbers XXIX: 11.

The subject is the Yom Kippur sacrifice, and the instruction in the *Talmud Bavli*[51] to sprinkle the altar once above and seven times below, counting in the following way: "One; one and one; one and two; one and three; etc." Benamozegh sought to understand the reasons for such strange behavior, engaging in a piece of close reasoning in the traditional style of Talmudic debate which showed remarkable subtlety and erudition. Having considered a dozen or so "classical" Jewish authors, he introduces ideas from Egyptology. The Egyptian number system, he points out, repeated the unit, thus rendering "three" as "one and two"; "four" as "one and three"; and so on. The Torah had been given to a people steeped in Egyptian culture, and their oral tradition reflected the fact. The doctors of the Talmud were no longer aware of the real background to traditions they had nonetheless preserved: that was to their credit.

This system of counting in units became a general principle he used to explain the repetition of certain words in some passages, where that seems to add nothing to our understanding; the Egyptian "forma mentis" was thus behind a stylistic oddity that had been explained in a thousand different ways.

Irrespective of the validity of this comment, it is instructive to compare it with the attempt by the famous Volhynia rabbi Malbim (Meïr Lœb Ben Jehiel Michael, 1809–1879) to explain the phenomenon of alleged synonyms in the biblical text. This antireformist rabbi interpreted a succession of words with apparently identical meanings in a juridical sense, case by case, in exhaustive detail.[52] It was his way of harmonizing written Torah with the oral tradition.

Benamozegh drew on the modern science of archaeology with the same aim. This illustrates both the similarities and the enormous differences in the intellectual horizons and the challenges facing two scholars, one working in eastern Europe where Jews were just getting their first taste of modernity, the other in a country that had for centuries been the locus of the most advanced—albeit strained—equilibrium between Jewish and Christian civilizations.

Concordism and Tradition

It is obvious that Benamozegh could not read the Bible merely as a scientific treatise in the way Ibn 'Ezra and Nahmanides (among other illustrious figures) had done at the start of their respective commentaries on Ecclesiastes and Genesis. He did not, for all that, renounce the theory of concordism, or agreement between the Bible and scientific truth. To do this, he did not use any figurative or symbolic interpretation, as, for instance, the Anglican exegetes did,[53] but took a route of his own.

Benamozegh was not looking for agreement between the Scriptures and science,[54] but between science and the rabbinic tradition. Numerous *midrashim* that had previously been regarded as obscure, or interpreted allegorically, were henceforth to be taken literally. Scientific discoveries gave the moderns hermeneutic possibilities which the ancients could never have imagined.

Such an approach had two results:

1. It confirmed the existence of a tradition not limited to the moral and ritual domains, the truth of which was beginning to be proved by scientific advances;

2. it retained the perspective of literal meaning (*peshat*) applied not to the Bible but to the *midrash*, which seemed to be the only approach possible, in keeping with the prevailing scientific atmosphere.[55]

The most meaningful application of this principle is offered in the interpretation of Genesis I: 5. A celebrated *midrash* relates God's creation and destruction of several worlds. The explanation usually put forward—wrote Benamozegh—was the one adopted by Leibniz in his best of all possible worlds theory: God had before him a range of different worlds from which he chose one, the one that was eventually created and in which we live. Ours is therefore the best of all possible worlds, since God is by definition good. It is an attractive explanation of the *midrash* that relies on a figurative meaning, "but in our day and age we do not need to take refuge behind a figurative meaning," since physicists and geologists had produced a theory of catastrophe that showed that the earth had been through a series of upheavals before coming to look the way we know it now.[56]

He added that without the support of tradition, the Torah was left exposed to easy, but fundamentally justified, attacks from scientific criticism. This is a sensitive point in Benamozegh's thinking. For the moment, let us simply note that he salvaged tradition—and the Scriptures with it—by taking a literal meaning and avoiding interpretations that relied on allegory or metaphor.

In Mantua, in the eighteenth century, Avi'ad Sar Shalom Basilea published a long essay in Hebrew[57] that undertook to demonstrate the perfect harmony between science (he himself was an astronomer and geometrician) and the teachings of Kabbalah, as found in the *Zohar* or the works of Moshe Zakut and Menahem 'Azariyah of Fano, both of whom came closer to recently discovered natural truths than Aristotelian philosophy did. Benamozegh thus had Italian Jewish precursors for his attempt to reconcile Kabbalah and the "new science."

Another comparison with Malbim provides an instructive contrast. We have seen how the eastern European rabbi attempted to integrate text and tradition through *halakhah*, and how Malbim sought perfect agreement between the legal tradition and the Bible, and thus between orality and Scripture. Such a project was manifestly impossible in western Europe, where the harmony had to be found on other levels. Benamozegh's would seem to be one such approach.

The new concordism espoused by Benamozegh is obviously impregnated with a positivism that suggests an original line of exploration which was not to be followed up.[58] Yet it must be recognized that for Benamozegh, the encounter between positivism and traditionalism produced the unconvincing result of dogmatism. The idea of a single, stable truth imparted to tradition and gradually revealed over time corresponded perfectly to a scientist program based on the uncovering of nature's buried secrets, a total trust in the methods of natural sciences—so typical of the end of the nineteenth century. Two ideas, concordism and scientism, that had been turned toward the past and the future respectively, ended up converging at this level as well.

Erudition and Philosophy

Em la-Massoreth, the great, lost *midrash* commentary, was intended to accompany *Em la-Miqra* "like a twin brother." The author included a long extract in his Torah commentary, and it is worth cursory examination for what it reveals about his working methods.

Under consideration is a *midrash* on Deuteronomy I: 13, which is found in two different anthologies. Rashi mentions the former, but omits the beginning: "Arius asked Rabbi Yossi, 'who may be defined as a wise man (*hakham*)? And what is the difference between a wise man and an intelligent one (*navon*)?'" The first part of Benamozegh's analysis is devoted to finding the right *midrash* text, since the two anthologies give different versions. Showing remarkable mastery of classical rabbinic literature—encompassing both *talmudim*, the *midrash*, the Tosafists, and several commentaries on Rashi—he manages to establish a text through internal criticism.

This is just the beginning of his research, however. After the textual issue, he addresses the historical one: he wonders whether this is the Arius who founded Arianism, as well as speculating on the likelihood of him ever having met Rabbi Yossi. Here too—after a succession of proofs—he finds an answer, in this case an affirmative one.

He leaves the philosophical level until last. What was the underlying meaning behind Arius's question? Benamozegh did not see the *hokhma* under discussion as an individual attribute, but the person of the Son in the Christian Trinity. The disagreement between the orthodox Christian position and that of what would become the Arian heresy concerned the position of the Son in relation to the Father, and in particular the issue of the eternal nature of each, or the latter's creation by the former. It was natural that on this matter, Arius would turn to someone from the Jewish tradition in which Christianity's origins lay.

These comments were not sufficient for Benamozegh. He finished the long passage in a characteristic fashion, with a comparison between several elements of Christian and Kabbalistic theology. It was his opinion that the entire Christological debate arose from the Christian fusion of two Kabbalistic triads, *keter—hokhmah—binah* and *hokhmah—malkhut—tiferet*. In both triads, the elements are called *Father, Son, and Holy Ghost* respectively, which leads to deep confusion in Christian theology. In contrast, in Kabbalistic doctrine, the first *Son* is eternal while the second is engendered. By not making this distinction, the Christians oscillated between the two hypotheses, which uncertainty threw up a stream of heresies and schisms.

To return to the *midrash* analysis: the erudite (rabbinical and historical) argument terminated in theological philosophy that eventually produced a theoretical and historical apologia of Kabbalah. This has become a familiar progression.

A review of the subjects to which Benamozegh devotes the longest digressions in *Em la-Miqra* reveals a Kabbalistic sensibility constantly at work, even if not always in explicit ways. This explains the number of pages—disproportionate to the overall length of the work—devoted to the angels, the evil eye, and the death of Enoch.[59] The author deploys his habitual astonishing erudition, reaching conclusions that do not seem to have elicited much response in the scholarly world. Let us consider one example.

In a 1907 essay on "Original Sin in ancient Jewish sources,"[60] the French scholar Israel Levi, who was one of the pioneers in critical research on the Talmud and *Midrash*, asserted that the refusal in the *Midrash* to accept the idea of Enoch's assumption into heaven (Gen. V: 24 states, "for God took him") was justified by anti-Christian polemic: the desire was to eliminate the Christian claim to see this episode as analogous to the assumption of Jesus. Levi attributes this insight to Friedländer; he does not mention Benamozegh, who had said exactly the same thing, albeit in conclusion to a fundamentally apologist argument.

This failure of scholarly communication may be justified by the very nature of *Em la-Miqra*, a dense, original work, but one in which the mixture of levels and registers formed an obstacle to its acceptance in the scientific circles of the day.

The Notes on the *Zohar*

In 1851—at the age of twenty-eight—Benamozegh played a part in a publishing operation of considerable importance. In collaboration with Shelomo Leoni and Yitzhaq Millul, he produced an edition of the *Zohar*, based on the earlier Constantinople edition, but involving an enormous amount of revision and correction.[1]

This "Livorno" *Zohar* was divided into five volumes, following the five volumes of the Torah; it was printed very clearly and crisply ("on paper as white as snow," according to the frontispiece), and was typographically elegant. Reprinted a number of times, its success was probably partly due to the critical apparatus, much of which was contributed by Benamozegh.

In fact, the young rabbi worked on the biblical references quoted in the *Zohar*—printed alongside the text—and, moreover, on cataloging all the places in the Talmud and *Midrash* where Shim'on Bar Yohai, the presumed author of the *Zohar*, appeared. He then linked these passages thematically with reminiscent passages in the *Zohar* and these quotations too were placed alongside the text.

This major work was based on the book *Ben Yohai* by the Hungarian rabbi Moshe Kunitzer,[2] but Benamozegh organized and incorporated it "drawing on the treasury of his knowledge of rabbinic sources."[3]

It is therefore not surprising that among Benamozegh's various projected but unrealized works, a book on the correspondence between rabbinic texts and the *Zohar* recurred with increasing frequency on the wish list. He had, after all, had a considerable volume of data at his disposal since his youth, and it had already taken up a fair amount of his energy.[4] The work that had already been done was in any case a substantial scholarly contribution, not to be surpassed or superseded for a century, until Reuven Margalioth produced his *Nitzotzei ha-Zohar* (*Sparks of the Zohar*).

The appendix to the Livorno *Zohar* contained two interesting new elements: a list of abbreviations found in the text and a compilation of *maftehot* (keys)—a sort of thematic index. The reader was thus able to orientate himself among the large number of technical terms and be sure of finding the location of a given subject, such as "creation," "the tables of the Law," and so forth. Each subject was accompanied by a brief description of the Zoharic statements concerning it.

The appendices show that the book was intended for a readership that might, on the one hand, need help in studying it, and on the other, expect to see a logical restructuring of the contents. Reading the *Zohar* was no longer necessarily only for specialists, where a teacher's guidance was indispensable; all that was required was a good linguistic grasp and enough familiarity with rabbinic texts, after which an individual could undertake private study of the monument of Jewish esotericism.

The thematic index met a similar need. The Israeli literary critic Gershon Shaked has commented[5] that works such as Hayyim N. Bialik's *Midrash* anthology, Hayyim Schirmann's anthology of Italian Jewish poetry, and Yeshayahu Tishby's *Zohar* translation and anthology (all works that appeared between the nineteen-thirties and fifties)[6] restructured traditional material for consumption by a largely secular readership. By collecting *midrashim* or passages from the *Zohar* thematically—for instance, the relationship between God and man; exile and the land of Israel; the family; daily life; etc.—the authors of these major works extrapolated the passages from their context and from the continuity required by traditional study. As we have seen, this fitted in with the new style of biblical commentary, which detached itself—even typographically—from the text, and was structured around "introductions" and thematically grouped essays.

In 1852 it was of course still inconceivable for an edition of the *Zohar* to be aimed at a readership that was not immersed in traditional culture; yet this is where Benamozegh's initiative was leading.

This provides a new explanation for the Livorno rabbi's intriguing statement that Progress consisted of gradually disseminating Kabbalistic knowledge and abandoning the esoteric aspect that made it the strict preserve of the initiated. The universalist theological motivation revealed in *Israel and Humanity* accorded with this position, which is even more meaningful when applied to this area: indeed, a spirit of research was imposing itself, not without difficulty, and for the time being within a theoretically traditional milieu, in one of the innermost recesses of Judaism.

PART TWO

Tradition, Orality, and Text

Issues in Play

According to some interpretations, the nineteenth-century intellectual consciousness culminated in a radical breaking with the past. This view holds that we should not be misled by the great flowering of historical disciplines, the popularity of which would actually represent a tendency to examine the past through documental reconstruction alone, seeing that as the only way to understand it. This in turn implies rejecting tradition as a source of meaning. The historian was obliged to attempt to recontextualize in order to comprehend the "truth" of the past, engaging in a process of artificial construction with no guarantee of success, and tradition, with its pretentions to be a vehicle for cultural data that had survived fundamentally unscathed over time, was comprehensively rejected. Despite some idealizing of mythical epochs—often worked up in support of nascent nationalistic ideologies—a very clear sense of discontinuity had taken hold.

It follows that oral transmission as authorized testimony was ascribed a strictly limited role and that the real traces left by the past were the written documents, the only ones that could be used in trying to reconstruct a time that was—forever—out of reach. Jewish culture seemed to take the same line. The German *Science of Judaism* (*Wissenschaft des Judentums*) movement aimed to represent both a beginning and an end: the beginning of a new approach to the Jewish past—whose developments were to be charted according to scientific criteria, identified as textual history—and the end of a living tradition, which it wished to see "buried with dignity."[1]

In this context, Benamozegh, for all that his work chimed with some of the key ideas of the times, seems to have been conducting a lone struggle as an inveterate champion of the oral tradition. He was able to set out his position in the course of a debate that raged in the European Jewish community on the question of Reform. The main issues primarily concerned matters of ritual, but they presupposed acceptance of the oral tradition as a source of inspiration and authority.

Benamozegh goes beyond this contingent framework to concentrate on analyzing the very crux of the problem; he examines tradition and orality in general, seeing them as a cultural unit from which the written word emerged as but one part. In his view the sacred texts especially did not have the preeminent role generally—and with little variation—ascribed to them in Jewish exegesis. As we shall see, he criticizes Maimonides harshly on this particular point, and even relativizes some assertions of the doctors of the Talmud, justifying them only in the light of the historical circumstances that gave rise to them.

Behind all this, obviously, stands Kabbalah, which for Benamozegh fulfilled the role of "cultural tradition": Judaism's dogmatic tradition, passed down by word of mouth, or in other words, the most typical expression of the theological "genius" of the Jewish people. On this definition he constructed his vision of Kabbalah as the manifestation of a living rather than a secret organism, hence his relatively limited esteem for text, an attitude that might seem unlikely for a Kabbalist. For Benamozegh, words did not conceal hidden meanings with regard to the world or the divinity, capable of being revealed only by a prophetic mind: they are, more modestly, the tangible marks of various doctrines that took shape in the natural course of a people's spontaneous development.

Several levels of analysis are therefore required to understand Benamozegh's intense "traditionalism," a position that at first glance seems unusual and without justification. His defense of orality does indeed go against the grain of much thinking of the period but it ends up circling round to where it joins another—equally major—stream of thought that comprised ideas such as the "genius of the people" and "spontaneous production."

Some aspects of his thinking were doubtless "untimely" even then, yet others marked him out rightly—and despite appearances—as a man of his day.

Tradition and Text

Between Enlightenment and Romanticism

This is the tradition to which I have the honor of belonging; it is an uninterrupted one whose roots are to be found in the Maghreb. Fathers acquired merit for their sons and study has never fallen silent in their mouths.

—Elijah Benamozegh, Introduction to Avraham Coriat's *Berith Avoth*

Our inheritance was left to us by no testament.

—Hannah Arendt, Introduction to *Between Past and Future*

In *Truth and Method*, the German philosopher Hans Georg Gadamer reminds us that the idea of breaking with the past came out of the Enlightenment and brought with it the gradual decay of tradition as a preferred means of understanding earlier ages. Thus far, this is a commonly held view in the history of ideas, but Gadamer's analysis goes farther in claiming that German historicism was not in this regard at odds with the Enlightenment but supported it in the essential points, even surpassing it in radicalism.[1]

One of the fundamental ideas in eighteenth-century enlightened circles was that humanity had finally outgrown its guilty minority, to use Kant's phrase, and could now look at the past from the heights of Reason; a vantage point attained only with great difficulty, but a sure and definitive one. The prejudices that had so long misled mankind were destined to disappear and be replaced by free examination undertaken in accordance with the immutable laws of natural reason. There was a strong sense of a break with the past. It was time to begin afresh, to build on the ruins of a past that had made too many mistakes and demonstrated too many weaknesses. Toward the end of the century, the notion of progress had been grafted onto this sustained rationalism, portraying the acquiring of consciousness and clarity—or, in other words, a transparency of objects and of people—as an infinite human task and the very law of human history.

In this context, the idea of tradition, defined as the passing down by word of mouth of truths authenticated by an institution, was inevitably cast aside and held in contempt. It was perceived either as an imposture that had held sway through ignorance, by dint of which it justified a political and religious order, or as a series of prejudices and superstitions with only the most distant relationship to the truth. There was a need to demonstrate the falsity of the claims of any doctrine or institution tracing its raison d'être back to the mists of time, where any accounts were by definition shrouded in a semi-mythical aura. The darkness of obscurantism had made possible the oppression of both bodies and souls; human freedom would be founded on the light of reason.

A new foundation; reason; freedom. These, then, were the key concepts of the Enlightenment. It is easy to imagine how texts that primarily derived their prestige from their antiquity were regarded. They were to be approached without bias, isolated from any explanatory system that tradition had built around them: in short, they would be looked at on their own merits. Trust in rational instruments led to decontextualization, insofar as it meant each and every individual had the intellectual wherewithal to understand a text's true meaning without the need for mediation.[2] It was a movement that distanced the reader from the text: by advocating a direct approach, it in fact broke the "naïve" magic circle that brought the two together in a relationship charged with meaning. The text became objectified, separated from and placed before a subject who could no longer rely on any but his own resources.

The philological—or critical—standpoint corresponded perfectly to this objectification and setting at a distance. It involved dissecting an actual thing in a scientific way, just as had come to be done with nature, avoiding preconceived opinions and rejecting implications that were logically unverifiable by reference to the object itself.

The Bible too was called before the court of rational criticism. The Book of Books was not to escape the scrutiny of a method dictated by disenchantment. Examining the Bible in this way naturally entailed serious risks for the worldview founded on it, which was still dominant at every level: that is why—after a radical, even belligerent start—biblical criticism proceeded with great circumspection.[3]

Spinoza had been the first to combine—in a thoroughly radical way in his *Tractatus Theologico-Politicus*—textual biblical criticism and the new, entirely rational ethics. The Scriptures, examined correctly, revealed themselves ill-suited to the task of justifying the doctrinal and political systems that were based upon them. They contained flagrant inconsistencies and were obviously the work of authors writing at different times.

The atmosphere seemed to change quickly. In the opening decades of the nineteenth century, the Romantics' interest in history brought about an apparent reevaluation of tradition. From a historicist perspective, the past reacquired relevance to the present, whether in the irrationalist version that extolled origins myths such as the "first Christians" or the "true" German people, or in the version that saw history as a long process in which every stage was necessary within an immanentist rational plan. Historicism took off: more than just one science among others, its spirit gradually came to pervade other branches of knowledge. The nineteenth was the century of the historical spirit.

A new element had been added to the Enlightenment's ideological thinking about the past: *recontextualization* as a means of comprehension. It was no longer a matter of reading documents from the past as they offered themselves up for scrutiny and judging them according to the laws of abstract, intemporal reason. Any idea or event could be understood only within its own historical context, reconstructing which was the task of the historian.

Did this focus on Becoming, on change, diminish the gap between the past and the present that had opened during the Enlightenment? Did the recontextualizing of historical data bring them any closer to the present?

Gadamer's analysis answers in the negative. In his opinion, for all its glorification of national traditions and its reassessment of a number of periods treated by the Enlightenment as obscure, Romantic historicism ultimately accepted the placing of the past at arm's length.

> The fact that the restorative tendency of Romanticism was able to combine with the fundamental concern of Englightenment to constitute the unity of the historical sciences, simply indicates that it is the same break with the continuity of meaning in tradition that lies behind both. If it is an established fact for the Enlightenment that all tradition that reason shows to be impossible, i.e. nonsense, can only be understood historically, i.e. by going to the past's way of looking at things, then the historical consciousness that emerges in Romanticism involves a radicalisation of the Enlightenment: for the exceptional case of nonsensical tradition has become the general rule for historical consciousness. . . . The whole of the past, even, ultimately, all the thinking of one's contemporaries, is seen only "historically."[4]

Contextualization—"historical understanding"—is therefore a subsequent stage in the process of distancing the past. The assertion that each manifestation of the past is understandable only when an effort is made to reconstruct the conditions surrounding its existence leads on to exclusion from the realm of sense of such immediate, "naïve"—at least in the "scientific" sense—contact as tends toward the truth. History as it was understood by the Romantics was a succession of moments, linked to one another yet distinct: it was not possible to turn to the past to find answers for the present, as each age raised different questions.

In contrast, a viewpoint centered on tradition denies Becoming the status of an untranscendable condition, possibly even seeing it as a problem to be confronted in preserving the truth. This worldview had, though, no legitimacy in the nineteenth century: with discontinuity being accorded precedence over continuity, understanding the past required a complex conceptual apparatus that ensured history became a discipline reserved for professionals. There was no longer any sense in listening to the ancients since the times were different. Transmission was impossible.

Recourse to the imagination as an instrument of historical under-standing can be seen as somewhat similar. Augustin Thierry and René de Chateaubriand allude to it explicitly.[5] Likewise, when Jules Michelet writes of the "exhumation of bodies" revived by historians,[6] he does no more than confirm with his voluntarism the lack of a present-day tradition to which to refer.

The written text would therefore seem to be an especially good instru-ment for penetrating the past, which presents itself to us primarily as Other. It is thus both irreplaceable and insufficient, and this gives rise to the notion of *interpretation* as a *necessary* yet always *uncompleted* task. Friedrich Schlei-ermacher (1768–1834), who is generally considered to be the founder of a new hermeneutic consciousness, embodied this position most coherently.

This way of relating to a text through the necessary but unsatisfying route of interpretation may be a new form of distancing. It is no longer a matter of considering an object placed before one and analyzing it solely with rational instruments, but of using personal involvement to bridge the gap between ourselves and an understanding of it. Distance from the text ceases to be a desirable condition, becoming instead an unfortunate necessity: separation is seen as a forced rip in the fabric of things that the individual must infinitely sew back together.

Yet, it is obvious that all personal engagement entails subjectivity; this is true even if the reader attempts to get closer to textual objectivity through a strategy of watchful passivity, receptiveness, and openness. He makes every effort to intervene as little as possible, allowing himself to be "penetrated" by what the text wishes to convey to him, an operation that cannot be assumed to produce absolute, definitive results. The work of interpretation consists in doing precisely that: by bringing the text closer to the reader, its fundamentally elusive character is decreed. The individual's appropriation is precarious, the text retains a certain—one might say a component—distance.

"Hermeneutics is based on the non-comprehensibility of discourse," Schleiermacher states at the very outset of his 1809 lecture on general herme- neutics.[7] What, then, are the means used to try to overcome this inherent problem of discourse per se? They are completely individual: interpretation is an *art* which requires both a profound *understanding of the context* that produced the discourse in question and also a matter of *intuition,* or the ability to grasp the irreducibly particular quality of the author. For the Protestant Schleiermacher the New Testament was no exception to this rule.

Alternating between an awareness of the general—the context—and the specific—the author—the interpreter can come close to full comprehen- sion. That, however, would require infinite knowledge, and, "Strictly, the task is therefore infinite and can only be done approximately."[8]

Interpretation is thus necessary, personal, and infinite. There is no tradition that can support and thereby illuminate the text. At the end of the day, Schleiermacher shares the sense of distance from the past that characterized the Enlightenment, writing,

> Any sacred book is merely a mausoleum of religion, a monument that reminds us that a great spirit once existed and does no lon- ger; because, were it still alive and active, how could we place this high value on the dead letters of such books that are but a pale reflection of it? Only whoever does not believe in a sacred book but does not need one, who—on the contrary—would be capable of producing one himself—only he has religion.[9]

Tradition and·Texts
for the "Science of Judaism"

Wissenschaft des Judentums, the movement founded in Germany in the first half of the nineteenth century by "enlightened" Jewish intellectuals shared the basic characteristics we have just described.[1]

The *Wissenschaft* scholars approached Jewish history with what were fully intended to be revolutionary principles and methods:

1. a "scientific" approach to Jewish history, which translated into the need for intellectual "refoundation";

2. the consideration of written text as a prime source of information;

3. the (implied) prediction of an imminent end to a living, autonomous Jewish culture which regarded continuity as a key concept.

The three are obviously interrelated and subscribe to a patent devaluing of tradition as an instrument of understanding.

The first two elements can be discerned in the opening article—a sort of group manifesto—in the first issue (1822) of *Zeitschrift für die Wissenschaft des Judentums*.[2] In "The Concept of a Science of Judaism," Immanuel Wolf wrote that the rabbis had so far always kept Jewish culture within the strict and restrictive bounds of what he called "scholasticism" and that this had in large measure been due to the marginalization forced upon it by the outside world. What, though, did he mean by "scholasticism"?

> This, then, is the essence of scholasticism: to follow to the letter a supposedly holy and untouchable tradition and to develop from it every aspect of every subject of human understanding and, in consequence, to fetter any free, individual, and living movement of the Spirit, making any rational and self-founded apprehension of the true, infinite idea impossible.[3]

Wolf immediately adds that to allow this rational principle to be deployed—or in other words, to enter the realm of science—required setting off on a new footing. In this regard, it is significant that he mentions Descartes and—more so again—Spinoza, the "great rebel" against the Jewish tradition. These two rationalists ended the age of scholasticism and inaugurated a new, self-founded philosophy. It was an approach that required all kinds of privileges to be given up and new foundations to be looked for on which the edifice might be constructed.[4]

The need for a scientific approach and for severance were, according to Wolf, strictly linked to a perception of literature as the only instrument for understanding the past. The other keynote to the program was the seeking of the Idea, the Living Principle of the Jewish people, from a typically Hegelian perspective:

> Judaism as it is represented here is *in se* and *per se* the object of a possible and necessary scientific examination: a whole that rests on its own internal principle and is *embodied on the one hand in a comprehensive literature* and on the other hand in the particular life and existence of a large class of people.[5]

Similarly, where the aims of this research needed to be indicated in concrete terms:

> As in any science, ours divides into several parts, according to the key differences in their subjects. . . .
>
> 1. Information on Judaism found in *historical and literary documents*.
>
> 2. Statistical information on contemporary Jewry in all countries. . . .
>
> The philology of Judaism equals the hermeneutic, critical understanding of *Jewish literature as that in which resides the particular world, life, and thought specific to the Jews.*[6]

According to the *Wissenschaft* historian Leon Wieseltier, the historiographic work of Leopold Zunz, the group's most eminent intellectual, was based on a philological model. When he drew up the program for the new Jewish historiography, Zunz had in mind August Böckh's 1818 *Encyklopädie und Methodologie der philologischen Wissenschaften*, a sort of general survey written for early-nineteenth-century philologists. That modern Jewish historiography was conceived as *Wissenschaft* (science) rather than *Geschichte* (history) and thus fell under the aegis of philology was not, for Wieseltier, without consequence.[7]

Zunz objectifies the textual account and places it at a distance by excluding its use as a method of orientation in the present: as a result, the whole of Jewish literature is an area for research rather than a pool from which value judgments can be derived.[8] But this attitude is related to the conviction that the philologist—like Minerva's philosophical bird—begins his task only as a civilization is coming to an end, this being the point at which it may be observed from outside as a scientific subject with a fixed form.

> Given that the Jews of our age—and we do not refer to German Jews alone—are turning with enthusiasm to the German language and culture and as a result—perhaps unwillingly or unwittingly—consigning Jewish literature to the grave, the Science of Judaism has arisen to evaluate what has been sealed.[9]

Leon Wieseltier comments that "the philologist looks backward."[10] We could add that this backward gaze affords him no indications for his own time, as embracing a tradition would do. His rational tools orient learned research toward the past, while his quest for core elements turns toward the future.

Whether from the perspective of rationalist "refoundation" or from that of Romantic historical examination, this context of abandonment of tradition as a point of reference is what gives us a deeper understanding of Benamozegh's work.[11]

In Defense of Tradition

True Judaism . . . lies in tradition and its organs, which, at the same time
as they accept the legacy of the Bible, dominate it from the lofty heights
of the superiority of eternal life over this momentary existence.

—Elijah Benamozegh, *Morale juive et morale chrétienne*

Tradition as a theme is omnipresent in Benamozegh's work: it is both a sort
of artery and an interpretative key. It is scattered throughout the hundreds
of pages of Pentateuch commentary—*Em la-Miqra*—as well as being found
in *Eimat mafgia'* and *Ta'am le-Shad*, the two books that formed a defense of
Kabbalah. It was also dealt with specifically in other works: the "General
Introduction to the Monuments of the Oral Tradition" (in Hebrew) published
in the newspaper *Ha-Levanon*[1] and "La tradition,"[2] which appeared in several
editions of *L'Univers Israélite*. This latter essay was in fact a reworking of
an unpublished chapter from the massive *Teologia*, much of which remains
unpublished. The *Midrash* commentary, *Em la-Masoret*, which has also never
been published and which seems to be lost, was apparently extremely interesting in its handling of the subject, as the various passages that found their
way into other works attest.[3]

But the notion of tradition is already present in the passionate commentary on the Psalms, *Nir le-David*, a youthful work that stands apart form
the body of Benamozegh's literary production, with its rather emphatic,
somewhat peremptory tone. In it, Benamozegh glosses Psalm CXLV: 4,
"Each generation will praise your works to the succeeding generation and
will recount your wonders," thus: The marvels of God and an understanding
of the Scriptures can only be perpetuated through tradition (*qabbalah*): it is
the basis for all faith and all knowledge.

Many of the "pathetic" themes in *Nir le-David*, such as the aspiration to
moral purity and the lamentations for exile, have disappeared entirely from
the later works. The same is not true of tradition, an idea that Benamozegh
reworks untiringly.

This degree of insistence needs a historical explanation. In reality, it is justified if we consider the various polemical "fronts" on which Benamozegh was engaged; they concerned the broader European culture and not just the specific Jewish milieu.

DEFINITIONS

We should begin by trying to grasp what Benamozegh meant by "tradition" and then proceed from there to examine how, in his thinking, this fit in with the written text. In the essay that appeared in *L'Univers Israélite*, he offered the following definition: "Tradition is all that which Moses, while he did not write it down, said or implied."[4]

What is meant by "implied"? For Benamozegh, it did not mean an explanation running parallel to the text—a sort of divinely inspired commentary like the written text, entrusted with elucidating obscure points and completing passages that looked unfinished. He labeled "vulgar" this definition of tradition, which, moreover, exposed itself to easy—and *well-founded*—criticism from those who detracted from the Bible as a unitary work.

It would be absurd to imagine that a text was delivered in such a way as to immediately admit of an "authorized" interpretation, in the absence of which it would remain largely incomprehensible. However, this was exactly Maimonides' position when he posited two simultaneous sets of teachings, one (oral) intended to explain and complete the other (written) one. Benamozegh opposed this idea, putting forward a more clearly articulated relationship.

> For our part, these objections [criticisms of the unitary vision of the Bible] make no sense. Tradition is not that which Moses knew and no one else knew; but at the same time what everyone knew, what only a few might know, and what nobody at all knew yet.[5]

The vulgar definition has tradition as some sort of *ex-professo* commentary, a scholastic doctrine formulated by Moses,[6] whereas tradition as Benamozegh saw it is very much not scholastic (we should, here, recollect Wolf's attitude). It is not the mechanical, authoritative appendix to a text, a sort of unique explanation given once and for all and necessary to correct understanding.

> Tradition for us is not deliberate and systematic but spontaneous and involuntary.[7]

It is identified with the very life of a people; it is the air it breathes, its very world.[8]

By stripping the text of its premeditatory character, Benamozegh is able to attribute universality to it. *All* texts, as such, presuppose and in turn generate orality. A text taken in isolation is an incomprehensible abstraction. It is the tip of an iceberg, the "epiphenomenon" of a larger, deeper reality.

Writing is ancillary and accidental.[9]

We have known for a long time that in truth it is tradition that carries the text and not the other way about.[10]

The text is therefore nothing more than the written trace of a "tradition that precedes and follows it";[11] that "encompasses" it, so to speak. It is only a very partial sign that refers back to much richer levels, like the letters exchanged by lovers—writes Benamozegh, with obviously Kabbalistic inspiration—which evoke tender, secret intimacies through small allusions. Other readers clearly grasp that love is involved, but necessarily miss many of the subtleties.[12]

This viewpoint already throws up a partial result—exclusion. The Bible is no exception to the interpretative rule laid down of the text's incapacity to justify itself. Whence the apparently paradoxical conclusion that the most severe opinions of biblical criticism are justified, if we restrict ourselves to the text alone. It must be recognized that the text contains manifest weaknesses and lacunae and is coherent only when integrated into a larger whole. Benamozegh has no problem accepting that the Bible's human origins can be established, its various parts dated and attributed to different authors; yet for him this flows from an erroneous approach, one that is purely and exclusively philological and textual. This is what dictates the hermeneutic, but also religious, exigency to call upon tradition: "An interpreter who tries to escape tradition falls inevitably into the trap of criticism."[13]

In giving pride of place to the oral, Benamozegh makes no claim to be an innovator. On the contrary, he asserts his connection to the ancient doctrines of the Sages of the Talmud, who maintained that some parts of Scripture merely offered support (*asmakhta*) and post hoc justification for the oral tradition.[14] This assertion leads inexorably to the refutation of another of the major interpretative principles of Judaism that stands in contradiction to the first: namely, the notion of a text that is the vehicle for all truth, being of divine inspiration. Talmudic hermeneutics is largely based—both as regards its ritual conclusions and its theological and ethical developments—on the presupposition that there is a meaning to be grasped from each word and nuance of expression. For the text is revealed and every word carries its freight. Hence, a hermeneutics was built up to excavate the text, break it down, and uncover within it meanings not immediately obvious to the naked eye in what might be called a "narrative" reading.

Of course, it is a matter of looking to see whether the conclusions reached by these delicate operations are really to be found in the text or whether they are the fruit of autonomous research (or part of the oral tradition), found afterward. In the first event, Scripture would, down to the smallest semantic unit, prove an inexhaustible mine of divinely inspired teaching; in the second, its authority would merely confer post hoc justification for conceptual constructions produced elsewhere.

Kabbalah pushes still farther the logic of the text as a treasure trove of truths. It is no longer the word alone that is scrutinized, but the very letters. Since nothing is accidental in the divine text, even constituent elements stripped of independent meaning are worth examining. Interpretative techniques such as *Gematria*—which calculates the numerical value of letters—*Temurah*—which creates correspondence between letters—and *Notariqon*—acrostics, claim to reveal even deeper levels of meaning. This obviously opens up a bewildering range of interpretative possibilities.

The seventy beginnings of the *Tikkunei ha-Zohar* that analyze the word *Be-reshit* in different ways provide a sense of what this hermeneutics involves. For Moshe Cordovero, the most "philosophical" of the sixteenth-century Safed Kabbalists, the phonemes of the Torah have their own spirituality, whether written or spoken, or even simply meditated upon.[15] The text thus undergoes a radical transformation: it loses its immediate narrative configuration (this, at a superficial level, retains its validity), reflecting instead a hitherto unsuspected metaphysical world.

This hermeneutic outlook is not really shared by Benamozegh, who—as I shall show—retains a typically Kabbalistic framework that he reworks in keeping with the historical and scholarly spirit of his age.

At the level of principle, Benamozegh is clear: text cannot lay claim to a status as hyperbolic as this kind of exegesis might suggest. In this he "dares" to contradict the Sages of the Talmud, despite their being the most loyal guardians of the oral tradition. According to a passage of the handwritten manuscript of his French essay on tradition, which, significantly, did not find its way into the final, printed version, the Pharisees afforded priority to the written text for reasons of contingency. The notion of a perfect parallel between the written and oral law ("everything is in the text") formed part of the struggle between Pharisees and Sadducees. We know that the former saw Jewish doctrine as an indivisible whole comprising text and tradition together, while the latter denied a divine source for tradition and, therefore, its authority. The polemic with the Sadducees occasionally led the Pharisees to attempt to find all of tradition in the Scriptures, resulting in labored efforts, sophistry, and the kinds of extralogical methods of reasoning that were nonetheless perfectly acceptable at the time. But, argues Benamozegh, since we no longer live under such limitations, we should certainly be able to renounce these kinds of artificial connections.[16]

The definition of tradition put forward by Benamozegh allows for multifaceted articulation. The method can be illustrated with a classic example, the meaning of the word *hadar*:

> The word *hadar* [citron]—in its popular meaning—was commented on by Moses; I maintain it to have been understood by everyone. The legal, sacerdotal, political, and theological details, only a handful would have known. The consequences of certain principles, their development and various applications, no one as yet could see.[17]

By defining tradition thus, with as much stress on Revelation as on the possibility of development, Benamozegh stayed true to his deepest inspiration, concerned both with finding stable anchoring points and postulating the need for change. Significant nuances are brought to light by closer analysis.[18]

What he meant in his definition of tradition by "*that which was understood by everyone*" was what we could call *culture*: the collected morals, language, and "sensibility" of a people. "The oral law [*Torah she-be-'al-peh*] is no more than all the customs of the nation since time immemorial," he wrote in his commentary, *Em la-Miqra*.[19] This explains why there is a literal meaning, *peshat*, and a secondary interpretation, *derash*, equating to the meaning of the word as it would have been understood by the contemporaries of Moses and justifying the value of historical and philological research.

This involved a semantic displacement of the term *derash*, which generally means figurative, or even allegorical interpretation and which in any case expands on the text's primary meaning. For Benamozegh, true *derash* corresponds to the task of the philologist who reinvests words with their original meanings. There was surely nothing new about the application of critical method to the Bible, even in observant Jewish circles; what was different about Benamozegh was his association of such methods with the most traditional interpretative standpoint. New science was connected to an ancient approach and completed it.

The second dimension concerns the *legal, sacerdotal, political, and theological details, what only a handful would have known*. Benamozegh was above all interested in the theological aspect. All his work centers around what he referred to as "the traditional philosophy of the Jews," which is none other than Kabbalah. I will consider this in greater detail later on.

The third dimension concerns the future, the *consequences of certain principles, their development and various application, [that] no-one as yet could see.* Here to "explain" (*parash*) coincides with to "extend" (*paras*);[20] this correlation was not a pedagogically minded word game but a genuine grammatical fact. Benamozegh takes words extremely seriously: he is not interested in playing with terms to produce pretty ideas but is concerned with dredging the linguistic sediment for a tradition of implicit thinking. Once again, he fuses the ancient with the modern, the Kabbalist's sensitivity toward words with the specific linguistic interest of the nineteenth century.

A number of controversies are explained by this third dimension of tradition. In principle, revealed doctrine leaves no room for discussion, which is why Maimonides and others excluded all controversial subject matter from tradition in an attempt to protect its monolithic character. Benamozegh reasons quite differently. Tradition is not a body of frozen data but a living organism that coexists with the future of the people. From this perspective, interpretation is embraced wholeheartedly within tradition: it represents its deductions and extensions.

> Maimonides and Ravad asserted that matters of controversy do not form part of tradition. They said this to sidestep the doubts of the Karaites, but they also denied an essential truth thereby. . . . I reject such an unfortunate apologia, which would drown half the ship in its efforts not to go under.[21]

The Written and the Spoken Word

The relationship between the written and the oral is expressed in that between the word and the voice. Consideration of this issue in the modern age has primarily been a Protestant prerogative. In *Institutiones Hermeneuticae Sacrae*,[1] the German theologian Johann Jakob Rambach (1693–1735) addressed the problem of the inadequacy of reading the Bible for understanding its original meaning, since, as we read, that which gave the words meaning and vitality—the speaker's voice—is missing. Without the inflection and nuancing of the voice, much of the biblical characters' true intention is lost to us and we may occasionally even make enormous mistakes.

It is easy to recognize that the question is couched in terms of lack, of want: allowing that the presence of the voice is required for correct understanding of the written text, and given that such testimony is obviously gone for good, it follows that the true, original meaning of the text is definitely and irrevocably beyond reach.

This leads to Schleiermacher's concept of interpretation as an infinite task, where there is no compunction about defining a sacred text as a *mausoleum of religion*, its *dead letters* as the *pale reflection of a spirit that once existed and does no longer*. Schleiermacher's proposed solution was individual: the truly religious person did not need sacred books because he was capable of living spiritual values within himself. Objectivity is replaced by subjectivity.

The mechanism whereby the text is set at a distance is thus pushed to its extreme: absolute moral and doctrinal reference is suddenly seen as useless testimony. Individual introspection fills the vacuum left by the rejection of the interpretative tradition.

Benamozegh's direct reference on the subject was probably the Spanish poet and philosopher Judah ha-Levi (1075?–1141?), whose *Kuzari* reached conclusions utterly different from those arrived at by the Rambach-Schleiermacher school of Protestants.

It is true, ha-Levi asserted, that listening has numerous advantages over reading a written text because the speaker's voice adds substance to the message and renders it more comprehensible. Yet, the absence of a voice does not equal silence, as the traditional *te'amim*—a kind of expressive notation applied to Biblical text to mark accentuation, pauses, cantillation—are intended to replace it. They are a sort of "directions" to the text, providing it with structure and pattern. This closeness between traditional reading and spoken language enables the true meaning to cross the centuries, making unnecessary, or even inadmissible, a subjective reading—presented as the only possible alternative—where the reader fills in the gaps left by the written text. It is significant that this passage from the *Kuzari*[2] is to be found in a context praising community—praise only possible because the text was inherited with indications that reconstruct the voice that uttered it, thus the true source.

By drawing on this approach, Benamozegh found himself opposed to the position that enjoyed the widest currency in his day. For, in the nineteenth century, the sense of rupture was uppermost, expressed through the irreconcilable distance from the "truth" of the text (which would later be transformed into a positive assertion of an infiniteness of interpretations as a proof of freedom). His emphasis on orality should therefore be understood as a contribution to an ongoing debate in which much was at stake.

In an astonishing passage from the introduction to the Biblical commentary "Writing and Tradition" (*Ha-Ketav ve-ha-Qabbalah*),[3] Ya'akov Zvi Mecklenburg of Königsberg (1785–1865) takes up the same problem and—in part—the same ideas, though nonetheless putting a different slant on them. Mecklenburg introduces a personification of the Torah that politely invites the reader to become more closely acquainted. A disquisition ensues on the virtues of orality:

> Children of Israel, well you know that words straight from the mouth have an advantage over what is written. With his organs of expression, a man reveals his thoughts. Now he speaks out clearly, now he whispers. He points a finger, nods or shakes his head from time to time; even his arms speak. There is no part of his body, from head to toe, that does not shed some light on the obscurity of his ideas.
>
> All this movement is like a light to the spectator's eyes; like keys in the hands of the listener, that allow him to unlock the doors of the rooms where the speaker's ideas reside.[4]

After extolling gestures and the spoken word, Mecklenburg moves on to examine written texts, which can never be properly understood without mastery of the interpretative criteria. This is a matter of even greater importance when the text is biblical. The key metaphor is used again:

You should know, children of Israel, that without these means, the gates of the house of wisdom will never open, but remain locked forever. Your eyes will see only the rust on the outside of the door, but never will you make your way inside if you do not have a solid understanding of the criteria [qnei-middah] for knowing me. . . .

For writing beside tradition [qabbalah] is as flesh to the soul . . . whoever separates the parts that join together [deveqim] restricts himself to appearances and his face shall never draw near to the hidden.[5]

Despite such preambles, Mecklenburg seems not to be aware of the primordial philosophical problem raised by Rambach concerning the possibility or otherwise of rendering a past discourse present. He restricts himself to statements of purely rhetorical principle, producing something perhaps typical of Jewish exegesis, with its lesser sensitivity to questions—especially those in the Protestant mould—on the author's intention and the ever vexed issue of the reader's understanding.

I have kept for you, who belong to the most recent generation, the same energy that I was born with. And with your children, I will be as I was when I left my parents' care.[6]

More sensitive to the rigors of philosophical thinking, Benamozegh first sets limits on the hyperbolic assertions of the perfect preservation of tradition, the very definition of which he then proceeds to inflect somewhat: it is not a body of data passed on as it stands, but a process of transformation and adaptation.[7]

It is impossible—he writes—to escape change, which is one of the guiding laws of the human condition. There is, however, an original kernel that can survive and be passed down: he calls this the "primitive spirit of a people," which is none other than the *Volksgeist* of Herder, Hegel, and the Romantics generally. This spirit is passed down more through the spoken than the written word; it can also be perceived through its manifestations, on condition that the appropriate instruments are used. The "fixed" word of the written form is no match for the variation of expression offered by speakers who use it to convey new ideas. However, the supremacy of the "flexible" oral text does not lead to an absolute assertion of difference at the expense of equality. Quite the opposite. It offers the best guarantee of keeping the original spirit in a dialectic of change and stability, progress and immutability, borrowing from the evolutionary—yet at root Aristotelian—model of a simple, original kernel growing toward complexity.

Benamozegh nonetheless seems to echo Mecklenburg when he states that

> [a]gainst the vagueness and indefiniteness surrounding any written word to a greater or lesser extent, tradition has a remedy: the voice, the gestures, the physiognomy, the gaze, in fact, any living commentary that plugs the gaps and dispels the shadows. But what can the naked book teach the reader aside from stasis, inertia, and strict literal meaning?[8]

The taking of such a clear stance in favor of *living commentary* is more comprehensible if three different contexts, moving from the general to the particular, are examined in depth:

1. the general context of European philosophy in the latter half of the nineteenth century and the degree to which a relativist, subjectivist mentality was widespread;

2. the debate that developed around the issue of religious reform in the western European Jewish community;

3. the polemic surrounding Kabbalah in scholarly and orthodox Jewish circles.

Polemical Context

TRADITION VERSUS SUBJECTIVITY

It has been said, and rightly so, that metaphysics is nothing other than theology in a soutane, and that it would not maintain its right of citizenship for long after religion has been definitively dismissed. Unfortunately, law, justice, morality, virtue, liberty, heroism, and sacrifice are none other than metaphysics in action; and we do not truly understand how such notions could still be held once their only source has run dry.

—E. Benamozegh, *Israël et l'Humanité*

One of Benamozegh's particular concerns, and one he shared with many religious thinkers of the age, was to ensure that philosophical relativism did not dominate. In his specifically philosophical works, Benamozegh demonstrated the necessity of unity between the True, the Good, and the Beautiful, as well as how they connected together concretely. These principles once accepted (independently of the actual matter concerned), deducing God was simple: stability as opposed to movement, certainty as opposed to uncertainty, and unity as opposed to plurality were the characteristics of God as opposed to those of the world. Upholding the necessity of absolutes implied recognition of a religious imperative. Combating gnoseological and ethical relativism ran parallel to combating secularization.[1]

Combat recurs as a metaphor in several places, in different contexts that are nonetheless linked by the antirelativist and antisecularist theme. He wrote, for instance, to the celebrated Italian idealist philosopher Terenzio Mamiani, stating that they were both fighting in the same army, if in different battalions.[2] In a preface to a highly traditionalist book by the Moroccan Kabbalist Ya'aqov Abihatzira, he wrote that he shared the author's fight against criticism that rejected Kabbalah on the basis of a purely literal reading.[3]

The opposition to the written text can be explained within this conceptual framework. Taken alone, a text is open to at least as many interpretations as there are readers because it is fulfilled only through the act of reading, without which it would be nothing. This idea is obviously unacceptable in a philosophy of the absolute, where it is inadmissible that a revealed text might allow all sorts of theoretical or practical deductions. A hermeneutics founded on individual reading cannot be defined as religious: there is a risk of mistaking an inner for an outer voice and subjectivity for truth. On the contrary, it is necessary to accept an extreme hypothesis that probably reflects the Kabbalistic aversion to immediate, or purely literal readings: "[T]he text taken alone is less than nothing; what is essential is the interpretation."[4]

Thus, in the juridical texts, a law cannot be considered absolute if it remains at the mercy of opinion. Rationalism is the offspring of scriptural-ism, and absolute rationalism not guided by tradition leads inevitably to subjectivism.

Gioberti had already linked Luther with Descartes. He maintained that the former had replaced "ontological" method in religion with psychological method, thereby severing the thread of religious tradition, and that the latter had done away with the continuity of scientific tradition centering on the gradual seeking of truth. Both prepared the ground for subjectivism.[5]

As we have seen, Hegelian philosophy, for all its emphasis on the ideas of the *necessity* of development and the *universality* of Reason was, to Bena-mozegh, at root subjectivism in a disguised form. It alluded to the concept of the relationship between Being and Becoming and the dialectics of the absolute that follows from it. The same ideas figure in hermeneutic debate.

According to Benamozegh, it is not acceptable to imagine that in a juridical text the letter alone is sufficient. In the case of a semi-juridical text such as the bible, many absurdities would follow: there would be too many inexplicable gaps, too many contradictions, too much inequality of length from one passage to the next. To this extent "textolatry"—idolatry of the letter—constitutes the fullest denial of probability and good criti-cism.[6] But above all, rejection of tradition leads to a degree of uncertainty and variability that cannot be tolerated in a text purporting to convey an absolute message.

> The science of criticism is changing, uncertain, long, difficult, and
> unusual; such that the moral, practical, and dogmatic conclusions
> it reaches must share the same faults. And yet, it would be the
> only criterion set by God for believing and observing![7]

With his gloss of Joshua I: 8 "This book of the law shall not depart out of thy mouth; but thou shalt meditate therein day and night," Benamozegh reaches for a theory of interpretation.[8] The subject for meditation, he argues, cannot be a book in the strict sense because if it is really familiar it does not need to be meditated upon; if it is not sufficiently familiar, meditation turns into a series of baseless fantasies. It is tempting to paraphrase Benamozegh as saying literary criticism is always either pointless or misleading. However, "meditation" of a verse is not at all about interpretation: it is, in fact, none other than the repetition of oral tradition that might otherwise be forgotten.

Does that mean it is a positive tradition whose content can be stated? Benamozegh oscillates between the need to preserve highly specific, eminently theological data, and a requirement for stability at any price, above and beyond any specific content.

One could protest that if the latter position dominates, we enter the realm of utilitarianism: tradition is only preferable to free criticism because it holds out a promise of stability—something of absolute value in a practical sphere. Yet, the relative weakness of the position defended by Benamozegh—mixing practical and theoretical spheres—is only justified by the extreme gravity of the situation. It was no longer a matter of defending a given principle or religion, but the very idea of certainty and stability.

In fact Benamozegh defines certainty, accessibility, and perpetuity as inseparable characteristics for any rule of faith. He does not assert them to be the best characteristics in an absolute sense, but that they are within the particular system of faith. One might therefore conclude that Benamozegh accepts in principle the legitimacy of fully secularized thinking and that he is content to offer landmarks once the basic principle has been accepted. The religious thinker's "retreat" thus seems to be well underway, and the frequently touted "line of resistance" about to crumble.

In this context it is instructive to analyze a passage from the manuscript on tradition which was not included in the equivalent article. Once again, the omission is significant. Benamozegh claims to prefer by far "free science" to "unwholesome" Judaism, by which he means a doctrine rife with compromise that retains external manifestations without being able to justify their basis. The "great expanse of the ocean" of free criticism, he writes, is more safely navigated than shores "strewn with obstacles."[9]

The fact that the manuscript was specifically intended for students merely confirms the scope of the assertion. Was the standard bearer of tradition about to cross the line?

There is, though, another way to interpret the positions taken, involving a version of what Gershom Scholem calls "pure transmissibility," an idea he broaches in letters[10] written to Walter Benjamin about the works of Kafka. With the gradual erosion of a traditional frame of reference, there remains only the bare notion of tradition itself, a vehicle for vanished content. The main challenge is thus not any given doctrine so much as the general principle of the possibility, or legitimacy, of an orally transmitted doctrine.

We must of course be careful not to ascribe to Benamozegh thoughts he did not hold. He would surely not have shared the "nihilistic" ideas of Scholem, for whom an esoteric tradition that cannot be conceptualized or formulated can with even less reason be transmitted, since at root its subject is nothingness and itself, strictly speaking, meaningless. Benamozegh openly states the existence of positive content, going so far as to suggest a systematic order for it. As far as conceptualization is concerned, not only does he hold it to be possible, but it is the very task he sets himself.

The context for Benamozegh's work is not post-Nietzschian Germany but nineteenth-century Italy, a place where religious thinking—Christian as much as Jewish—had not renounced its claim to a central position based on positive theological content.

CRITICISM OF MODERNITY AND A NEW APOLOGIA

In nineteenth-century Italy, Jewish apologia—which had traditionally focused primarily on anti-Christian polemic—was forced to change radically. Secularization, not Christianity, was now the strongest adversary: Jews and Christians joined forces against a common enemy. Christian theology was still obviously not viewed as similar to Jewish doctrine, but differences were laid to one side in the face of more urgent problems. Samuel David Luzzatto admitted to disliking engaging in polemic against Christians. He wrote on the subject of his discussions with a Catholic theologian:

> If I am attacked, I respond. The swords are still there; they have
> not been beaten into plowshares. So, he has not come. But be
> a good Christian and let each of us concern himself with his
> native beliefs.[11]

Luzzatto described Alessandro Manzoni—the author of *The Betrothed*, and the living glory of nineteenth-century Italy—as a "Catholic whose faith is above suspicion." He was even more explicit when he went so far as to state that to refute Christianity—even in defense of Judaism—would be immoral as it would contribute to the spread of antireligious sentiment, then the gravest danger facing Christians and Jews alike.[12]

For his part, one of Luzzatto's colleagues at the Padua Rabbinical College, Della Torre, upbraided a French Jewish scholar for the excessive virulence of his discourse regarding Christians: Christianity was no longer the same religion as the one that had produced the medieval burnings at the stake, and the new spirit of tolerance should be taken into consideration.

As for Benamozegh, while he wrote a brilliant apologetic work on the comparison of Jewish and Christian morality, he selected—as we have seen—the Catholic Vincenzo Gioberti as his philosophical mentor.

These authors thus battled against modernity, or at least against a modernity that would have the effect of marginalizing religion and traditional morality. Their fight was more a question of resistance, interesting primarily at a documentary rather than a theoretical level. Yet, these conservatives shared a vision of the ongoing changes that was only possible because exacerbated by a clear sense of an adversary. Let us regard them as the privileged witnesses to a time of profound upheaval.

In a long, three-part Hebrew poem called *Derekh Eretz, o Attitzimus* (*Morality, or Atticism*),[13] Luzzatto develops a number of themes typical of this conservative viewpoint, in addition to several drawn from his stance on Judaism. The work is suffused with an ironic spirit: he lists the successes of modern civilization and its reasons for being proud, only to demolish them immediately afterward. It is highly reminiscent of the approach taken by his compatriot, the poet Giacomo Leopardi, who mocked the unbridled optimism of his age and derided its dogmatic belief in "the magnificent, progressive destiny of Humanity."

The modern spirit's absolute trust in its own strength was the first target of Luzzatto's polemic: according to his contemporaries, everything that belonged to the past was to be thrown out, since for them history involved a gradual march out of darkness and into light, from ignorance and violence to the cultured delicacy of morals. The position is summarized by a parody of Ecclesiastes: "There is no remembrance of former times: *everything* is new under the sun."

The poem continues to level a series of accusations against "the spirit of the century," all in the same ironic vein. Civilization, identified as a Greek spirit (or "Atticism"), preaches freedom but favors anarchy. Its alleged finesse is none other than softness, grounds for all sorts of hypocrisy.

> This generation's strength is lost,
> Its hands have become soft;
> There are perhaps no bears or tigers living,
> But the adders and vipers are breeding.
> Which would you prefer—
> A hidden foe or open enemy?

The utilitarians' algebra of pleasure is condemned as being a non-absolute morality that loses any value when divorced from social control and which tends at the end of the day to come down to the exaltation of money, for according to this particular view, money is more than ever what contributes to man's greatness.

All in all, these are fairly commonplace remarks.[14] Luzzatto was far more original and effective when pointing up the tyrannical and exclusive nature of modernity, to which he ascribes ten new commandments:

> I am Atticism, who has brought you out of the darkness of ignorance and into the light of reason and civilization. . . .

> Thou shalt worship no other god: for I the Lord thy God am a jealous God.

Dynamism was an essential, necessary characteristic of this modern deity:

> Desire not the peace and calm of honest men:
> it is a deadly calm and the peace of the grave.
> Desire not the peace and calm of the dove or the lamb;
> for I must grow, and raise myself up,
> and cast down all resistance.

From Luzzatto's perspective Judaism was the primary—the sole—barrier to the disastrous triumph of the spirit of the age. Hence the somewhat simplistic contrasting of "Greekness" and "Jewishness" at the core of his historical philosophy, whereby the latter represented the heart, interiority, simplicity, and stability, in latent or overt contrast to reason, external beauty, superficial redundancy, and energy at any price as manifested by the former. Atticism can charm while Judaism may be off-putting, but once in a while, Man turns away from his infatuation with the changing and the ephemeral and recenters on the values of the heart.

It is superfluous to state the extent to which this view deprives Judaism of any specific connotations by making it into a vague, undefined religion of sentiment. Luzzatto in effect plasters the label of Judaism onto an antiprogressive viewpoint. His apologia of Judaism is actually that of a certain conservative stance also adopted by many contemporary Christian thinkers and polemicists.

Lelio Della Torre also chose poetry to address the same issues. *The World Upside Down*[15] is an extremely elegant Hebrew poem nearly four hundred lines long, whose lexical richness verges on virtuosity. The opening lines give a flavor of the work:

> 'Olam hafukh, 'olam ha-pukh,
> bi-zmirotai aria' lakh
> [Upside down world, made-up/cosmeticized world,
> I shall acclaim you through my song]

This work too was an indictment of modernity conducted, like Luzzatto's, in an ironic voice. Besides the themes typical of conservative thinking—denunciation of hypocrisy, of the loosening of social bonds and society's adulation of the external—it is interesting to note an awareness of the changes occurring in the field of critical methodology. Research was the true religion of the modern age:

> The God of research has enlightened us,
> he separates us from the perplexed.

Its approach involved systematic dissection and unremitting claims to reveal all secrets.

The most recent generation, wrote Della Torre, *nani super humeros gigantium*, were contemptuous of their setting: instead of thinking of themselves as part of an unbroken continuum, their attitude to the past was destructive and dogmatic. They saw themselves as the offspring of a real, final birth after a pregnancy that had lasted throughout history until their appearance.

To look for major references to Judaism in this brilliant polemical work would be to read in vain, though there are obviously various sociological comments on contemporary Jews, such as a description of their thirst for recognition after a long period of marginalization. As for references to the abandoning of heritage, they are so general as to be applicable to tradition in its widest sense rather than to any specific faith. The polemical arrows are aimed not at the enemies of Judaism but at the heralds of modernity, supporters of progress who were scornful of tradition, and at individualism without points of reference.

THE DANGER OF INDIVIDUALISM

The other face of relativism was individualism. Tradition, according to Benamozegh's thinking, could not be conceived of outside an *ecclesia*: Jewish tradition was identified with the *Knesset Israel*—the entire Community—which was not only its guardian but also its source of inspiration and motor of development. Free, undirected reading, as the cause and effect of a rationalist approach, also resulted in the dissolving of community ties. In the act of private reading, the written word took on meaning and fulfillment, certainly, but it had a life only within the reader-text relationship, outside of which it remained—at core—incommunicable. This made it all the more incapable of inspiring moral or political rules and meant it was unsuited as the cultural foundation for a group.

This was a preoccupation of many nineteenth-century European intellectuals concerned about the way the economic and social practices of the bourgeoisie were dissolving community ties. We need look no further than Renan—for all Benamozegh considered him a thinker who "fluctuated" between idealism and skepticism—who wondered in 1890 if it was now possible to draw up a "catechism" for all mankind.[16] Before him Lamennais, in his *Essai sur l'indifférence en matière de religion* (1817), had advanced tradition as an antidote to the indifference of individualism, though this was not a specific, positive tradition but the body of "general reason" or common sense accumulated by mankind.[17] Benamozegh's conclusions were similar, though closer to the idea of a national tradition. What distinguished him, however, was his explicitly Kabbalistic inspiration. The *sefirah malkhut*, the last before the created world, is defined in the *Zohar* as both oral tradition and the community of Israel, which is but one proof among many of how conceptual systems from apparently very different contexts can be applied.

This system related not only to space, but to time as well. A hermeneutics that gives priority to text separates both men and their times: it isolates the present from the past and the future, restricting itself to a single moment that has not yet occurred and which will not occur again. It denies the legitimacy of interpretative continuity. The reader who approaches a text while claiming to elude the collective culture leaves no inheritance for later interpreters. Textual criticism that is intended to demystify tradition is in fact connected to a notion of timelessness and refoundation. The rationalist reader must start afresh every time, and sees this as a way of guaranteeing freedom from dogma and prejudice. Yet, at the same time, Benamozegh reminds us, he renounces any possibility of social communion or considered cultural transmission.[18]

These fears obviously related to a very real historical situation, and a traditionalist would have seen them especially clearly. With all due circumspection, and seeing it as no more than a simple interpretative hypothesis, we may take the story of the Reggio-Michelstaedter family, from Gorizia in Italy, as an eloquent illustration of this process of estrangement from tradition. Avraham Vita Reggio (1755–1846) was a noted Kabbalist. His son Isaac Samuel Reggio was an adherent of the "Science of Judaism" and resolutely hostile to Kabbalah, though he remained closely tied to religious traditions. Isaac Samuel's grandson on his mother's side was the philosopher Carlo Michelstaedter (1887–1910), a rare Italian existentialist, who committed suicide at an early age. It is worth noting that Michelstaedter's father was scandalized by his son's subjectivist and relativist ideas, which he refuted with an absolutist ethics that, at its core, lacked any positive content of its own.[19]

The positions successively held within a single family were thus as follows: adherence to Kabbalah as a "strong" tradition; a rationalist attitude that did not reject the notion of tradition; antisubjectivism without a defendable basis, and—finally—a philosophy that championed the primacy of existence and action. It is too tempting not to see such a succession as having historical meaning. Benamozegh stood at the center of this debate, between Kabbalah, the dogmatism of Luzzatto, and the first stirrings of a kind of religious existentialism.

JEWISH REFORMERS AND TRADITIONALISTS

In his 1860 commentary on the *Sifra* (compendium of rabbinical *midrashim* on the book of Leviticus), the Bucharest rabbi of Russian extraction Meir Leybosh, better known as Malbim (1809–1879), wrote:

> In 1844 cries of misery were heard. . . . The *Torah* has been betrayed by her friends, for which she laments, since the rabbis, scholars, and cantors came together at Brunswick, in the valley of demons.[20]

Forced to move from one town to another due to his intransigently orthodox positions, the rabbi was attacking a rabbinical conference organized in Germany as a response to the increasing secularization of European Jewry. The organizers felt that a new situation that had arisen with the civil emancipation of the Jews in a number of countries and their rapid assimilation with the surrounding culture required a certain adaptation in rites and doctrine.[21]

The Brunswick conference was the first of three such annual events, for which Avraham Geiger was the driving force. The decisions reached concerned—among others—the homily, the formulation of the Yom Kippur *Kol Nidrei* (cancellation of vows), and intermarriage between Jews and members of other monotheistic faiths. In all three cases the rabbis had expressed themselves in favor of modifying the rite. Intermarriage was permitted, for instance, on condition that the civil law of the country involved allowed the children to receive a Jewish education.

The bitter controversy in fact centered on the importance of the oral tradition. The rabbis convened in Brunswick, and later in Frankfurt and Breslau, maintained that some rituals—as well as some of those surrounding mourning—were no longer in tune with contemporary sensibilities and should be scrapped as obsolete. From this viewpoint, many of the traditions that had grown up around the biblical text were based on matters of historical contingency and could therefore be abandoned without impinging on the theological and moral heart of Judaism.

Malbim's reaction could not have been more explicit, or more determined to resist an outrage:

I have therefore armed myself like a warrior and begun writing my works on the Bible. . . . As regards oral teaching [*Torah she-be-'al-peh*], I have built a rampart with a keep and battlements. . . . It is this very work that will combat the enemies of tradition [*qab-balah*] before the gates, with a quiver full of powerful arguments; it will show that everything with regard to oral teaching was in fact given by heaven and is firmly anchored and printed in the literal meaning and the depths of the language.[22]

This champion of the eastern European orthodox resistance was fighting the same battle as Benamozegh, but their conception of tradition seems to have been fundamentally different. To the former, tradition was implicit in the text, which served as a sort of repository; textual support (*asmakhta*) was to be understood in the strongest possible terms, as the source and root of orality. From this follows his assertion that the literal meaning (*peshat*) and the interpretative meaning (*derash*) were related and indivisible.[23]

The latter went farther in his contemplation of tradition, making it all but independent of the text. The written word was to him simply the record of a wider reality; *asmakhta* had pedagogical value and the parallels between text and tradition had been exaggerated for quite other reasons.

Benamozegh's exegetic approach, as we have seen, was both tradition-alist and antidogmatic. He rejected interpretation of the Bible on the basis of unprovable assumptions, including the strict relationship between text and orality. Yet, at the same time, through his historical and philosophical approach, he was able to confirm various rabbinical statements and even, on occasion, to see them from another angle. The partial divorce between text and tradition in no way detracted from the worth of the latter. On the contrary, Benamozegh brings to bear considerable erudition in a range of areas—from natural sciences to comparative philology—in proving the solid basis of many *aggadot* generally regarded as being odd or obscure. For a nineteenth-century Kabbalist, taking words seriously meant justifying them in a scientific way. Benamozegh offered a "modern" response to "modernist" attack; he used new tools to buttress and support tradition.

A phenomenon similar to that of the German rabbinical conferences, though on a much less influential scale, was taking place among Italian Jewry. There, assimilation with an older and more markedly Christian society was unfavorable to reforming movements. Italian rabbis were intellectuals steeped in the humanistic tradition; connoisseurs of "belles lettres," they were generally well disposed toward the national culture. This kind of intellectual leadership was bound to regard the changes as less dramatic.

Michael Meyer, in *Response to Modernity: A History of the Reform Movement in Judaism*, interprets the lack of interest in the reform movement using the customary psychological categories of individuality and lightness as the natural prerogative of Italians. This is easily understood from statements such as "Italian Jews' personal preference was to move away from religious institutions rather than assume the burdensome responsibility of creating new ones."[24]

The changes in the lifestyle of Italian Jews were nonetheless at least as big as those happening in other European countries, though they took place with less upheaval because—at least for a large segment of the population—the ground had been prepared long before.[25]

Possibly the most outstanding difference between the modernization of the Jewish studies movement in Italy compared with the equivalent process in Germany, or even to some extent, France, lay in the fact that in Italy the protagonists were—with a few exceptions—orthodox scholars and rabbis. In Germany, the *Wissenschaft* encountered the Reform movement; in France, rabbis allied themselves with the scientific movement that was being introduced at least in part by German immigrants. Whether we ascribe it to an inability to recognize the seriousness of the crisis, to the weakness of academic oriental studies, or to the relative harmonization between traditional and secular disciplines, the fact is irrefutable: Reggio, Luzzatto, Della Torre, Eude Lolli, Marco Mortara, and Benamozegh were all either rabbis or scholars who were faithful to the religious tradition, and in the main they held positions of responsibility within their communities. David Castelli, as professor of Hebrew literature at the University of Florence and a researcher with a positivist perspective, and Salvatore de Benedetti, Hebrew professor at the University of Pisa, were exceptions: but the former studied with Benamozegh, and the latter had been the director of Jewish studies in the community of Livorno.

This continued to be the case in succeeding generations. The eminent historian and biblical scholar Umberto Cassuto was the erudite orthodox heir of Samuel David Luzzatto; Dante Lattes—a writer, popularizer of the first order, militant Zionist, and probably the highest profile Italian Jewish figure of the first half of the twentieth century—was ordained by Elijah Benamozegh.

One exception was Mosè (called "Maestro") Soave (1820–1882), a Venetian scholar who attempted to found a reformed Judaism that would allow religious dogma to be harmonized with moderate progress. Soave drew a clear distinction between the dogmatic and the ritual and legal aspects: the former was immutable and represented the very essence of Judaism (as for any religion), whereas the latter were time- and location-specific, and thus liable to the same changes as the other realities of life. "Ultra-orthodox" unconditional loyalty to religious practices was an obstacle to the Jew's ambition to "sit down at the banquet of communal life without seeing himself as a foreigner among his compatriots and fellow-citizens."[26]

Soave abandoned the idea of the Jewish nation. For him, "Israel [was] no longer a people; it represent[s] only a religious principle,"[27] and any hope of national regeneration was merely a pious dream the realization of which depended on God alone. The political sphere lay outside the scope of Judaism.

The harmonization of stability and progress and the central role given to the dogmatic side of Judaism was also a core part of Benamozegh's religious thinking. His solution, however, prescribed absolute faith in traditional ritual, grounded in a profound, complex dogmatic tradition vital to mankind. For Benamozegh, Judaism was a whole that could not be dismembered. Compromise was not only unjustified but also doomed to fail: it was better to choose—freely—between total acceptance of tradition and the freedom—also absolute—to criticize.

Making use of the powerful navigational metaphor already adopted by Benamozegh, Soave stated the exact opposite: "An experienced captain may throw part of the cargo overboard to safeguard the ship. Imitate him, if you wish to avoid shipwreck"[28]

Italy also saw attempts, at the initiative of Marco Mortara (1815–1894),[29] to organize a rabbinic conference like those that had been held in Germany. Mortara, a rabbi in Mantua from 1842 and a disciple of Samuel David Luzzatto, exemplified a liberal current in Italian Judaism and shared certain key ideas with the Reform movement. As far as dogma was concerned, he advocated a kind of return to biblical religion involving the relinquishing of a fair amount of tradition. This was seen as a creation of the Talmudic rabbis, contingent on a particular set of historical circumstances and not in a position to aspire to being absolute and constraining.[30] Mortara extolled a "return to Mosaic origins" within Judaism, at the same time as he held the Mishnaic-Talmudic developments in the highest esteem. In particular, he stated that at the time these great works were composed, the danger of geographical fragmentation and the lack of any central authority made it necessary to write down traditional rituals that had previously been transmitted orally. The same logic applied to the drafting of codes by Yitzhak Alfassi and Maimonides. Later on, a spirit of religiosity and a sense of conservation incited the Jews to add significantly to the number of rituals. This period being past, it was a question of conserving the *spirit* that had nurtured a centuries-old literary tradition rather than mechanistically sticking to outdated precepts.

We need to choose. Either we continue in the lethargic sleep of the Middle Ages, or we take the living work of the Talmudists up again. We must decide between the fruitless attempt to save a system that is now only history and the titanic task of restoring our rituals in a progressive spirit.[31]

For Mortara, as for the German reformers and the *Wissenschaft* scholars—though for the latter at a more strictly intellectual level, less closely implicated in social practices—there was a need to identify the deep reason of Judaism, its "essence." In this, there was general agreement that Israel had a religious mission to spread monotheism among the nations, and the Jewish diaspora could be seen as providential since it favored the dissemination of this message.[32]

The national idea of Judaism contained in this proposal was gradually abandoned along with any thought of restored political centrality for the land of Israel. Jewish eschatology lost its nationalist connotations and retained only the spiritual and religious dimensions.

Mortara's attempt failed: no reforming conference was held in Italy.[33] However, his ideas continued to hold dangers for a traditionalist such as Benamozegh, who saw fit to react with a long article that appeared in Livorno's *L'Israelita* newspaper in 1866.

The tone of the article was firm yet respectful: it was a far cry from the virulence of Malbim. Mortara was an adversary to be respected for his knowledge and his sincerity, and Benamozegh responded with a line of arguments that strongly expressed some of his central tenets. Firstly, he sketched out a theory of religion as an organism forming itself around a core, intended to resolve the tension between progress and immutability; secondly, he restated his unwavering agreement with the methods and ideas of the Talmudic rabbis, echoed throughout his writings, exegetic as well as historical.[34]

However, he concentrated his polemic on another aspect, rejecting the negative historical assessment of what Mortara called the Jewish Middle Ages, and that he claimed had begun with the great codifications of the rites. According to Mortara, Alfassi, Maimonides, and their successors had prevented any development due to their preoccupation with stability, which had led to a living spirit becoming a dead letter. This was also the position held by the leading members of the *Wissenschaft*: for Leopold Zunz, Marcus Jost, and Abraham Geiger, medieval Jewish culture was closed, dogmatic, and best forgotten. For them, it was crucial to dispense with this legacy if "Jewish literature" was to take its place in universal literature.

Benamozegh countered that between the great eleventh- to thirteenth-century Jewish authors and the Geonim, and between them and the Talmudic and Mishnaic scholars, there was a continuity. If criticism was in order, he maintained, it was more appropriate to direct it toward the instigators of this chain of tradition rather than drawing on cultural categories that belonged to an entirely different context. There was—in temporal terms—no Jewish equivalent to the Christian Middle Ages, in the sense of an age of obscurantism.

One of the key elements in his criticism was the definition of normative Judaism. As was his habit, Benamozegh expressed the choice to be made in clear terms. There was, notably, no third position between traditional Judaism and thoroughly free criticism. There was no point in hiding the fact that Judaism without ritual would be no more than simple deism—"socinianism," to use his term—in which a vague feeling of belonging would conceal total freedom or "established arbitrariness."

> We must either be more or less hidden deists, or persevere as
> Israelites. For our part, the choice has been made. it is now up
> to the reader to do the same; and may the whole world recognize
> the infinite merit of this excellent author, who has expounded
> the problem in its purest and clearest terms.[35]

Once again, alongside attempts to demonstrate the necessity and superiority of a philosophy of the absolute, we glimpse a possible legitimation of a set of opposite values: to Benamozegh, both options seem equally coherent, with the choice lying ultimately with the individual rather than being preordained.

Yet we should also note the degree to which Benamozegh shared the ideas and conceptual instruments of the Reform Jews. He denied that monotheism had been the primary concern for the doctors of the Talmud, as many reformers claimed, yet at the same time he made it the main theme of his ambitious *Israel and Humanity*. He affirmed Judaism's eminently political character, which had in part resulted in a certain dogmatic negligence,[36] but for him—as for the reformers—the children of Israel had a spiritual and religious task that had been facilitated by diaspora.

Benamozegh's insistence on tradition—ritual as well as dogmatic—was nonetheless sufficiently great to set him apart from the reformers on this crucial issue.

During the same period (1866–1888) he published a long article in Hebrew in the Paris newspaper *Ha-Levanon* on the possibility of using a biblical text to prove the existence of an oral tradition. The underlying argument was clear and can be summarized thus:

1. the entire Torah was initially oral;

2. it was written down, not in one but several stages;

3. everything that was not written down remained in the oral state, and since the completion of the Talmud this corpus resurfaced at irregular intervals. "Tradition would come back from time to time and then disappear again: [its] comings and goings at the speed of lightning."[37]

This tradition replaced the centrality of written text in times of weakness and forgetfulness, when a book might remain dumb where answers are needed. Of its nature it would be historical, ritual, and theological, but it is the last of these qualities that most attracted Benamozegh's notice.

Using the tree metaphor—as Hellenistic as it was Kabbalistic[38]—Benamozegh wished to convey the indivisibility of the various aspects of Judaism and at the same time establish a hierarchy:

The truth is that Judaism is one, homogeneous and indivisible; its dogma is the roots; the service, morals, literature, and history are the trunk, branches, leaves, and fruit; and when storm and devastation ravage the tree, its life can retreat into the roots of dogma.[39]

Jewish rite was certainly complex, and in fact neither the Mosaic text alone, nor rational criticism, were capable of supplying a fully satisfying explanation. This should therefore not lead to it being abandoned, but rather the opposite: a search should be made for a doctrine complex enough to justify it. This doctrine was, naturally, Kabbalah.

DEFENSE OF KABBALAH

Polemic in Italian Judaism: S. D. Luzzatto's Dialogues on the Kabbalah

From the fifteenth century on, the debate surrounding Kabbalah had been one of the most interesting areas of Italian Jewish culture. It was in Italy that the first doubts about the dating of the *Zohar* were raised in a critical spirit, and it was above all there that Kabbalah found opponents who felt it to be a dangerous "foreign"—in other words, Christian inspired—doctrine.

Yehuda ben Yehiel called Messer Leon and Elia del Medigo provided this opposition in the fifteenth century; the Venetian rabbis Leone Modena and Simone (Simhah) Luzzatto later also tried—unsuccessfully—to oppose the spread of the Kabbalah produced in Safed, for which Italy was one of the main centers for study, and dissemination to the Jewish communities of the West.[40]

As to the nineteenth century, a historiographical question must first be addressed. How was it possible that a culture that was esoteric and irrational at a theoretical level, and close to popular belief at a practical one, continued to be present—in the modern day—among the Jews of the peninsula? They had—or were about to—become legal equals with Catholic Italians, which represented the culmination of an integration process started long before. Kabbalah, with its generally exclusive discourse—around the *essential* specific-ity of Israel—was hard to reconcile with the then widespread trend toward finding a common religious ground with compatriots of other faiths.

Furthermore, from an intellectual perspective, throughout western Europe, including in Italy, Jewish science had in large part become a histori-cal science. Manuscripts were published, forgotten aspects of Jewish cultural history were rediscovered, and a critical assessment of them engaged upon, in accordance with the century's own imperatives of distance. Even those scholars who were personally orthodox in their religious beliefs were obliged in their research to demonstrate scientific objectivity. Their audience had also expanded considerably: much of their work was written in Italian or other European languages, and was therefore addressed at the "universal" scientific community, which was not supposed to hold preconceived dog-matic positions.[41]

Like other aspects of Jewish tradition, Kabbalah had ceased to be a doctrine experienced and invented from inside, and become an object of critical analysis. Efforts were made to determine its origins, and to find a non-Jewish context that could have given rise to a mode of thought seen as unlike the rest of the tradition, and above all as being hard for the rational mindset of the time to accept.

This relative weakening of Kabbalah had in fact commenced much earlier, in all likelihood around the second half of the eighteenth century, with the death of talented theologians such as Yosef Ergas and Moshe Hayyim Luzzatto, and of methodical thinkers like Immanuel Hay Ricchi and Avi'ad Sar Shalom Basilea. One gets the impression that after the great explosion of the early seventeenth century, Kabbalah continued to be very present in Italy, but only at the level of popular belief and practice; its development from that point concerned mainly the eastern European and North Afri-can communities. Until emancipation, the Italian Jewish intellectual elite concentrated its creativity on literature and linguistic studies, a trait that had long been present. Probably the most important figures of that time were the writers and poets inspired by the classicism of Pietro Metastasio,

Efraim Luzzatto (1729–1792), and Samuel Romanelli (1757–1814).[42] In this regard the education of Anania Coen (1757–1834) is interesting. He used his traditional training—which implies familiarity with Kabbalah—in a context of prescientific research, especially in the fields of Hebrew rhetoric, grammar, and lexicography.[43]

As a subject for scientific study in the nineteenth century, Kabbalah in Europe faced severe historical and philological as well as theoretical criticism. These criticisms were combined by the most virulent detractors, for whom the esoteric Jewish doctrine, which according to its partisans went all the way back to the Revelation at Sinai or—at the latest—to the time of Shim'on Bar Yohai (second century CE), belonged in fact to a far less mythical time and place, having its roots in late-thirteenth-century Provence and Spain. The content was generally deemed superstitious and obscurantist.[44]

The debate that took place in Italy was based on the same assumptions: philological certainties had been acquired, and it was impossible to go back on them. Only a few people were caught up in the debate, but it effectively combined a certain critical and philological attitude, characteristic of German scholars such as David Heymann Joel[45] or Adolf Jellinek, with a philosophical analysis developed by the Frenchman Adolphe Franck in particular. Thus, throughout the nineteenth century, Italy was the setting for one of the closing chapters in a dispute that had rumbled on for centuries: the polemic surrounding Kabbalah, whose new protagonists were Reggio, Luzzatto, and Benamozegh.

Traditionally, criticism of Kabbalah centered on three areas:

1. the *authenticity*, and by extension the authority, of the founding texts of Kabbalah. To critics, the doctrine was not—as its adepts believed—revealed, but wholly invented, and, moreover, invented comparatively recently;[46]

2. the *obscurity* of the doctrines, often expressed in incomprehensible terms, and which at any rate eluded rational analysis, a fact explicitly admitted by the Kabbalists themselves;

3. the danger of *heterodoxy*, above all in connection with the doctrine of the *sefirot*, which weakened the absolute unity of the divinity, and the anthropomorphic representations of God. This was not a purely theoretical controversy, but had social repercussions, since any perceived similarities between Kabbalah and Christianity might push Jews toward conversion.

Each of these three points received more or less emphasis from the Kabbalah's Jewish opponents, as dictated by the needs of the time. For a long while, the second point was probably the most important, and it formed part of the debate on rational and philosophical attitudes. At about the time when the effects of the great Sabbatianist disturbance began to wear off at the start of the eighteenth century, two of the most important works of Kabbalah to be published in Italy were produced. They were Yosef Ergas's *Shomer emunim* (*The Guardian of the Faith*) (1736) and Moshe Hayyim Luzzatto's *Hoqer u-mequbbal* (*The Philosopher and the Kabbalist*) (circa 1730), both written in the form of dialogues. In each case the Kabbalist's interlocutor is an intellectual—described as a philosopher or Talmudist—who is wedded to a purely natural logic, and who finds Kabbalistic ideas obscure and verging on the heterodox. I. S. Reggio's position, a hundred years later, was totally different.

The evolution of Reggio's position is interesting. In 1827 he devoted a chapter of his (Hebrew) book *Torah and Philosophy* to the relationship between Kabbalah and "rational enquiry." Issues of expediency meant that the chapter was refused by the publishers, and it was self-published separately by the author seventeen years later, in an anthology with other previously unpublished works.[47] In it, he expresses both admiration for the greatness of Kabbalistic doctrine and doubts as to the reliability of its sources. Overall, he suspends judgment, but attributes that to his own avowed incompetency. As an unconditional supporter of the literal interpretation of texts (what he called "the dry bread of *peshat*"), Reggio remained respectful of, and faithful to, the central idea that it was not necessary to resolve every uncertainty or mystery at any price. This was in fact what pushed him to condemn the dissemination of Kabbalistic ideas to the uninitiated masses. He argued that anthropomorphic or material images were only indispensable where the idea was too abstract to be comprehended other than through tangible representations: the more abstract and spiritual the subject, the simpler and the more material the representation should be. Consequently, the relationship between the object and the description must necessarily remain allusive.[48]

Misreading can therefore throw up insidious misunderstandings. Yet, despite serious reservations—including ones relating to the Kabbalists' boundless imagination, which could only be tempered[49] by philosophical discipline—Reggio's conclusion was that

> as we can read in the *Zohar*, when Israel was in its own land, in a state of purity, it could devote itself to secret doctrines. But now, impure and in exile, it should keep a certain distance. . . . We must therefore take care to show prudence regarding this knowledge, for the combined reasons of the depth of the subject, the inadequacy of the person studying it, the risk of errors arising out of the discussions of the Kabbalists themselves, alterations to

the texts, and a lack of the preparation needed truly to understand them. It is thus no surprise that a number of weak-minded individuals have been caught out by their desire for marvelous and secret things, which has led them into heresy. From their ruin, we should learn to lay aside the secret, hidden dimension of this learning, as its name indicates. Its analysis should remain a closely-guarded secret until such time as God has pity on the people of Israel, and pours pure water onto us to wash us of bodily impurities and stains of the soul; only then will he illuminate our eyes with the secrets of his sublime Science; soon, in the near future.[50]

According to Reggio, it was thus too early to be considering Kabbalah: its study was to be put off until the—mythical—time of total knowledge. It should be mentioned in passing that the opinions of Luzzatto and Benamozegh on the matter differ considerably. Luzzatto demonstrates caustic irony: we may well wait for the people of Israel to open their eyes, but it will only be to realize the inanities of the Zohar and Kabbalah in general. Benamozegh, in contrast, felt that the dissemination of secrets and the transformation of the esoteric into a public doctrine was related to the gradual coming of the messianic age.[51]

In 1854, Reggio adopted a drastically different point of view. The Kabbalists, he wrote, did not reason for themselves, but were content to follow in others' footsteps: they made amulets and practiced sorcery; they added strange dogmas according to their wishes. This offended God, tarnished man's nobility, and favored all kinds of mental aberration. Even anthropomorphism, which he had seen a few years before as a theoretical and linguistic necessity, was now denounced as a harmful invention that could turn the most balanced of individuals into a fanatic.[52]

What lay behind such a change of position on Reggio's part between 1827 and 1854? The cause is actually easy to find, and lies in the powerful influence of Luzzatto, which had already made itself felt with the 1852 publication of Dialogues on the Kabbalah and the Zohar; and on the Antiquity of Punctuation and Accentuation in the Hebrew Language,[53] a work that had been in a drawer for over twenty years.

We must first and foremost remember that Luzzatto was an implacable anti-Kabbalist, despite tendencies that could be discerned in members of his family (testimony, incidentally, to the extent to which Kabbalah was still the cultural "bedrock" for Italian Jews in the nineteenth century): his father was so imbued with popular Kabbalah that the rabbi of San Daniele del Friuli, "misinformed, felt he had to tell his parents that he exorcised angels."[54] For his part, the young Samuel David refused to obey his father

when he wanted to initiate him into the mysteries of "Kabbalistic meditation" and teach him to pray "with the Kabbalistic *Kavanot* . . . And I, who
no longer believed in those doctrines, refused to comply."[55]

His cousin Samuel Vita Lolli, who had a prodigious knowledge of
biblical text (it was said that he could identify a verse from its cantillation
signs [*te'amim*] alone), wrote Luzzatto a very long, concerned letter when
he heard of his doubts about Kabbalah, in which he exhorted him to think
carefully before disclosing his ideas and "discoveries."[56] Writing to Reggio,
Lolli expressed his perplexity as a traditionalist believer faced with the conclusions of the then twenty-one-year-old Luzzatto. "I have chosen the faith
and the Torah, which in all its signs and *te'amim* corresponds to the names
of God, and which was given by the same shepherd. I am still waiting for
you to give me proofs that will force this detractor into silence." In the end
it was the "detractor" who succeeded in swaying Reggio with the soundness
and richness of his arguments.

Luzzatto's *Dialogues on the Kabbalah* is actually an important text in
stylistic as well as a content terms. Reggio's Hebrew was rich and supple,
allowing him to adapt biblical expressions to other contexts, in the finest
stylistic tradition, He did not, however, step outside that tradition, and his
writing now appears irreparably dated. As for Luzzatto, who was frankly
conservative in his ideological position, he wrote in a Hebrew that was
contrastingly vivid and "modern."

The *Dialogues* are true dialogues rather than an artificial production
that, under the semblance of an exchange of comments, hid a treatise by
a single narrator. There is a psychological—even existential—dimension
to the work's two characters, the "author" and the "guest." They also have
biographies. Both of them contain elements of Luzzatto's own personality: the guest, in his open, critical spirit and the extent of his knowledge;
the author, in his love of linguistic and grammatical studies, his dignified
poverty, and great sense of hospitality. The scene was not neglected either.
The text drops us *in media res*, opening on a synagogue the night before
Hosha'nah Rabbah. An unknown individual, who we learn has arrived from
Poland, falls asleep, showing his obvious lack of interest in a Kabbalistic
rite. There follows an animated exchange on the legitimacy of sleeping in
specific situations, based on rabbinic sources, immediately after which the
discussion of Kabbalah begins to get heated.

The dialogue is dynamic. Sometimes the speaker is interrupted as arguments are refuted; the characters are continually on the move, entering and
leaving the synagogue and the author's house; they stop their debate to eat,
and so on. The many textual quotations are made after the relevant book
has been taken out of the library, and opened to the right page. The debate
is presented as a kind of journey through a great library. The reading of a

prayer of Kabbalistic origin triggers a series of criticisms from the guest that alternate between irony and brusqueness, drawing on grammatical reasons one minute and theoretical observations the next. The whole passage is a little masterpiece of polemical literature. A reputedly holy text is held up to ridicule, reduced to an assemblage of superficiality, contradictions, and crass errors.

Luzzatto was intensely hostile to the Romantic literature of his age, which he saw as symptomatic of its frivolity and decadence.[57] He himself, however, had the potential in Hebrew to be an author, narrator, or playwright, though Hebrew literature in Italy had by then reached the end of its creative phase, and was looking instead to eastern Europe for its future.

The *Dialogues'* "author" is a fervent Kabbalist who finds himself in trouble. Faced with the urgent questions of his interlocutor, his replies are generally fairly weak: he frequently resorts to the formulae *ignoramus* and *ignorabimus* in view of the greatness and complexity of the doctrine:

> The author: When we study the texts of the Great Lion (Yitzhaq Luria) and the lion-cubs, his disciples, we are not in a position to understand. We should therefore restrict ourselves to a reading of the words.

> The guest: And so, please, I would like to understand how it happened that there have never been so many books written.[58]

According to the author, only the great—and in particular those who have been initiated into tradition—are in a position to understand: finally, authority is the principle on which he calls, which is why the Kabbalist is regarded as an obscurantist.[59] In a letter he wrote at the age of twenty, Luzzatto's criticism of Yitzhak Luria and his disciples has about it the flavor of Voltaire. He calls them "lazy beardies," and accuses them of having added a considerable weight of folly to the prejudices of the past for no other purpose than to confound good sense and, by misleading their audience, to live in opulence.[60]

Luzzatto's comments in the *Dialogues* fall into three categories:

1. theoretical and general criticism: Kabbalah is founded on a medieval way of thinking and is inspired by Judah ha-Levi's (twelfth century) *Kuzari*;

2. criticism centering on the dating of vowels in the Masoretic texts, on which certain Zoharic arguments are based: it can be deduced that the text must be later than the vocalization (eighth century),

and thus much later still than the time of the *Mishnah* (second
century), to which the tales refer;

3. linguistic analysis of the *Zohar*: the text displays numerous linguistic
   anachronisms, including words of Castilian origin, and other such
   flaws.[61]

After this violent attack, Luzzatto never returned to the subject. He
saw it as being outdated and no longer current, in view of the fact that in
any case "the century [was] too material for the effects of mysticism to be
harmful to Mosaism."[62] Furthermore, the polemical target of this remarkable
book lay not in Italy at all, but in eastern Europe, and it was Hassidism. If
he decided to publish the work twenty-six years after the time of writing, it
was because of what he called "the dangerous effects" that Hassidism, "the
enemy of all culture," was still having among the Jews of those areas. It was,
however, not worth wasting too much effort on ideas that had already run
their course in most of western Europe, being far more urgent to grapple
the rising tide of atheism than to combat mysticism.

In his response,[63] Benamozegh analyzed occasional comments by Luzzatto, without succeeding in doing more than making some of his conclusions
appear slightly less assured. His interest was more religious and philosophical than philological;[64] in this sense, Benamozegh's position regarding the
religious crisis was at root similar to Luzzatto's. All his philosophical and
critical work is presented as a response to subjectivism and its corollaries,
theoretical skepticism and indifference to religion. However, he overturns
Luzzatto's assumption: the crisis in Judaism was indeed a consequence of
its neglect of the dogmatic/philosophical side, and its reduction to a set
of practices whose only purpose was to remind the faithful of the ancient
national character of Israel, and bring them closer to the idea of monotheism.
The "material" or "practical" Judaism advocated by Luzzatto was, according
to Benamozegh, ensured a quick and certain demise: thus conceived, it was
bound to lose its specific character early and be transformed into a vague
deism, destined to be succeeded by calm indifference. For adhering to the
Luzzatto viewpoint meant saving the body but sacrificing the soul, keeping
the act but rejecting the thought that informed it. For Benamozegh, the
soul—the very mind—of Judaism lay in Kabbalah.

Benamozegh played on the ambiguity of the term *qabbalah*, which
means "tradition" in a general sense, as well as *Kabbalah*, meaning a corpus of esoteric Jewish knowledge. He never employed expressions such as
hokhmah nisteret (hidden science) or *torat ha-sod* (secret teachings), habitu-
ally used by followers to indicate the latter meaning. This derives from
two presuppositions:

First, tradition is unique, and there are no clear demarcations between the ritual or Aggadic oral tradition of the Talmud and *Midrash* and the metaphysical tradition that culminated in the *Zohar*. They are two sides of a single phenomenon, with different modes of transmission.

Second, Kabbalah is not a secret doctrine. If it is shrouded in mystery, it is because its complexity necessitated precautions. There is no longer any reason for this; on the contrary, it should be made clearer so that the greatest possible number of people can benefit from it. As we have already seen, Benamozegh goes so far as to say that the gradual dissemination of Kabbalah to the Jews needs to be the spiritual corollary to the material progress of civilization.[65] The metaphors used to indicate that the task of modern Kabbalists consisted in making the doctrine clearer and more intelligible are especially interesting: it was a matter of "removing the rust of centuries which has made it into vain formalism";[66] of clearing a forest where the finest fruit trees were choked by undergrowth;[67] finally, to spread waves of light to bring order to a chaotic whole.[68]

THE INADEQUACY OF LITERAL INTERPRETATION

Along with rationalists and reformers, Benamozegh shared the view that there was a decadence to nineteenth-century Judaism, by which they meant a loosening of community bonds, a steady loss of language and culture, and—above all—a falling away of religious practice and feeling. The Jewish people's raison d'être was eminently religious: by connecting the Romantic idea of *Volksgeist* with the biblical notion of electedness, Benamozegh emphasized the priestly role of the Jews. Judaism was the religious soul of the world; it had a necessary but not exclusive role in the "spiritual economy" of the peoples. Other nations were assigned the task of spreading the philosophical, political, and aesthetic spirit.

This religion did not, however, boil down to a simple set of practices. Interpretations of Judaism as a doctrine of action that left free range for all sorts of theoretical justifications, in short, as a-dogmatic orthopraxy, were the product of weakening and oversight. The interpretation successfully adopted a half-century later by the likes of Martin Buber and Franz Rosenzweig, which resembled existential philosophy, was condemned as soon as it made its first, tentative appearance.[69]

The champions of this idea were, according to Benamozegh, acting in complete good faith, since they were faced with a set of practices that seemed to have no overall, coherent meaning, and thus were open to all manner of speculation. Yet, practice was merely the outer casing, and the complexity of the ritual no more than implied that of the underlying dogma,[70] which was, however, partially lost, since it in fact concerned tradition in the true sense, that is, the personal transmission of difficult, subtle doctrines from master to pupil and generation to generation. This was the case for Benamozegh himself, as he discreetly acknowledged in a footnote.[71]

The *pashtanim*—the interpreters who emphasized the literal meaning of the biblical text—were therefore the victims of a misunderstanding. They nonetheless bore a heavy responsibility for the crisis the Jews were experiencing.

> Those who give primacy to the bare letter reduce tradition to nakedness. . . . For them, the goal of human existence is to accomplish an infinite number of tasks with hands, feet, mouth, eyes, and ears: in other words, with every part of the body except the highest—the brain—or the best of its faculties—the intellect.[72]

> He who wishes to avoid the beliefs of tradition (*qabbalah*) must fall into the trap of criticism: there is no escaping it.[73]

> No other choice is possible, between the Kabbalists and the demolishers (*mefareqim*).[74]

The refusal to acknowledge the existence of a doctrine parallel to the written text opened up a crack through which a critical spirit could penetrate, with inevitably skeptical premises and conclusions. The text alone, being partial and incomplete, could not sustain critical objections. It necessarily referred to something else, which underlay and completed it.

If traditional explanations are rejected, the Bible is reduced to a simple, inconsistent text. How, for instance, is the "resemblance" between man and God described in Genesis I: 26–27 to be understood? If the hyperbolic hypothesis—Kabbalistic in origin—of a real correspondence between High and Low is discounted, either the opinion of Luzzatto must be adopted, whereby the Bible was couched in simple anthropomorphic terms because the vast majority of people were incapable of abstract thinking, or it must be accepted that in antiquity a minimum of corporeality was attributed to even the highest of beings. This is both inadequate and absurd.

In the traditional, metaphor-rich style that characterized much of his Hebrew writing, Benamozegh wondered:

> What seduced so many scholars of Israel to follow vanity and become vain themselves? The work of the Kabbalists, or of those who interpret literally, who believe only in the superficial

meaning produced by the union of letters and words, and in the results of scientific enquiry?[75]

An entire universe is revealed behind the text: the religious people par excellence necessarily disposes of a profound doctrine from which it draws its inspiration and conviction. A spirit truly committed to research cannot be satisfied with a doctrine of action in which theory is optional and of secondary importance, nor with the "puerile" reasons invoked by the rationalists:

> There are people who are not content to observe practical com-
> mandments, because their souls yearn to walk in the garden of
> divine wisdom, graze its gardens and gather its roses, the flowers
> of wisdom and knowledge. And so long as they have not under-
> stood things to their truest extent, they will constantly be tossed
> by the storm that howls unceasingly in their souls.[76]

Tradition, both in the general sense of oral teaching and Kabbalah proper, sheds light on the Scriptures: it does not create things, but renders them visible.[77] The Scriptures taken alone, out of context, are ephemeral enough. For Benamozegh, true Judaism involves accepting the Bible, but as part of a larger whole by which it is overshadowed "as eternal life [over-shadows] the existence of an instant."

The positions of Luzzatto and Benamozegh could not be farther apart. The former saw the lies of Kabbalah as an impediment to a pure view of Juda-ism and liable to lead to it being corrupted and abandoned. This risk needed to be confronted urgently as the number of skeptics was rising fast.[78]

Benamozegh in contrast claimed that neglecting Kabbalah would pro-duce an unnatural situation such as only the most ill-intentioned sorcery could achieve, in conjunction, obviously, with the devastating effect of time on the delicate mechanisms of transmission. If a prophet of evil had wanted to strike the Jews with the most calamitous curse possible, he would have opted to divide the Torah into two parts, one practical and the other doc-trinal. The latter would have been forgotten over generations, leaving only a set of empty instructions covering prohibitions and permissions.[79]

It is not hard to see how Luzzatto came to reply thus to Benamozegh's overtures of friendship:

> Are you not opening a terrible gulf between us? Do we not find
> ourselves diametrically opposed? . . . So consider whether or not
> we can be friends.[80]

He added ironically that he considered himself as a friend of anyone who sought the truth unalloyed with fable:

> Anche coi misticisti
> Anche coi gesucristi
>
> (Even with mystics
> Even with the jesus-christs)

To which the Livorno rabbi retorted that the longevity of Judaism was above all due to "the metaphysics intermingled with its institutions," adding,

> Please don't imitate Napoleon in his antipathy towards ideo-logues! He wielded a sword, so it suited him well enough, but for you—who wields a pen?[81]

KABBALAH AND PHILOLOGY

At a time when the text held a central position as testimony to the past, Benamozegh upheld the centrality of the oral tradition. True Kabbalah was not written down, but passed on by word of mouth. Indeed, the key texts of postbiblical Judaism, the *Mishnah* and the Talmud, were put into writing only very late, for reasons of contingency. There was no reason to regard Kabbalah differently: on the contrary, the reticence that made it so suitable for oral transmission was inherent in its complexity. The vertiginous characters of the divine world could only be expressed in more or less tangible terms, with all the attendant risk of unfortunate misunderstanding.

If the doctrine was ancient and resolutely oral, the major texts could still have been written much later.[82] This was true of the *Zohar*, which Benamozegh, in accordance with the findings of philological criticism, dated to the thirteenth or fourteenth century. In his opinion, Kabbalah was a sort of *midrash*, a collection of doctrines that kept pace with the existence of the Jewish people. His analysis went farther regarding the historicity of Kabbalistic doctrine, which he saw as having developed gradually: there had been no sudden birth of a rigid and immutable thought system. Thus, there was gradual revelation up to the *Zohar*, which represented an end point rather than a beginning.

Benamozegh traced this progression as a growing, uninterrupted spread of light:

From the beginning of the process whereby the oral *Torah* was written down, the East was illuminated by rays of majesty that rose up to the celestial canopy, when a thread of mercy was drawn from the sun of Kabbalah and began to shine on earth; it was fine and weak, since it was but the beginning of the dawn. But it grew slowly lighter and lighter: to start with, a slight allusion behind a thickness of veils, later on explicit ideas. Thus, as far as the *Talmud Bavli* and *Yerushalmi*, which abound in stories and allusions stamped with Kabbalah. . . . And then came the books of Kabbalah, which also used hidden language; up to the *Zohar*. Then, the small ray of light took the shape of the constellations of Taurus, the Pleiades, Orion, and the whole diaspora caught fire like a torch.

Between the time of Shim'on Bar Yohai, the author, and that when his work the *Zohar* was disseminated, there has never been a gap: . . . there has been a thread, pulled to varying degrees of tautness, but ever-present.[83]

Kabbalistic tradition, by nature doctrinaire, was not comparable with ritual tradition, which was juridical in nature. It was too delicate, and therefore needed many conditions to be met before its study could be undertaken; it was too complex to be summarized and popularized. The limited number of people who had cultivated it had necessarily led to problems of transmission.[84] Little by little, Kabbalah had ceased to be studied with the appropriate instruments.

It was reduced to mere form, and it is easy to see why enlightened minds refused to take it seriously, given the state it was in. Denied its traditional base, it appeared to be a ragbag of superstitions and absurd, abstruse beliefs: this was the conclusion Benamozegh reached. Thus, for the good of Judaism—of which Kabbalah was the soul—as well as for the good of the whole world, for whom the Jews were the religious heart, it was important to breathe life into the apparently dead edifice that looked so heavy and impenetrable.

The nineteenth-century cabalist takes up the theme of another great Italian Kabbalist of a century earlier, Moshe Hayyim Luzzatto, who was already denouncing that the doctrine (or science; the Hebrew word *hokhmah* can mean both) had been reduced to a collection of hollow terms that one read without understanding, as if one was limiting oneself to merely reading the book's table of contents.[85]

The thinking of Elie Benamozegh, the last Italian Kabbalist, brings together the different intellectual demands of the Kabbalists in Italy in the early eighteenth century, when the esoteric doctrine was still strong enough to ward off the rise of rational thought. During a final blooming, remarkable authors such as Immanuel Hay Ricchi (1688–1743), Avi'ad Sar Shalom Basilea (1685–1730), Yosef Ergas (1688–1730), and Moshe Hayyim Luzzatto (1707–1746) wrote works that would have a key place in Kabbalistic literature. Benamozegh defended the Kabbalah against rationalist pretensions, as did Basilea, a writer with whom he shared the idea of a substantial identity between the rabbinic tradition and the Kabbalah but also—more original—the notion of a fundamental accord between the sciences, which unveil the truth in the course of time, and the knowledge of the rabbis, keepers of timeless truth, by denouncing the pretensions of philosophical systems posing as absolute and definitive. With Ergas, Benamozegh shared a concern for transferring Kabbalistic notions from a rhetoric narrative and allusive context to the discursive and systematic context of philosophy. Both undertook a philosophical reading of key passages in the *Zohar* or books inspired by Yitzhaq Luria, while distinguishing clearly between the theoretical status of philosophy and the Kabbalah. The most famous of these eighteenth-century authors, Luzzatto, postulated that the passage of time and the Kabbalah's imperfect handing down had made understanding it almost impossible. He saw himself as the man who could render its venerable doctrines understandable again by formulating them clearly and precisely. This was exactly the aim of Benamozegh, who considered himself to be ridding the ancient science of the "rust of centuries."

Benamozegh was therefore the heir to an Italian Kabbalistic culture which had already begun to embrace the challenges of modernity.

REASON AND DIVINE TRADITION

The relationship between Kabbalah and philosophy is far from simple and cannot be seen as unambiguous. Historically, both standpoints have provided instances of conflict within the Jewish intellectual construct. Some authors point to an oscillation between the two: rationalist excesses led to a reaction from those most resistant to such an approach.[86] Georges Vajda remarked with subtlety on the paradox contained in many Kabbalists' connecting of intuition and tradition.[87] For his part, Charles Mopsik tried to reincorporate what has often been called "Jewish mysticism" into the history of Jewish thought. "For many aspects," he wrote, "the Kabbalists' intellectual work is of greater philosophical interest than the Aristotelian drivel that saturates Jewish books of philosophy."[88]

Naturally, there was another line of Jewish thinkers who rejected both camps, considering them strangers to "genuine" tradition. One of the most famous, and most intransigent, representatives of this school of thought—as well as an epigone—was Samuel David Luzzatto. He saw the philosophical spirit as having entered Judaism through Arab Aristotelianism in the Middle Ages, adding nothing but confusion to the austere structure of Judaism. Moreover, philosophy imposed its principles in the exegetic domain: allegorical interpretations that sought to uncover reasoned truth from biblical stories were in fact arbitrary violations of the text.[89] Seen this way, Kabbalah and philosophy are one and the same dream.[90]

In contrast, the Kabbalist's relationship to philosophy was extremely complex. A key to understanding it might be that he shared the spirit, but did not approve of the tools. A philosophical mindset is required to comprehend Kabbalah, for all that it is considered as a revealed doctrine rather than the product of rational enquiry.

The distinction was made very plain from the earliest period of the *Zohar's* dissemination. The definitions drawn up by Yosef Ibn Waqar, who lived in Toledo in the first half of the fourteenth century,[91] were adopted by all who took up the subject: philosophy is based on argument, whereas Kabbalah is a tradition supposedly derived from the prophets, and thus claiming to be authoritative. The former is acquired by the correct use of logic to identify sure premises and draw the necessary conclusions from them. The latter is knowledge learned from a teacher who provides his students with both principles and exegetical methods.[92]

For Moshe Cordovero, rational enquiry could access partial truths which were completed by revelation, for which tradition was the vehicle. Logical deduction draws ever nearer to reality, but cannot entirely reach it.

In a very clear apologue he shows that the work of reason is founded on doubt and exclusion: Shim'on, Levy, and Yehudah see Reuben pass by, bent double under the weight of a heavy bag. Observation and reflection allow them to form hypotheses as to the contents of the bag, with an escalating probability of accuracy, but only Reuben, who filled the bag, really knows what it contains.

If the contents are known, what then is the work of the interpreter? Cordovero wrote:

> For all that we are the inheritors of the true tradition, we still need to commit ourselves to really understanding the verses of our Torah, and the reasons for the commandments it contains, for we know that there are secrets within the secrets, and hidden things within the hidden things, and that our comprehension has not the capacity to plumb such depths of secrecy.[93]

Two centuries later, Moshe Hayyim Luzzatto raised the same question. In *The Philosopher and the Kabbalist*,[94] he is virulent in his rejection of free enquiry, which he accuses of appropriating the name of Science, whereas only Kabbalah, as a revealed doctrine, can claim the term.

> Philosophy and research are continually wronging this great Science (*hokhmah*, or Kabbalah), like an insolent servant trying to dominate her mistress. It is a kind of leprosy that has really spread in Israel because of our many sins; for the children of Israel it has been a powerful obstacle that has caused wise men with a love of learning to stumble.[95]

Despite the severity of these antiphilosophical remarks, Moshe Hayyim Luzzatto establishes the traditional distinction between the two kinds of knowledge: his polemic concentrates not on the legitimacy of philosophy—within a clearly delimited terrain—but on what he perceives as its arrogance. Throughout the work, the questions of the philosopher elicit explanations from the Kabbalist; they are, in a way, the preamble to them, and as such useful (true Science is revealed in nature and prophetic in origin), if not necessary. At any rate, they were not mutually exclusive.

Benamozegh's intellectual training came from two directions: his Jewish knowledge derived largely from his uncle, the famous Moroccan Kabbalist Yehudah Coriat, while in secular matters he was in the main self-taught. It should be remembered how in his autobiography he describes hiding Gioberti's books under the counter of the warehouse where he worked, and in another passage describes how as a child he read all the way through the *Zohar* twice with his teacher.

In truth, the Moroccan milieu that had produced Coriat was not conducive to a rationalist philosophical approach. Coriat himself, although a member of Moroccan Judaism's enlightened faction,[96] was harshly outspoken about rationalism.[97] The illustrious Ya'aqov Abihatzira, who was published by Benamozegh, and esteemed in the popular imagination as "holy," held an even more extreme position: recourse to rationalism to resolve the basic problems of mankind and the world was for him nothing short of comparable with the instinct to evil (*yetzer ha-ra'*).[98]

If this were the basis for Benamozegh's Judaism, it is easy to see why he felt the urge to beg the reader's indulgence toward his youthful work on the Psalms, for all that he did so with a barely concealed dose of irony:

> You must understand that I have rolled a little in the mud of philosophy, and am not yet entirely cleaned of its stain. My reason [*kelayot*] suggested several times that I remove myself from its environs, but until now I have not had the heart [*libby*] to do so.[99]

A few years later he had thoroughly embraced the philosophical dimension, without losing faith with his traditional education. He then wondered about the relationship between the two, managing to draw a distinction: the "search for truth" was not the same thing as "true tradition"; "philosophical induction" was not synonymous with "kabbalistic deduction."[100] Yet, he saw the former as an indispensable preliminary to the latter: "The true Kabbalist must be a philosopher."[101] Kabbalah invested philosophical space; Shim'on Bar Yohai, the putative author (or inspirer) of the *Zohar*, is described as a "master of the *Mishnah* and philosopher."

Nonetheless, Benamozegh's attitude to the matter is not devoid of ambivalence, regarding both style and content. On the one hand, he can write that without Kabbalah, which is the divine Science (*hokhmah*),

> we, the cherished children of the Creator, who have pledged
> with him an alliance that will never be abolished, would once
> again become like blind men, feeling our way through the
> dark, searching for the smallest chink or tiniest spark of light
> to illuminate us.[102]

On the other hand, he refers to Plotinus as a "brother, close to the Kabbalists," and as "standing out from the throng" because he held ideas that accorded with those of the Kabbalists. Likewise, he notes the great similarity between the "divine Science" (meaning Kabbalah), Pythagoreanism, and Platonism.[103]

Earth would never have known the secrets of heaven had the latter not turned its attention on it,[104] writes Benamozegh, exalting the role of (Kabbalistic) revelation. Elsewhere, he places these same secrets on a level with the truths brought to light by human reason: this is the meaning of the equivalency he establishes between the *sefirot* and Platonic ideas.[105]

At the end of his intellectual path, there remains no doubt about Benamozegh's statements: Kabbalah is an intuitively expressed metaphysics, and attempts to interpret the former using the methodology of the latter are not only legitimate, but essential.

> Each time a somewhat idealistic philosopher elevates the expression of his thoughts, we seem to hear the reasoning of a Kabbalist, the clear proof that we are not the plaything of illusion in seeking to interpret the one through the other.[106]

In his final publication he writes: "To recognize the relationship between Kabbalah and philosophy, you only need to have a pair of eyes and an acquaintance with both disciplines."[107] Elsewhere, he brackets them together as sciences of first principles.[108]

In the eighteenth century, the works of the likes of Yosef Ergas and Moshe Hayyim Luzzatto still shared an entirely Kabbalistic perspective. Their aim was to disseminate the divine science clearly and systematically: philosophical arguments were put forward only to be rejected.

One hundred and fifty years later, Benamozegh was forced to step beyond these boundaries. Himself the student of a prestigious teacher, and thus perfectly representative of the model of the directly taught Kabbalist, that chain of transmission ended with him. He therefore directed his knowledge outward, attempting to insinuate the Zoharic tradition into the European philosophical debate. In his French and Italian writings, he tried to make seemingly obscure concepts clear to an educated Jewish and non-Jewish audience by couching them in current philosophical terms.

His desire for recognition allied to a genuine commitment to the values of independent research pushed him a long way in that direction. Significantly, his *Credo* concluded with a panegyric to doubt. Doubt alone, he wrote with some solemnity, could engender true understanding, since religion—like philosophy and science—demanded research and impartiality.[109]

In other texts intended for other audiences he asserted a belief in the fundamental value of keeping commandments, the "intrinsic virtue" of it in Kabbalistic terms. In the economy of the universe, every religious gesture has value; movements here below influence the upper realms.

Moral, national, and historical reasoning was all valid in his opinion, assuming an awareness of its inadequacy and pedagogical purpose. However, the gestures of faith are larger and more resonant, as Benamozegh the "philosopher" poignantly states in a letter to Luzzatto:

> Tomorrow you and I will hear the sound of the *shofar*. What will it mean to you? Doubtless, nothing more than one pretty but puerile explanation among the thousands to be found for it outside of Kabbalah; and to hear it with devotion will require you to make an extraordinary effort of faith. For me you know it is quite different. Every note has its importance, as every atom of matter is a mystery, as each body has its place and worth in creation. For me the Torah is a model of the world, it is the world in divine intention, the real Word incarnate in practical commandments. What do you think of that? Am I a friend of material Mosaism, or am I not? Though it seems to me, in a way that differs slightly from your own.[110]

A single individual thus combined the philosopher who extolled rational impartiality and the Kabbalist who believed in the "cosmic" efficacy of action.[111]

The latter doctrine finally found a place in a complete philosophical system adapted to the European sensibility. The enthusiastic comments of youth, in which the beauty of kabbalistic ideas was seen as evidence of their truthfulness, gradually gave way to arguments more in keeping with the critical spirit of the time. Yet even when he wished to be scientific, his hermeneutics and criticism remained strikingly original.

SCIENCE, METHOD, AND TRANSMISSION

As for you, dear reader, know and understand that the words of the Science of truth may either be perfectly understood so as to seem as clear to the eye as the sun is, or else completely misunderstood, and they are then as strange as it is possible to be.

While they are pale and insipid to those who learn them without understanding properly, he who studies and understands them will find them to be a deep science, compared to which the other sciences are as nothing.

—Moshe Hayyim Luzzatto, *Hoqer u-mequbbal*
(The Philosopher and the Kabbalist)

One cannot understand a book of Kabbalah by leafing through it, because it is a science that requires to be studied systematically, beginning with its premises and basic principles. This attitude is also valid for every other science.

—Yosef Ergas, *Shomer emunim*

It is hard to understand the work of Benamozegh without being aware both of his passionate, sincere participation in the European scholarly research centering on philology and the distance that separated his approach from that of other scholars.

Throughout the hundreds of pages of his historical writings, commentaries, and polemical works, Benamozegh followed interpretative strategies that marked him out from the current of scholarly thought around him. We may hazard the suggestion that his hermeneutics was that of a passionate individual who *lived* the doctrines he analyzed. The consequence of this is not the perpetration of violence upon texts with the intention of revealing preconceived ideas, but the emergence of new and surprising meanings. At times Benamozegh manages to captivate the reader with the rashest of hypotheses because he writes as one who is himself convinced.

Long expositions on the rites and beliefs of ancient Egypt and their similarities to Kabbalistic ideas (which look like an easy target for the mockery of historians), reveal themselves to be fascinating. Seemingly fantastic deductions end up looking convincing. Benamozegh's outlook, steeped in Kabbalah, vibrates in harmony with ideas uncovered in Egyptian mythology, as well as Platonic and neo-Platonic ones, and leads him to explore paths that no one else in scholarly circles would dare to tread.

This is not the place to offer an opinion on the correctness or otherwise of Benamozegh's theories on the "inverted symmetry" of Egyptian mythology and Kabbalah,[112] nor the relationship between it and original Christianity,[113] even if some contemporary debates, such as the polemic surrounding the Dead Sea scrolls or the antiquity of Kabbalah confer on them at least some degree of legitimacy.[114] What must be made clear is the dissonance of this voice in nineteenth-century historical and philological research, and the fecundity of that dissonance.

Briefly to survey one significant example, Benamozegh studied the myth of Isis and Osiris in the minutest detail, and went on to establish parallels with what it is easy to call "Kabbalistic mythology." The similarities found are enthusiastically delineated, as demonstrating the mythologies' shared origins, and—above all—the antiquity of Kabbalah.

Thus, the acts of Isis and Osiris are compared with the Kabbalistic representation of biblical characters (Jacob and Rachel, Moses and Miriam) and their metaphysical meanings. In Benamozegh's philosophical translation, Osiris is the Egyptian version of the *sefirah tiferet*, the ideal, the infinite, the formal and final cause, while Isis corresponds to the *sefirah malkhut*, the real, the limitation imposed on the infinite, the material cause. In the Egyptian myth their union is frustrated by Typhon, the Kabbalists' Sammael, the original serpent who defiled Eve as Typhon married Isis after having murdered her husband Osiris. We know that for the Kabbalists this was only an anthropomorphic representation of the fracture at the heart of the divinity itself, and that the goal of all religious action was actually to repair that fracture.[115]

This is not the place for a detailed examination that would require skimming through vast tracts of ancient mythology and Kabbalistic doctrine. What interests us is to note that Benamozegh's argument combines a philological and a philosophical approach, and the course of his research is ultimately dictated by the latter. Benamozegh is interested in the conceptual: since the value of words lies in their conveying ideas, the "philosophical" critic will reach his goal faster than others who content themselves with external analyses. A philosophical sensibility is the cognitive tool that allows such erudite questions to be resolved. "It is useless to dwell on this overmuch, he wrote in the middle of a display of erudition, since any sensible person will surely *feel* (*yargish*) what is concerned here."[116]

This aestheticist hermeneutics is certainly a considerable deviation from scientific criticism, for which the neutrality of the scholar toward the subject was one of the cornerstones: an impossible neutrality, according to Benamozegh, for each act of knowledge implies a value judgment.[117]

However, this sensibility obviously exposes Benamozegh to the dangers of a somewhat crude hermeneutic circle: the sensible person feels and understands; but only the person who feels is really sensible. It is thus impossible to understand properly a given symbolic system from outside; this is what stands out from his remarks:

> Every science includes—in addition to its subjects—a manner, and a form (*Metodo*) [in Italian in the Hebrew text] suited to it that distinguishes it from the other sciences. Likewise, Kabbalah should contain within it the manner which any person who is interested in it must learn. In fact, it is useless to approach it with the instruments of rational enquiry without taking into account its own interpretative rules: these are an essential part of it.[118]

Every science thus needs to be studied according to its own method, writes Benamozegh, citing Aristotle,[119] and this method is never neutral. The same approach cannot be adopted for every discipline: the type of analysis is dictated by the subject. To understand Kabbalah requires something of the Kabbalist in order to accept its principles and observe it from inside. Only then can be perceived the beauty that is the best proof of its truth. This brings us back to the interpretative circle described earlier, which can also be expressed in terms of the preeminence of experience over the scholar's scientific neutrality.

To use Wilhelm Dilthey's now classic terminology, Benamozegh lies along the dividing line between *explaining* and *understanding*.

Max Vexler, who reviewed *Israel and Humanity* for the *Revue des Etudes Juives*, was distinctly French in his defense of clarity and distinction. He admitted to being disconcerted:

> It must be admitted that Benamozegh appears never to have been able to distinguish between real history and theological interpretation, religious speculation and metaphysics. In this respect, his mind is a strange thing indeed. There is both ancient and modern within him, and the mixture is disconcerting. Alongside scientific and philosophical knowledge, he contains unmistakable elements of the *aggadist* (exegete) and *darschan* (preacher). . . .
>
> He is an odd and powerful character in which two periods of history meet strangely.[120]

Taking a closer look, these allusions to method bring us back once again to the issue of tradition. This method, which should accompany any kind of study, and which should be attuned to the subject in advance, is none other than a modern version of the Kabbalists' traditional warning not to approach reading the doctrine alone, but to get a teacher, failing which there is a likelihood of not understanding or—worse still—of misunderstanding. The teacher here is obviously the living voice of tradition; a direct, unmediated approach to the text produces superficial and misleading results. Understanding is based more on transmission than on intuitive communication between text and reader, an approach Benamozegh calls "Protestant" when writing in French and Italian, and "Karaite" in his Hebrew work.

S. D. Luzzatto, himself a standard bearer of the spirit of clarity, waxed ironical on Benamozegh's criticism of his own *Dialogues on the Kabbalah*: "Surely you don't believe you have put up a serious argument against me," he wrote condescendingly.[121]

It is true that *Ta'am le-Shad*—the work devoted to criticism of Luzzatto's anti-Kabbalistic dialogue—was not a refutation in the true sense of the term. The real thrust of the book is historical, given that it is above all about the antiquity of Kabbalah, yet Benamozegh gives the impression of choosing a terrain slightly different from Luzzatto's own: he effectively shifts the confrontation from a linguistic to a conceptual level. Above all, he recommends avoiding dogmatism, and instead ventures into paths that may seem impassable but which require courage to explore, even at the risk of intellectual isolation.

He wrote to Luzzatto in the clearest terms:

> Do you know that if the truth did not prevent me, I would be capable of conceding that the *Zohar* is false from start to finish, and despite that, force you to accept that Kabbalah is ancient? What has the *Zohar* to do with Kabbalah, or the bibliographical question to do with the critical or theological one?[122]

Samuel David Luzzatto, like Isaac Samuel Reggio, and Elia del Medigo and Leone Modena long before them (to stick to examples from Italian Jewry), attacked Kabbalah primarily for its pretensions to representing an authentic tradition extending back to Moses: in other words, the polemic was focused on a documentary plane. Benamozegh, however, while he did not leave out philological counterarguments, moved the debate onto different territory. When he wrote that the temporary disappearance of Kabbalah was due in part to "its excellence and loftiness"[123] which made transmission difficult, he incorporated a value judgment, The ultimate argument for the truth of Kabbalah's truth and antiquity seems to be its beauty and depth: according to him, whoever tastes of its delights cannot continue to deny its transcendent origins.[124]

Between these two positions, one scientific/empirical and the other metaphysical/intuitive (though deeply traditionalist), no dialogue would seem to be possible. It must be added that the anti-Kabbalists did not get into doctrinal details, and generally restricted themselves to noting Kabbalah's lack of originality and bizarre formulations. The Kabbalah they attack seems to be a caricature of that described by Benamozegh. The Kabbalist of their imagination is a narrow-minded, dogmatic individual who rejects research and is content to read without understanding the words.

Thus, Reggio published Del Medigo and Leone Modena's anti-Kabbalist texts with the addition of extremely severe glosses which criticized contemporary Kabbalists as enemies of research (*mehqar*) who hid behind the notion of an unexplained—and inexplicable—"revealed secret."[125] S. D. Luzzatto's Kabbalist in the *Dialogues* admits that he personally does not understand the esoteric commentaries at all, but that he nonetheless believes them to be true because great authorities from the past have declared them to be so.[126]

There could not have been greater incomprehension: Benamozegh's "philosophical" Kabbalah had no chance of being taken seriously in European intellectual circles, except possibly by some German and Italian idealists. He was perfectly familiar with Molitor's work, but claimed he wanted to avoid easy modishness. To Western Jews at the time, Kabbalah was a term particularly associated with Hassidism, itself a byword among the enlightened for obscurantism and superstition.[127]

Benamozegh shared this aversion for the form Kabbalah had taken among nineteenth-century Hassidim, and referred to it in the harshest terms, speaking of abuses committed in the name of Kabbalah, superstition, and contempt for human science. The theology professor found himself poles apart from the "thaumaturgical rabbis of Russia and Poland, whose practical Kabbalah lies behind the widespread hostility to speculative Kabbalah."[128]

It was thus a misunderstanding, but one that was too deeply rooted to allow the virtual heir of Italian Pythagoreanism to make his authentic philosophical voice heard.

RELIGION IN THE FEMININE DECLENSION

Benamozegh's position on the relationship between textuality and orality did not conform entirely to that of the *Zohar* and most of the other major Kabbalistic texts. For these texts, the Torah was not a dead letter: it was a hidden one. Orality was the explanation necessitated by the weakness of human sight, distanced from the sources and in need of commentaries that in their turn created even greater distance. This recalls the anthropologist Clifford Geertz's notion of "thick interpretation."

The idea that one day the oral tradition would be placed on the same level as the written Torah—just as the moon would be as luminous as the sun—meant in fact that the Scriptures would regain the transparency they initially had in the eyes of Moses.[129]

This motif is totally absent from Benamozegh's thinking. By emphasizing the correlations between *Shekhinah*-People of Israel, *Malkhut*-the Real, and *Torah she-be-'al peh*-oral tradition, he demonstrates in the purest nineteenth-century style the relationship between the people and the living tradition. He eschews the dramatic vision of a lost or hidden sense rediscovered in favor of one of cultural continuity.

This idea is expressed in what might appear to be a technical detail of secondary importance, but which in fact represents a total overturning of the traditional Kabbalistic viewpoint.

Benamozegh transforms the relationship between *tiferet*, the ideal, the written Law, and *malkhut*, the real, the oral Law. According to the classical definition, the second *sefirah* is subordinate to the first: the oral tradition is no more than the necessary accompaniment to the written tradition, a necessity that arises from the loss of the text's original meaning, It is the lesser light—the moon—compared to the great light of the sun. In the future, each will be of equal importance: their unity will be perfect because the text will not need its interpretative crutches any more, and will be clear in its own right.

Benamozegh, in contrast, saw the *sefirah tiferet* as not simply superior to *malkhut* ("that which engenders" compared to "that which is engendered"), but at the same time inferior to the *sefirah binah*. He points out that a parallel also exists between *binah* and *malkhut*, with the former being called "Higher Mother" and the latter "Lower Mother."[130]

This extended view of the *sefirah binah* enables Benamozegh to base his interpretation of tradition on Kabbalistic foundations. Orality was no longer only the daughter of textuality—its consequence, a contingent necessity destined to be reabsorbed—but also its origin. Moreover, *tiferet* and *malkhut* constantly aspired to reunite, completing Benamozegh's schema, and justifying it every step of the way. The oral tradition produces the text (as *binah*), accompanies it (the union between *tiferet* and *malkhut*), and is ultimately its product as well (as *malkhut*).[131]

The comments of the Italian historian Pier Cesare Bori in an essay on Christian sacred hermeneutics and its secularization allow us to make the transition between this selective aspect of the theory of *sefirot* as developed by Benamozegh, and some of the key moments in Romantic hermeneutics. Bori points out that the extension of sacred hermeneutics to all texts—represented as "secularization," or as the accomplishment of the task of sacralizing literature, depending on the viewpoint—occurred in proto-Romantic circles at the beginning of the nineteenth century.

A vital element of this extension was the application of the "infinite interpretation" principle to any work of art. Originally applied only to the Bible, whose different meanings were inexhaustible due to the fact that they derived from God, who is infinite, the principle was gradually extended to works of human art, which were seen as having the same potential. The infinite could be manifested in the finish of a painting or a poem; detail could throw up an infinitely rich set of meanings. The departure point for this expansion was the passionate debate surrounding Raphael's Sistine Madonna, hanging in Dresden, conducted among German authors (Herder, the two Schlegels, Goethe, Schiller, Von Kleist, Schopenhauer, etc.) and Russian authors (Pushkin, Herzen, Tolstoy, Dostoyevsky, and Bulgakov).[132]

Benamozegh also defined tradition as the developments that grew out of a text, and identified this aspect of tradition with the *sefirah malkhut*. Although *malkhut*, as we have seen, is called the "Lower Mother," Benamozegh—and he is obviously not alone—regards this *sefirah* as the origin of the Christians' Virgin Mary: *malkhut* is the immanent God, the feminine principle, the *sha'ar* (gate) that corresponds to intercession, of which Mary is the instrument.[133]

Bori noted that during this "secularization" of sacred hermeneutics, the role of the Virgin became alternative to Scripture, and wondered whether this was accidental or rather the resurfacing of an ancient antithesis between mother-goddess religions and religions of the book. This antithesis was brought up to date by the Romantics, who derived from it a feminine figure to oppose the "masculinity" of the biblical text, thus moving from the immanence of the Word of God in Scripture to the immanence of the divine in Nature.[134]

The parallel between the two processes is arresting. The Romantics escaped the exclusivity of the biblical text through the image of Mary: Benamozegh saw in the *sefirah malkhut*, the "Lower Mother," the incessant changes of a transition that bears rather than is borne by Scripture.

Cloaked in the form of an esoteric and seemingly distant doctrine, Benamozegh's thinking was, even in this case, in accord with the mainstream of European culture.

This "feminine declension" of religion is clearly shown in various, and very different texts by Benamozegh. Firstly, in the introduction to *Morale juive et morale chrétienne*, he describes his astonished delight when, as a youth, he realized that the science of his age was in perfect harmony with the Torah and Kabbalah as he had been taught them. This is an example of the unifying tendency we have already encountered in his thinking, though the passage contains something else as well. Benamozegh discusses the writing of *Morale juive*, shortly after the death of his mother:

> The work to which I devoted myself was like a precious balm to me. I found in it a food pleasing to the spirit, a delicious return to the late nights of long-ago, when at the side of my loving mother, and after the hours devoted to worldly works, I thrilled with the naïve pleasure of perusing the books I had ordered from Paris, seeing widen before me ever wider horizons which my eyes delighted in measuring, and seeing finally the thousand knots which tied my maternal religion to science: so much so that when I closed the books and heard again my mother's voice, I did not feel disoriented, and I said to myself, "This voice holds nothing but love."[135]

Benamozegh refers to "maternal religion," then to his mother's voice as a "voice of love," with no apparent link to the rest of the passage. Then again, why might he have felt disoriented after his reading? Possibly the return to the real world could be seen as a contrast with the inner concentration of reading? But in that case, why would his mother's voice have warded off such disorientation? Probably because Benamozegh's religion was in a certain sense "maternal," implying—it is tempting to suggest—a feminine connotation or tonality. The return from the intellectual journey that had led him far away occurs within the heart of his—feminine—religion.

It is not only the real mother who holds an important place in Benamozegh's life and thinking. There is another mother, one who is mainly present between 1847 and 1861, the years of the Italian nationalist *Risorgimento* movement. The "Motherland" of Italy acquired a religious status in the passionate speeches of this young rabbinical preacher that is rarely found in European Jews. This "mother" is occasionally placed immediately below God.

> Therefore love [Italy], love her next after God, above any earthly attachment; love her with the desire of the child who after a long abandonment presses into his mother's arms with trembling love.[136]

A year later, the motherland would actually take the place of God in a daring formulation (verging on the blasphemous) that set it at the very heart of the core Jewish religious declaration, the affirmation of the oneness of God, the *Shema' Israel* (Hear, O Israel):

> Yes, O Israelites, in this Temple where you have often voiced your woes to the Eternal consoler, where many of you have cried over the loss of a mother or a brother; where today you recognize in Italy a mother and in all Italians your brothers in love; swear, before the beloved scrolls we venerate, swear, O Israelites, that you will always love Italy, that you will love her *with all your heart, with all your soul, with all your mind.*[137]

Earlier, addressing God, Benamozegh claimed that the "Italian soil" had been "engendered by the thought of your love," a definition suitable for a divine emanation, or *sefirah*.

Beyond historical comments on the level of participation in national destiny by a Jew—one, moreover, of Moroccan extraction—it must be recognized that some of his expressions were certainly inspired by his Kabbalistic training. In any case, whatever the reason—be it his intellectual training or the early experience of losing his father—certainly the effect was an attenuation of the "masculine" character of Jewish monotheism, in which the bulk of the Law refers back to the figure of the Father. This trait is consistent with all of Benamozegh's thinking.

PART THREE

Style as Witness

"THE ORIENT, TO ORIENT ONESELF"

If for some thinkers, style is one of the reasons behind their success, for Benamozegh the exact opposite is true: his marginality is largely the consequence of a writing style that did not appeal to the cultivated milieus he intended to address.

There was certainly a formal progression in the successive use of Hebrew, Italian, and finally French. The youthful texts, composed in a very traditional Hebrew, with Aramaic phrases and biblical and Talmudic quotations throughout, gave way to major philosophical works in Italian and French that required a different tone. There are, however, a number of stylistic traits that can be discerned throughout his work. A brief survey of these unchanging elements sheds further light on his intellectual character. Benamozegh's writing is rich, but often redundant; it is passionate, but occasionally pompous; his arguments are clearly articulated, but at times verge on the verbose.[1]

The lack of a summarizing or systematic mind is compensated for by the great conceptual coherence that did not wane throughout his career. If it is true that Benamozegh expressed himself more in oratorical tones reminiscent of natural speech than with strict regard for order, all his writing is nonetheless conceptually dense, with the totality of his thinking being represented at the level of each page, rather as a single cell figures in miniature the form of the entire organism. His style is circular, and he returns again and again to the same themes, deepening and enriching them, adding new arguments and unexpected affirmations as his thinking and reading progressed.[2]

All these aspects are to be found in the earliest books. In *Eimat mafgia‘* the prose is so emphatic as to become poetry in places, or at least, to become rhymed prose (*melytzah*) in the kind of traditional cadences that had long been abandoned by Western Jewish writers. It involved a repetitive melody based on a number of elements, often sets of synonyms, or successive sentences with minimal semantic variations. It is a style that obviously required complete mastery of the language, and of the canonical texts of Hebrew literature. A Western ear may find the result surprising, or amusing, but rarely beautiful.

Benamozegh was conscious of the characteristics of his style. We know this from a text written in odd circumstances, in which he described his own way of writing. It was in fact a statement presented to the judges of Livorno's civil court as part of his defense against an accusation of having slandered a rival Hebrew publisher in a series of letters to a mutual customer. Since the letters were in Hebrew, Benamozegh entered into a stylistic examination of rabbinic Hebrew in general, and his own in particular, with the intention of explaining the scope of some allegedly insulting phrases. It is clearly a subjective opinion justifying a partial position, but one that is consistent with other statements made in more neutral contexts. It should be noted that here, as elsewhere, Benamozegh shows his capacity—we might even go so far as to say, his need—to reach a general conclusion from a specific, contingent occurrence.

Hebrew, according to him, was an absolute language lacking the subtleties in which European languages abounded. For example, while it had the concepts and words for *true* and *false*, it was incapable of indicating the *probable*.[3] Its outstanding rhetorical devices were hyperbole and redundancy:

> The language in which my letters are written is as far removed from ours . . . as East is from West. It is one of the oldest Oriental languages—in fact the oldest—which, like its sisters, possesses a certain genius, a style, special qualities. . . . Among these qualities, the most marked are hyperbole, redundancy, exaggeration of the concept, a . . . temperature, in so many words, that matches the climatic temperature of those regions where it was spoken, and with which it has truer and more intimate affinities than one might imagine.[4]

These qualities also rely on Hebrew's condition as a nonspoken language, one that condemned it fatally to impoverishment and approximation.[5] Redundancy, a tendency to exaggeration, and an absence of precision are thus the traits of postbiblical Hebrew. This was in itself a controversial statement, when the typical style of Italian Jewish authors until the nineteenth century was characterized on the contrary by an effort toward clarity and preciseness, even toward concision.

For an idea of the stylistic model of some of Benamozegh's contemporaries who were more deeply rooted in Italian Judaism one must look to the extreme clarity of Reggio and Luzzatto, the inheritors of a culture where lucidity and elegance were absolute necessities of erudite prose. The following statement by Reggio could in a sense be seen as their motto:

> The more the author manages to summarize what he has to say and the more he avoids saying everything at any cost, the better the service he renders to the reader.[6]

Over the next few years, while never attaining a satisfactory level of restraint—except where it was imposed by editorial dictate[7]—the tumultuous style leveled off somewhat. It did, however, continue to pose problems of accessibility in tackling subjects that were complex enough to start with, and contributed to the impression of a brilliant, but difficult author.

All of this may surely be laid at the door of individual temperament. Benamozegh was a generous and passionate man who believed deeply in what he wrote, and who allowed himself to be swept along by what he was saying. The distance Luzzatto kept between them disappointed without offending him.[8] His intellectual sincerity was such that he did not shy away from admitting oversight, capable of candidly writing, "I do not recall where I read that,"[9] and occasionally making the appropriate correction in his next work. This approach certainly raised a few eyebrows among the scholars of the time.

Yet, the psychological explanation is not sufficient; Benamozegh's style was also the product of his culture. It is worth noting a few details about his father, and comparing them with what we know about Luzzatto's father. In an act of filial piety, at one point in his Bible commentary, Luzzatto quotes his father, who, while not by any means a scholar (he was a carpenter), knew Hebrew well, and had a fine linguistic sensibility. It was these qualities that allowed Luzzatto senior to understand a poetic verse (Gen. XLIX: 18) that had troubled many an exegete.[10]

The description of Elijah's father, Avraham Benamozegh, as left by Sabato Morais (an illustrious representative of the Italian, and later the American, rabbinate), is quite different.

> Benamozegh inherited from a long line of ancestry a marvelous aptness for Hebrew knowledge. I remember to have heard from my saint teacher, Chief Rabbi Abraham B. Piperno, that Benamozegh's father, who emigrated from Fez, Morocco, to Leghorn, fitted Biblical sentences into his ordinary conversation so cleverly and with such spontaneity as to create amazement. But with the ability to speak and write the sacred language faultlessly, the son inherited also a fondness for mysticism which prevails in Africa and, alas! in Palestine and Eastern Asia, too, among our brethren.[11]

These are two very different attitudes to language, typical of the Italian and North African Jewish traditions respectively. Indeed, Benamozegh never denied his "Oriental" character. Addressing an Italian audience, he remarked:

Your positive, analytical, western European thinking cannot without difficulty picture the bold, brusque transitions and sudden shifts from the proper to the improper meaning of a word. It can with even greater difficulty take in at once the infinite set of applications and ramifications whereby the mother-idea is gradually transformed; increasingly hidden from view, virtually enveloped in a loose, opaque mantle.[12]

It is therefore necessary to "turn occasionally to the Orient, to orient oneself,"[13] and also to reenergize, since it is the locus for the memory and the hope of Israel. All of Europe needs to pump this invigorating water to displace the stagnant water of indifferentism and positivism.[14] The Orient is faded but religious, he writes in the introduction to *Israel and Humanity*, and the Western world is progressive, but without any religion. Judaism is a synthesis of both because it is Orient at the time of Western world.

It should also be noted that the advancement of knowledge was matched by a larger space for mystery ("the mother-idea . . . is increasingly hidden from view . . ."): the more we know, the more aware we become that the thing we call God is unknowable. Benamozegh the Kabbalist proposes a fundamental variation on a Western idea of progress in which he was nonetheless a fervent believer.

If Benamozegh wrote his final works in French, the European cultural language par excellence, he still continued to publish the works of rabbis from North Africa and Palestine, often adding introductions, notes, and comments expressing a degree of admiration and agreement that went far beyond formal tribute.[15]

Benamozegh's more intuitive than analytical style of thinking had definite consequences on his aesthetic choices. This is why for him Kabbalah, though it shared some content with the philosophy of Spinoza, was infinitely superior to it *not least* because of its style, which was not merely an external form, but intrinsic to a way of thinking.

Kabbalah sang its dogmas whereas Spinoza demonstrated his; the one is a powerful harmony, a continual hymn, while the other has produced nothing but a web of definitions, axioms, and corollaries; the former has revealed thoughts in the manner of the poets, with their free cadences and flights of daring, while the latter has set them out after the manner of the surveyor.[16]

Quoting the doctors of the Talmud, Benamozegh points out that the entire Torah is in fact a poem.[17]

SOLITUDE: "I LIVE IN THE BOEOTIA OF JUDAISM"

Nobody has been a better embodiment than Benamozegh of Gérard Genette's statement about authorial notes and the way they belong to the text, extending and modulating rather than commentating it.[18]

The freedom Benamozegh got from owning a publishing house does not fully explain the extraordinary number and length of the notes he added to the end of his works. Dozens of pages enlarging upon the text, focusing more intensely on a given aspect of it, or supporting it with additional examples, are to be found even in his Italian writings published by others.

One could say that his work is a *work in progress*: if by chance an idea or discovery came to light just before the book went to press, it had absolutely to be included. Some of Benamozegh's notes are longer than the text to which they refer; others are genuine articles in their own right.

Are we forced to conclude that he was incapable of logically ordering his thoughts and marshaling arguments? He often creates the impression that he is asking questions and then answering them. It is a kind of moving soliloquy, probably arising from an absence of interlocutors whose existence might have resulted in a more ordered discourse. There were many who had heard of him and his works, and their compliments were occasionally hyperbolic, calling him master or genius.[19] However, those who could truly claim to have read his books and understood them were few indeed. He was sadly deprived of dialogue.

This informed his half-bitter, half-ironic complaints. He wrote to Luzzatto asking him to keep him abreast of developments in the Jewish sciences to pull him out of the "holy apathy" which seemed his inevitable lot.[20] Otherwise he was afraid he must resign himself to being a "citizen of the Boeotia of Judaism,"[21] and he went on:

> Here I live in near perfect solitude, and aside from the company
> of my books, my children, and my new students, I see almost
> no one, and keep no company. Moreover I live in a villa, and
> am an all-year-round *villano* [peasant].[22]

In a letter to Angelo De Gubernatis (1840–1913), director of the *Rivista Orientale* and prominent scholar of Oriental studies in Italy, Benamozegh declared: "Unfortunately, if there is torpor everywhere, here there is lethargy. Whoever has a bit less chloroform in his veins is shouted down as crazy; and maybe he is."[23]

Despite his fame and his status as a public figure well known even beyond the Jewish community (in Livorno he was seen as a literary object of pride, and a city-center square was named after him), he was exposed to intellectual solitude almost all his life.

There is something almost pathetic about the following lines from *Israel and Humanity*, a work that was not published until fourteen years after his death:

> If I have chosen to write in French it is only because of the need to be read. . . . I accept any criticism in advance, provided that anyone deigns to listen to me.[24]

THE NEED TO SPEAK

The length of Benamozegh's texts certainly put his readers to the test, and the same was true of his correspondents. The letters he sent to Luzzatto are on average five times longer than the (occasional) ones he received in reply. He had a lot to say. He had what amounted to a virtual compulsion to write, to try to convince, to argue. He felt he possessed a wealth of material, and it is easy to believe him. Yet he experienced constant anxiety that he would not be able to use it all.

> "Stop," advise friends and typographers. "You cannot say everything. Abandon some of your ideas somewhere far away; the sun and the wind will take them." I followed their advice and restrained myself. This is the result: desiccation and melancholy.[25]

Once you realize that the formula, "Unfortunately I must be brief" is generally followed by a digression several pages long, it is easy to understand how a reader of limited motivation might be discouraged.

Benamozegh was not a man to do things by halves, as he says himself in the introduction to *Morale juive et morale chrétienne*. He was equally convinced that the task facing him was infinitely weighty and important, being in fact that of rediscovering the harmony between science and traditional (Kabbalistic) Judaism, which had been lost in the Middle Ages. Such overarching ambition could scarcely fail to provoke sentiments of impotence, solitude, and lack of fulfillment, with the effect that Benamozegh occasionally seems to lose confidence. He believed people were not yet ready to accept the new order to which he had devoted all his energies. In *Ta'am le-Shad* he described his project of defending Kabbalah by scientific methods as a task nobody had undertaken before, and which he was obliged to pursue alone. In his hyperbolic Hebrew, he wrote of himself as like a simple dove who chirps and moans [a pastiche of Hosea VII: 11 and Isaiah XXXVIII: 14] without getting any answers . . . like the first man, who tills and sows, harvests and mills, kneads and bakes though no one has ever done these tasks before him; not like the other sciences in which each chooses a terrain and cultivates it . . . and, adding his labor to those of all the others, kindles the flame of truth: many are they who stir themselves, and abundant the knowledge.[26]

Furthermore, the enterprise of reconstructing a vanished harmony required an eclectic approach that widened both horizons and the range of disciplines taken into consideration, but did so at the occasional cost of a desirable simplicity. The resulting impression of a lack of methodological rigor belied the author's commitment and the depth of his ideas.

Benamozegh was aware of this, and attempted to remedy the situation, though he ended up tacitly acknowledging the impossibility of imposing order. Such is the case of the argument "keys" intended to orient the reader, which he appended to *Em la-Miqra*, and which contradict the decision to provide facing-page text and commentary. Another example is the rapidly abandoned attempt to issue his unpublished manuscripts by subject order.

THE IMAGINARY LIBRARY

Benamozegh's literary fecundity is the proof of his unquenchable thirst to communicate. As well as the many printed works published during and after his lifetime, many hundreds of pages have never seen the light of day, and some have been entirely lost.

There is yet another category of works: those he planned out but never wrote. They constitute an entire library of intentions, the subjects and even in some cases the titles of which their author left behind.

The project that recurs most often is the notion of a comprehensive anthology of references to Kabbalistic doctrines in Talmudic literature. This most clearly centers on *Les noms de la Sagesse et ses livres dans la littérature rabbinique*: it is not hard to conjecture that this would have been a comparative study of the notion of wisdom in Kabbalah, Gnosticism, Neo-Platonism, and Christianity.[27]

He had the outline and much of the information for his planned *Traces des doctrines juives dans les religions païennes*.[28] There was also a *Bilan du prosélytisme israélite dans le monde gentil, en tant que préparation au christianisme*, a subject suitable for "a major work."[29]

He would also have liked enough time to write about the relationship between Ibn 'Ezra and Kabbalah;[30] lastly, he was attracted to works on the linguistic connections between the Torah and the Prophets,[31] and between Josephus and the rabbis.[32]

The range of arguments and the plethora of ideas not only dizzy and potentially overwhelm the reader, but they have the same effect on the author, who admits with his usual frankness that he has a great many documents "swimming in chaos."[33] This mix of enthusiasm and disorder are the blessing and the curse of a tremendously talented but almost entirely self-taught man. It would be unreasonable to expect him to possess the calm detachment of an analytic mind. The effort required to move from the traditional culture of Moroccan Jewry to the intellectual world of Italy and Europe probably made a full synthesis impossible. It should be remembered that his immediate antecedents were Moroccan, and that he quickly passed through all the stages of assimilation with the intellectual world of Italy and Europe.

This assimilation was so complete that one Italian critic recently saw him as a potential representative of the deepest current in Italian thought—Pythagoreanism—though no more than potentially, as he was either too far ahead or too far behind his time, making dialogue with the philosophical milieus of Italy impossible.

The sclerotic formulas of scholastic Hegelianism did not admit significant deviation, it has been said, and Benamozegh was "an unbridled intelligence forced to keep pace with the lame."[34]

FROM ORIENT TO OCCIDENT

It is appropriate to give the protagonist of this text the last word, in the form of an extract from *Storia degli Esseni*. This book shows a certain "nostalgia for the Orient" as well as an attitude toward nature that denied it any autonomy, subjugating it to God. This powerful idea, which removes man from direct contact with nature, probably belongs to the Western tradition. Once again, the double belonging of Benamozegh stands out.

In this work, the author compares Jewish religious practices of his own time with those of the Kabbalists of Safed, in the sixteenth century. Using the formulae of Giambattista Vico (the "poet-theologians"), Benamozegh draws a demarcation line between a religion of nature and one in which the primary relationship is that between man and God, and in which the view of nature derives from that relationship. At the same time, he sketches a religious aesthetic that is in some ways the counterpoint to the Romantic, elucidating the relationship between God and Beauty in interesting ways.

Yet it was also an appeal for the rejuvenation of contemporary Jewish culture, a position that anticipates those arrived at forty years later in Russia and Israel by writers such as Aharon David Gordon, Yosef Hayyim Brenner, and Hayyim Nahman Bialik.[35] It is remarkable to find an appeal to leave the spiritual ghetto coming from an "Oriental" rabbi with a training in Kabbalah so long before the proponents of "Jewish modernity" took up the cry.

O, how different are modern times! Persecution, imprisonment, and tyranny have certainly done much harm, more even to minds than to bodies; for if Religion was preserved in the ghettos, it was at a high cost, the cost of becoming rickety, atrophied, impotent, ungenerous; the cost of losing the noble, imposing, poetical, emotional demeanor that was its own.

It is true that the ghettos have crumbled and men have hurried from them. However, they left the precious stone of religion behind. Religion is still in the ghetto, in distress and darkness, in the mud of those dreadful lanes. The adherents of Islam are far happier, for they practice in the open, fearlessly; they also indirectly show what the Jewish faith is, and could be.

The Kabbalist Pharisee who climbs a mountain to welcome the holy day of *Shabbat* is imposing to whoever hears him and has not lost the sense of our institutions. He is greater than a Byron confiding himself to the storm-tossed sea as a spectator and potential victim of angry nature, wishing to get a close enough taste of death to be able to describe it. He is greater than Iacopo, Foscolo's creature,[36] who seeks powerful emotions in steep slopes and chasms.

Why do I say greater? Because the poets seek the sources of Beauty in nature and its great scenes, whereas the poet-theologians of Judaism bring Beauty into nature and spread it around. They do not seek big ideas and grand effects but introduce them, because they are infused with God, the creator of nature, the supreme source of the beautiful and the sublime, which means they relate as judges, rather than spectators, of created Beauty.

In a word: poets receive the rays of God reflected in nature while the poet-theologians of Judaism spread the rays of the divine as reflected in their souls over nature. Nature makes the poets divine, does it not? But the poet-theologians of Judaism make nature divine.[37]

Notes

INTRODUCTION

1. Aimé Pallière, *The Unknown Sanctuary. A Pilgrimage from Rome to Israel*, trans. Louise Waterman Wise (New York: 1928), 178. In the same text Pallière expressed most succinctly the contrast between Pope Leo XIII and Elijah Benamozegh, both of whom he saw in the course of a single trip to Italy. Of the former he wrote, "I shall never forget the diaphanous old man's hand that Leo XIII held out to me and the extraordinary brightness of the eyes he fixed me with. That blinding vision of serene grandeur has remained with me," and of the latter: "I must admit I was surprised and even somewhat disappointed by him when he arrived. I was no longer before the Kabbalist rabbi in a *tallith*, listening, rapt, to the strident sound of the *shofar*, but in the presence of a little old man, hesitant in manner and unkempt in attire, who introduced himself humbly, without glamor and apparently without even interrupting the flow of his meditations, his gaze remaining fixed on some place of inner concentration." But Pallière was forced to conclude, "When I listened to Benamozegh I was convinced I was in the presence of a man of God, one illuminated—to use the Catholic expression—by supernatural light" (168, 170, 177).

2. Antonio Silvio Scarlatti, "Sul rione dell'Origine (curiosità ottocentesche)," *Il Telegrafo*, Livorno, February 15, 1942, 4.

A FEW BIOGRAPHICAL POINTERS

1. Avraham Ytzhaq Laredo, *Les noms de Juifs du Maroc—Essai d'onomastique judéo-marocaine* (Madrid: 1978), under the name "Ben Amozegh."

2. *Autobiography*, in Nahum Sokolow, *Sefer ha-zikaron le-soferei Israel ha-hayyim ittanu ha-yom* (Contemporary Jewish writers' memorial book) (Warsaw: 1889). Italian trans. D. Lattes in E. Benamozegh, *Scritti scelti*, ed. A. S. Toaff (Florence: 1955), 17.

3. Jean-Pierre Filippini, "Livourne et l'Afrique du Nord au XVIIIe siècle," *Revue d'Histoire Maghrébine* 7–8 (January 1977); id., "Livorno e gli ebrei dell'Africa del Nord nel Settecento," in *Gli ebrei in Toscana dal Medio Evo al Risorgimento. Fatti e momenti* (Florence: 1980); id. "Juifs émigrés et immigrés dans le port de Livourne

pendant la période napoléonienne," *East and Maghreb*, IV (Ramat-Gan: 1983); Renzo Toaff, *La Nazione ebrea a Livorno e a Pisa (1591–1700)* (Firenze: 1990).

4. Elijah Benamozegh, "Introduction" in Avraham Coriat, *Berith Avoth* (*The Alliance of Fathers*) (Livorno: 1862); Sabato Morais, *Italian Hebrew Literature* (New York: 1926), 213.

5. Benamozegh married Rachel Coriat, his cousin's daughter. Cf. Bruno Di Porto, "Due lettere familiari di Elia Benamozegh," *Il Tempo e l'Idea* VIII (2000): n. 18, 19, 20, 147. Cf. also *La verità sulle due tipografie Tubiana e Benamozegh svelata al Tribunale e all'opinione da Angelo Finzi* (Livorno: 1861), 15.

6. *Autobiography*; for the genealogy of the Coriat family, see Haïm Zafrani, *Les Juifs du Maroc. Vie sociale, économique et religieuse* (Paris: 197), 36.

7. Cf. Isacco Rignano, *La Università Israelitica di Livorno e le Opere Pie da essa amministrate* (Livorno: 1890); Michele Cassandro, *Gli ebrei di Livorno nel 1600* (Milan: 1983). Mid-nineteenth century, there were 4,500 Jews in Livorno, which had a population of 90,000. See Michele Luzzati, ed., *Ebrei di Livorno tra due censimenti (1841–1938). Memoria familiare e identità* (Livorno: 1990).

8. For an incident of the hostility between the Sephardic and Italian Jewish communities, see Renzo Toaff, "Livorno, Comunità sefardita," *Rassegna Mensile di Israel* XXXVIII (1972): 7–8.

9. *Vessillo Israelitico* 24 (1876), 334, Italian trans. by P. Perreau, from a series published in *Jüdische Presse*, July 15, 1874.

10. *Autobiography*.

11. *Nir le-David*, (*The Splendor of David*, from I Kings XI: 36) (Livorno: 1858), Introduction.

12. Cf. Guido Sonnino, *Storia della tipografia ebraica in Livorno* (Turin: 1912). David Verner Amram, in *The Makers of Hebrew Books in Italy* (Philadelphia: 1909), 407, recalls Steinschneider's fulsome praise, "It is a pleasure to see a Rabbino predicatore and author not disdaining to work with voice, pen and press. Would that German presses came into such competent hands!"

In 1857, Benamozegh requested from the authorities the right to publish a review in Hebrew for the Jews of Egypt, Persia, and the Maghreb, in which news from the Tuscan press would be translated. However, the review was never published. See Archivio di Stato di Livorno, "Governo," 380, 1433. I would like to thank Ms. Liana Funaro for providing me with a photocopy of this request.

13. On Livorno's Rabbinical College cf. G. Sonnino, "Il Talmud Torà di Livorno," *Rassegna Mensile di Israel*, X (1935–36): 183–96; A. S. Toaff, "Il collegio rabbinico di Livorno," ibid. XII, no. 7–9 (1937–38): 184–95; Id. "Cenni storici sulla Comunità ebraica e sulla sinagoga di Livorno," ibid. XXI (1955): p. 355–68, 411–26. See also A. Berliner, art. cit. in *Vessillo Israelitico* 333. Note the study of Latin alongside more traditional subjects. The oft-repeated assertion that the Livorno Rabbinical College was a center for the dissemination of mystical studies should be modified substantially. The only "mystical" teaching was to be found in Benamozegh's theological lectures and even there it was contained in a philosophical framework. Benamozegh would teach the treaty *Avoth* with his comments and the *Lezioni sabbatiche* by Lelio Della Torre (to practice the exposition of the Torah and the rabbinical tradition in Italian) three times a week, from midnight until

two in the morning (Livorno Jewish Community Archives, October 24, 1873). I would like to thank Ms. Liana Funaro for providing me with a photocopy of the programs of study. On a parallel institution—the Padua Rabbinical College—which, with a degree of effort, can be seen as an alternative to the Livorno model, see the monograph by Maddalena Del Bianco Cotrozzi, *Il collegio rabbinico di Padova. Un'istituzione religiosa dell'ebraismo sulla via dell'emancipazione* (Florence: 1995), with an extensive bibliography. Cf. also Riccardo di Segni, "I programmi di studio della scuola rabbinica italiana (1829–1999), *Rassegna Mensile di Israel* 3 (1999): 15–40. For the cultural background, see Alfredo S. Toaff and Aldo Lattes, *Gli studi ebraici a Livorno nel XVIII secolo* (Livorno: 1909).

14. *La Gazzetta Livornese*, February 6–7, 1900.

15. In Yoseph Colombo, *Vivere per un'idea* (Milan: 1958).

16. On the meeting between Benamozegh and Pallière as described by A. Pallière, see *Le sanctuaire inconnu*. See also A. Guetta, "Due lettere di Aimé Pallière a Elia Benamozegh," in *Gli ebrei in Toscana del Medio Evo al Rinascimento* (Florence: 1980), 49–63. After Benamozegh's death Pallière published *Israël et l'Humanité*, which the rabbi had considered his *magnum opus* and also undertook the work of spreading his spiritual master's doctrines. He was later to play an important role in the Liberal Jewish community in Paris. On this subject see the interesting comments by Gérard Haddad, *Benamozegh, Aimé Pallière, Lacan et la "vraie religion,"* in *L'enfant illégitime. Sources talmudiques de la psychanalyse. Suivi de Lacan et le judaïsme* (Paris: 1996), 320–46. Benamozegh had already intervened to prevent another conversion, though this time from Judaism to Christianity. The episode appears in a Hebrew poem by Israel Costa, in *Ki na'ar Israel (For Israel is Young)* (Livorno: 1881), 42.

17. *Vessillo Israelitico* XLVIII (1900): 161.

18. Arrigo Lattes, "In memoriam. Elia Benamozegh," ibid. 49 (1901), 47–48.

PART ONE: PHILOSOPHY AND KABBALAH

Kabbalah and Progress

1. *Grand Dictionnaire Universel Larousse du XIXe siècle* (Paris: 1866–1879), under "progress": "The idea that humanity is become daily better and more prosperous is one particularly beloved of our century. Belief in the law of *progress* is the true faith of our times."

2. On this subject Gershom Scholem wrote that the Jews of western Europe who were close to European culture dismissed Kabbalah as foreign and embarassing, and thus quickly to be forgotten. (See G. Scholem, *On the Kabbalah and Its Symbolism*, trans. Ralph Manheim, foreword Bernard McGinn [New York: 1965], 1 and id., *Encyclopaedia Judaica* [Jerusalem: 1971], Vol. 10, col. 648). Heinrich Graetz, the author of the monumental and indispensible Heinrich Graetz, *History of the Jews* (Philadelphia: 1891–1898), *passim* defined Kabbalah as "pseudo science," "a source of superstition" that "had infected Judaism with its poison."

3. On the topic of Kabbala in Morocco, see Moshe Halamish, "Al sugey ha-yetzirah ha-qabbalyt be-Maroqo" ("On Different Kinds of Kabbalistic Creation in Morocco") *Pe'amim* 15 (1983): 29–46 (with bibliography).

4. *Teologia dogmatica e apologetica*, Vol. I: *Dio* (Livorno: 1877), 1.

5. The name of Jules Simon (1814–1896) should be added to this list. His *Théologie naturelle* (Paris: 1866) is so strikingly similar to Benamozegh's *Teologia* (Benamozegh knew and cited it at several points) that it is reasonable to wonder whether the Italian did not use the French philosopher's book as a model for his own.

Theology and the Discovery of the Unconscious

1. *Bibliothèque de l'hébraïsme* (Livorno: 1897), 16. See also *Teologia*, 271: "The ego itself, insofar as it is potential, is elastic, so the potential can be transformed into actual and consciousness increased in extent. Increased in extent, it naturally encounters the most extensive consciousness; thus it comes into closer proximity with God; progressively it becomes divine."

2. *Israël et l'humanité* (Paris: 1914), 256, 330.

3. In *Von den Wurzeln des Bewusstseins, Studien über den Archetypus* (*Les racines de la conscience*, French trans. Yves Le Lay [Paris: 1971]), 467, Carl Gustav Jung described the transition of this idea from the realm of philosophy to that of psychology, which would as quickly become the kernel of psychoanalysis. Jung's text contains some remarkable ideas on the subconscious in the religious thought of the Middle Ages. Lévinas's thinking can, on the other hand, be seen as a reaction to this vision of history as a process of *progressive understanding*: "Consciousness then does not consist in equalling being with representation, in tending to the full light in which this adequation is to be sought, but rather in overflowing this play of lights—this phenomenology—and in accomplishing *events* whose ultimate signification does not lie in disclosing" (E. Lévinas, *Totality and Infinity; An Essay on Exteriority*, trans. Alphonso Lingis [Pittsburgh: 1969], 27–28).

4. Wilhelm von Humboldt, "On the Historian Task," in Leopold von Ranke, *The Theory and Practice of History*, ed. Georg G. Iggers and Konrad von Moltke, trans. Wilma A. Iggers and Konrad von Moltke (Indianapolis: 1973), XX: "It is possible and necessary that the quintessence of humanity, the depth contained in its limitations, shall gradually attain the clarity of consciousness, and that the mind, by striving toward this and succeeding in part, shall absorb the Idea of humanity and (like a You produced by the ego) that of the divinity." For Vincenzo Gioberti, cf. *Protologia* (Turin: 1924), 34 and *passim*. As for Ludwig Feuerbach, cf. *The Essence of Christianity*, trans. George Eliot (New York: 1957). Here Feuerbach's program of reducing theology to anthropology is interpreted as a process of reappropriating the essence of humanity by increase or clarification of consciousness. Friedrich Nietzsche, *Human, All Too Human: A Book for Free Spirits*, trans. R. J. Hollingdale (Cambridge and New York: 1986): "The new, conscious culture kills the old culture . . . it also kills the distrust of progress: progress is possible." On this subject, see also Gennaro Sasso, *Tramonto di un mito. L'idea di "progresso" fra Ottocento e Novecento* (Bologna: 1984), 90.

5. Ernest Renan, preface to *L'avenir de la Science* (Paris: 1890).

6. On the theme of the subconscious in European thought, cf. George Gusdorf, *Les origines de l'herméneutique* (Paris: 1988), 357–59. Cf. also Henri Bergson, "Fantômes de vivants," in *Œuvres*, ed. André Robinet (Paris: 1984), 860–78.

7. Eduard von Hartmann, *Philosophie des Unbewussten* (Berlin: 1869). English translation *Philosophy of the Unconscious; Speculative Results According to the Inductive Method of Physical Science* (London, New York: 1931).

8. *Teologia*, 268. An important consequence of these two differing visions is the weight accorded to the freedom of human intervention in history. For a Kabbalist such as Benamozegh, man was not merely the master of his own destiny but could affect the universe, and condition God himself through his actions. For his part, Hartmann saw history as dictated by unconscious (but not blind) necessity, and man's true freedom for him consisted in his gaining awareness.

9. *Teologia*, 144 and 148.

10. Moshe Cordovero, *Pardes rimmonim* (Cracow: 1592), Gate II, chapter 7. On the same model of concentric emanations, see also Hayyim Vital, '*Etz Hayyim* ("Tree of Life") (Tel Aviv: 1960), first "palace," third "gate," third chapter and Id. *Otzroth Hayyim* ("Treasures of Life") (Tunis: 1813), Gate of Circles. The *ein sof* from which the *sefirot* emanated was called the "soul of the soul," an expression reminiscent of Benamozegh's description of God as the "*consciousness of consciousnesses.*"

11. Georges Vajda, *Le commentaire d'Ezra de Gérone sur le Cantique des Cantiques* (Paris: 1969), 26.

12. G. Scholem, *Origins of the Kabbalah*, trans. Allan Arkush (Philadelphia: Jewish Publication Society; Princeton: 1987).

13. Mircea Eliade, ed., *The Encyclopedia of Religion* (New York: 1987), Vol. V, 566–79. The authors of the articles on Gnostics relevant here are Gilles Quispel and Ioan Petru Culianu.

14. Cf. *L'origine des dogmes chrétiens* (unpublished in French; Italian translation by Marco Morselli [Genova, 2002]), Part 1, ch. 7 and 8, *passim*.

15. Cf. Gilles Quispel, *Gnostic Studies* (Istanbul: 1974), Vol. I, 14.

16. The same kind of variation from classical neo-Platonism is to be found in Gioberti.

The Universal Relationship

1. *Zohar*, III, 65b, section *Ahareyi moth*. See also G. Vajda, *Recherches sur la Philosophie et la Kabbale dans la pensée juive* (Paris and The Hague: 1962).

2. Exodus III: 14.

3. The translation is by Adolphe Franck, *La kabbale, ou la philosophie religieuse des Hébreux* (Paris: 1892; fist edition Paris: 1843), 143.

4. *Teologia*, 81–84.

5. If *Asher* was one of the names of God, *Asherah*—the Canaanite fertility God—was a distorted derivation of it. Drawing on the *Zohar*, Benamozegh came up with the idea—which we will examine later—of a resemblance between Judaism and other ancient religions. These retained certain aspects of the truth that was fully revealed in the Jewish Kabbalistic tradition. See *Teologia*, 231.

6. Cf. Auguste Comte, *Système de politique positive*, Vol. IV (Paris: 1854), 530. English translation, *System of positive polity* (London: Longmans, Green, 1875–1877).

7. Interpreting Exodus XXXIII: 23

8. Hayyim Vital, *Peri 'etz hayyim* (*The Fruit of the Tree of Life*) (Koretz: 1785); cf. Moshe Idel, *Kabbalah, New Perspectives* (New Haven: 1988), 294, note 79.

9. *Teologia*, 164, 191.

10. Ibid., 157, 184–85. The expression is Malebranche's. Renan appropriated it with reservations in *L'avenir de la Science*, 527, note 191.

11. *Teologia*, 163. The idea of *relationship* for Benamozegh was very different to that voiced by the great Kabbalist Moshe Hayyim Luzzatto in the eighteenth century. In *Hoqer u-mequbbal* (*Maamar ha-vikkuah*) (in *Sefer Sha'arey Ramhal*, ed. H. M. Friedlander [Bnei Brak: 1989], 29–94) (*Le Philosophe et le cabaliste*, French trans., intro., and notes Joëlle Hansel [Paris: 1991], 155–56), Luzzatto used the term *relationship* to describe that between God and his creatures, which are the only objects accessible to thought. The object of this reflection is the *divine*, by opposition to reflection about *God*, which is an impossibility. The refusal to be concerned with essence and the deliberate decision to concentrate on relationships is significant in comparison with the modern, almost pre-Kantian potential of a certain esoteric line of thought.

Conditioned Progress

1. On the need for this dual analysis, see A. Guetta, "Elie Benamozegh, la rencontre de deux traditions," *Revue des Etudes Juives* 156, no. 3–4 (July—December 1997): 471–80.

2. Paul Bénichou, *Le temps des prophètes. Doctrines de l'âge romantique* (Paris: 1977), 162

3. Ibid., 101.

4. Ibid., 162. Bénichou cites both Lamennais's works: *Essai d'un système* (Paris: 1906), 221 and *Esquisse d'une philosophie* (Paris: 1840), 10–11 and 58.

5. It should be noted that the term *disclosure* corresponds exactly to Martin Heidegger's definition of truth as a manifestation of the Being (*a-letheia*). This is not the only common ground between the German philosopher and the thinkers who concern us here. The subject of tradition, so dear to Benamozegh, is, for example, central to the thinking of Heidegger's pupil, Hans G. Gadamer. A hundred years have, however, sufficed to see the disappearance from European thought of the idea of movement as progress and the perspective of infiniteness coexistent with human finitude. The philosophy of the twentieth century is principally founded on a crisis in the idea of progress and the affirmation of finitude as a unique, insuperable horizon. Thus, the theosophical thinkers of the nineteenth century assist us, *a contrario*, to better understand our age.

6. Vincenzo Gioberti, *Della filosofia della Rivelazione* (Naples: 1871), 13. The word *palingenesis*—literally "new birth"—was used in the modern period (after appearing in the *New Testament*—Matthew 19: 28; Epistle to Titus 3: 5—and in the context of alchemy) by Charles Bonnet, who hypothesized a theory of the origins of life combining elements of creation and evolution in *Palingénésie Philosophique*

(Neuchâtel: 1783). Benamozegh knew this work: cf. *Ta'am le-Shad* (Livorno: 1852), 134. For Friedrich Schleiermacher, Christ was the prototype (*Urbild*) of man plunged into history. Cf. *Die Christlische Glaube nach den Grundsätzen der evangelischen Kirche* (Berlin: 1836), 29 ff. (in Vol. IV of the *Sämmtliche Werke*). See also *Zohar*, I, 181a–182a: the text speaks of the "renewal" of the world.

7. *Israël et l'humanité* (Paris: 1914), 318 and 320; *Israel and Humanity*, trans. Maxwell Luria (New York: Paulist Press 1995), 168, 170.

8. Ibid., 320. Hegel, *Phenomenology of Spirit*, trans. A. V. Miller (Oxford: Clarendon Press, 1977).

9. The Venetian rabbi Leon Modena (1571–1648) in his *Magen va-Herev* (*The Shield and the Sword*, ed. Shlomo Simonsohn [Jerusalem: 1960], 39–40), a work critical of Christianity, established a parallel between the revelation on Sinai and the incarnation of Christ.

10. *Teologia*, 268–69.

11. Cf. for example Sa'adiyah Gaon, *Sefer emunoth we-de'ot* (*The Book of Beliefs and Opinions*), Hebrew trans. Yosef Qafih, fourth ed. (Jerusalem: 1995), Introduction, ch. 6, 27–28. English translation by S. Rosenblatt, *The Book of Beliefs and Opinions* (New Haven and London: 1948), 31–32.

12. Cf. *Enciclopedia Cattolica* (Vatican City: 1952), Vol. VIII, col. 1188–96 s.v. "Modernismo."

13. *Della filosofia della Rivelazione*, 142. Lamennais wrote of a "general instinct directing the progressive movement of peoples." Letter dated, November 2, 1835, to Baron Vitrolles, in *Correspondance inédite entre Lamennais et le baron de Vitrolles*, 291, in Bénichou, op. cit., 170. Victor Cousin for his part considered the distinction between intuition and reflection in both individual psychology and history as being of an "inexhaustible fecundity." Cf. Victor Cousin, *Préface aux fragments philosophiques* (Paris: 1862), quoted in *Dictionnaire des philosophes* (Paris: 1984). Cf. Franz Joseph Molitor, *Philosophie de l'Histoire ou "de la Tradition"* (Frankfort: 1827), French trans. by Xavier Quris (Paris: 1934), 118, on the post-exile history of the Jews: "The era of intuition was over: analysis replaced synthesis."

14. "Mavo kelali le-khol sifrei Torah she-be-'al-peh" ("General Introduction to the Monuments of the Oral Tradition"), *Ha-Levanon* 3 (1866): 235.

15. Cf. Auguste Comte, *System of Positive Polity*, op. cit., and Charles Darwin, *On the Origin of Species by Means of Natural Selection, or The Preservation of Favoured Races in the Struggle for Life* (London, 1859).

16. Friedrich von Schiller, *On the Aesthetic Education of Man, in a Series of Letters*, trans. Elizabeth M. Wilkinson and L. A. Willoughby (Oxford: 1967 [i.e., 1968], 31–43.

17. Cf. Franz Joseph Molitor, *Philosophie de l'histoire ou "de la tradition,"* 167: "The debilitating process [of contemporary philosophy] may continue for a long time yet, attacking life in the deepest and most destructive way, but the living seed of the world's future regeneration exists already and it will reunite and breathe new life into what we had earlier separated and killed."

18. On this subject, cf. Ernest Renan, *L'avenir de la science*, 259: "To understand these extraordinary apparitions, we need to be hardened to miracles: we need to raise ourselves above our age of reflection and slow devising, to contemplate

human faculties in their creative originality, as, scorning our laborious procedures, they drew the fullness of the sublime and the divine. That, then, was the age of psychological miracles." Victor Cousin, for his part, described thought as a spontaneous development, and that spontaneity as "a true revelation. This spontaneity constitutes religion." Quoted in H. Maret, *Essai sur le panthéisme dans les sociétés modernes* (Paris: 1840).

19. *Israel and Humanity*, 173–75.

History and Truth

1. Georg W. F. Hegel, *Encyclopaedia of the Philosophical Sciences in Outline, and Critical Writings* (New York: 1990), 50. This opinion was echoed in France by Cousin, who spoke of "religion giving birth to philosophy in pain," while also maintaining that both "distinguish themselves without being exclusive of one another in the mind of the true philosopher." See *Cours de l'histoire de la philosophie* (Paris: 1841), Vol. 1, lesson 2, 42–43. (English translation: *Course of the History of Modern Philosophy*, trans. O. W. Wight [New York: 1853], lecture 2). Gioberti commented ironically, "For Cousin, religion is philosophy in a smock." See Gioberti, *Considérations sur les Doctrines Religieuses de M. Victor Cousin* (Italian ed. 1840, French translation by V. Tourneur, Reims: 1844).

2. Georg W. F. Hegel, *Phenomenology of Spirit*, 479.

3. The same cannot be said of the post-Hegelian debate on the relationship between religion and philosophy. Generally speaking, discussions dissipated into a mass of details and tended to be more apologetical than theoretical. On the debate among Christians, see Karl Löwith, *From Hegel to Nietzsche: The Revolution in Nineteenth Century Thought*, trans. David E. Green (New York: 1964), and among Jews, see Gershon Greenberg, "Samuel Hirsch: Jewish Hegelian," *Revue des Etudes Juives* CXXIX (1970): 205–15; Irene Kajon, "La 'filosofia della rivelazione' di Samuel Hirsch," *Archivio di filosofia* LXII, no. 1–3 (1994): 382–91.

4. Emil L. Fackenheim, "Samuel Hirsch and Hegel. A Study of Hirsch's 'Religionphilosophie der Juden' (1842)," *Studies in Nineteenth-Century Jewish Intellectual History*, ed. Alexander Altmann (Cambridge, MA, 1964), 171–201.

5. Georg W. F. Hegel, *Reason in History; A General Introduction to the Philosophy of History*, trans. Robert S. Hartman (New York: 1953).

6. Vincenzo Gioberti, *Protologia* (Turin, 1924):. 34: "The hypothesis may be gratuitous, whimsical, arbitrary or quite logical and natural. [. . .] Hegel proceeds through arbitrary hypotheses as he admits of an absolute democracy of truths."

7. *Teologia*, 144. In *De antiquissima italorum sapientia* (1710), (*On the Most Ancient Wisdom of the Italians*, trans. L. M. Palmer [Ithaca: 1988], ch. III), Giambattista Vico had already noted that the only way to prove the existence of God would be—as for geometrical objects—to produce him, becoming in so doing, God's God. He obviously excluded such a possibility, which he regarded as impious.

8. Georg W. F. Hegel, *The Philosophy of History* (New York, 1956), ch. II, Christianity, 318–31.

9. *Teologia*, 117: "The absolute, the necessary, must contain the whole of being. Hegel, on the other hand, makes human thought—a finite entity—the most perfect form of being, that which includes the being par excellence. This is the

absurdity of a nonabsolute absolute." Gioberti, in *Protologia*, 77: "Hegel, for all his pretentions, is a psychologist."

10. *Teologia*, 118.

11. *Em la-Miqra*, Genesis (Livorno: 1862), 52a: "All eras and all beings form a continuum and a path to Beth El [the house of the Lord, a reference to Judges XX: 31 and XXI: 19]." The sentence is completely isolated in an apparently unlikely context. See also *Israel and Humanity*, 166–67.

12. *Protologia*, 163. The word *mimesis*, meaning imitation of ideas by material things, was used by Plato, notably in *Phaedrus* 74a and *Republic* III 409b. "Metexis," meaning participation of material things in ideas, occurs in *Phaedrus* 100c, *Republic* V, 4, 76c, and *Symposium* 29, 211b. (English translation, Cambridge: London: 1977–1986).

13. *Protologia*, 181.

14. *Teologia*, 181: cf. 41: "We walk before God '*Hitalekh lefanai*' (as the last and the end of all), beside God '*Et ha-Elohim hitalekh Noah*' (as the middle and the connection between things) and behind God '*Aharei Adonai Eloheikhem telekhu*' (as the first)." Cf. *Talmud Bavli*, tractate Shabbat, 104a.

15. *Protologia*, 163.

16. Ibid., 11; *Teologia*, 137; *Israel and Humanity*, 159–60. See also *Em la-Miqra*, Deut. 72a and especially Exodus 20a, where Benamozegh drew a laborious comparison between the Indian and Chinese word *Tao* (meaning "divinity" and "way"), the Hebrew *Shadday* ("God"), and its Kabbalistic transposition to *Derekh* ("way"). The source is once again almost certainly *Talmud Bavli*, tractate Shabbat,104a.

17. *Protologia*, 190. "The aim of the universe is thus continually present and continually displaced and removed: it is like the judgment of Christ announced to his contemporaries as present and not yet come." Bénichou, on Lamennais, spoke of "man's continual, not to say asymptotic, tendency toward God" (*Le temps des prophètes*, 165). For the Benamozegh passage, see *Vessillo Israelitico* XXIV (1876): 17. On this subject see Georges Vajda, *Le commentaire d'Ezra de Gérone sur le Cantique des cantiques* (Paris: 1969), 265, the chapter entitled "Le monde qui vient."

18. *Filosofia della Rivelazione*, 13: "Christian supernaturalism tends to become rationalism and mystery, evidence. . . . The revelation of mysteries is thus a beginning of rationalism: the veil is slowly lifted, but it is not torn aside."

19. *Protologia*, 19.

20. *Teologia*, 117.

21. In places Gioberti nonetheless seems to have been tempted by the idea of "the end of time." See *Filosofia della Rivelazione*, 33 and 154.

22. Pierre-Simon Ballanche, "Formule générale de l'histoire de tous les peuples appliquée à l'histoire du peuple romain," *Revue de Paris* (May 1829), cit. in Bénichou. See also Chateaubriand's famous remarks in *Mémoires d'outre-tombe*, Livre 44, ch. 8, Bibliothèque de la Pléiade (Paris: 1958), 936: "I found myself between two centuries as at the confluence of two rivers: I plunged into their troubled waters: regretfully leaving the ancient strand where I was born, and swimming hopefully towards the unknown shore where new generations will land" (trans. A. S. Kline, 2005–07).

23. *Teologia*, 117 and 176. On p. 146 Benamozegh quotes an article by Adolphe Franck which brings in an assessment by Auguste Comte of the impossibility of explaining the superior by the inferior. A strange but significant encounter between

an orthodox, Kabbalist philosopher, a secular "scientific" connoisseur of Kabbalah, and the founder of positivism.

24. Lévinas accentuated the break with history as it had been conceived by Hegel, interpreting it as a *whole* that corresponded to the return of the self to the self. This is the Lévinasian theme of *eschatology*, or "meaning without context" that has broken free of the jurisdiction of history. The distance can be measured between the thinking of Benamozegh, centered on harmony between history and the absolute and that of Lévinas who, a century later, demonstrated in his own way that the "philosophies of history" were exhausted. Cf. *Totality and Infinity*, 22–23.

"Pantheism: The Great Error of Our Age"

1. In many respects, Gioberti's philosophy may be considered as a sort of Neoplatonism that replaces the ascetic individual movement of return to the One with universal progress. Likewise, in the ideology of progress in general, and the notion of expansion of consciousness in particular, may be discerned an adaptation of the traditional philosophical tendency toward self-knowledge. On this, cf. *Encyclopédie philosophique universelle*, vol. *Les Notions Philosophiques—Dictionnaire* (Paris: 1990), under "Progrès," contributed by G. Almeras.

2. *Teologia*, 116. Gioberti characterized Hegel's philosophy as "exquisite pantheism" (*Protologia*, 144).

3. Cf. Samuel David Luzzatto, *Vikkuah 'al khohmath ha-qabbalah / Dialogues sur la Kabbale* (Gorizia: 1852). See the second part of the work. Cf. also Paul L. B. Drach, *La Cabale des Hébreux vengée de la fausse imputation de panthéisme par le simple exposé de sa doctrine d'après les livres cabbalistiques qui font autorité* (Rome: 1864), a dense and brilliant work written, among other things, to counter the theories laid out by Adolphe Franck in *La Kabbale, ou la philosophie religieuse des Hébreux*, 7 (Eng. trans. *The Kabbalah; or, The Religious Philosophy of the Hebrews*, trans. I. Sossnitz [New York: 1926]), which saw "pantheism at the bottom of all the doctrines of the Kabbalah."

4. *Teologia*, 77.

5. "Spinoza et la Kabbale," in *Univers Israélite* 19 (1864): 36, 130, 161, 274, and 364; see also *Bibliothèque de l'hébraïsme*. On Spinoza's reception in Jewish circles, cf. Zeev Levy in *Studia Spinozana* 6 (1990): 251–78. For an effective critical summary of Spinoza's relationship to Judaism, see Mino Chamla, *Spinoza e il concetto della tradizione ebraica* (Milan: 1996), 107, 130, 178, and 186, which also devotes a few comments to Benamozegh.

6. *Teologia*, 177.

7. Ibid., 117. Cf. Hegel, *Encyclopedia of the Philosophical Sciences*, 69: "This pure being is *pure abstraction*, consequently that which is absolutely negative, which is to say, if we also take it immediately, nothingness."

8. *Teologia*, 129, 173. Cf. Hegel, *Phenomenology of Spirit*, 23.

9. *Teologia*, 103. The same conceptual framework is applied at a gnoseological level, in a Platonic scheme. Knowledge of the infinite precedes (in intuition) the fragmentary knowledge of the finite (in reflection), and is finally recomposed in the infinite object. See *Teologia*, 148.

10. See *Zohar*, III, 250b and I, 24a.

11. Ibid., part I, 3a: "All unions come under the sign of the letter *aleph*"; cf. *Tikkunei ha-Zohar*, 15b: "The letter *aleph* alludes to the All."

12. *Teologia*, 182, 200.

13. *Protologia*, 144.

14. *Israel et Humanité*, 213–14. See also Benamozegh's own addition to the work of the Moroccan Ya'aqov Abihatzira, *Elef binah* (Livorno: 1890), 67, which he edited: man's task consists of "harmonizing opposites."

Moderate Idealism: A Tendency toward Union

1. See *Teologia*, 148; *Israel and Humanity*, 189–94; *Bibliothèque de l'hébraïsme*, 90. Art was also perceived—from the idealistic angle—as "a retreat from nature [effected by man] toward the eternal standards of ideal beauty." Benamozegh saw therein a Pharisaic-Kabbalistic principle: man's duty to correct the abnormal parts of created things, which he referred to as "co-creation." Cf. *Storia degli Esseni* (Florence: 1865), 465.

2. On the Kabbalistic inspiration of Christianity see Franz-Joseph Molitor, *Philosophie de l'Histoire, ou "de la Tradition,"* 197 and ff. On the relationship between the real and the ideal, see 135, 164, and 167. The German author made use of the concepts of "intuition" and "analysis-synthesis," examined above, as they formed part of the European philosophical "koinè" of the first half of the century. He applied these categories to Jewish history: the period of return, after Ezra, was forced to replace synthesis with analysis. Cf. 118.

3. Molitor and Benamozegh also shared the conviction that Christianity was the offspring of Kabbalah.

4. *Bibliothèque de l'Hébraïsme*, 90. See also Renan, *L'avenir de la science*, 526, n. 182. The writer sees parasites on a plant and does not intervene: "But now I see that I was wrong; I should have killed them; for the work of man in nature is to reform the ugly and the immoral."

5. Benamozegh's reference is to *Midrash Rabbah* 8, ed. Albeck (Jerusalem: 1956), which interprets Daniel VIII: 12. The biblical text offers an allegory of the power of Antiochus Epiphanes and his immoral conduct. The *midrash* reads it as though referring to the story of man's creation. In this interpretation, Truth opposes the creation of the first man, seeing his descendants as liars. God cuts short the debate and throws Truth to the ground, or sends Truth down to Earth, from heaven. Benamozegh understands the *midrash* differently: for him the phrase alludes to the presence of the infinite within the finite.

6. Here the reference is to the interpretation found in the *Zohar*, part III, 74a, of Lamentation II: 1. "Rabbi Yehudah said: when the wise abound in the world, the community of Israel [= *sefirah malkhut*] gives forth a sweet smell, receives the blessings of the Holy King [= *sefirah tiferet*] and its face is illuminated; but when the evil are numerous, the community of Israel does not give forth a sweet smell and tastes the bitterness of the Other Side [*Sitra akhra*]. It is for these circumstances that it was written 'He sent (back) down from heaven unto the earth. . . .' " *Malkhut*—the earth—was chased out by *tiferet*—heaven.

7. *Em la-Miqra*, Deut. 147a.

8. Particularly noteworthy is the example of Filosseno Luzzatto, the son of Samuel David and thus of the "second generation" researcher, compared to the religiously inspired intellectuals of the first generation. Young Filosseno, who died at the age of twenty-five, was a distinguished scholar of Sanscrit, Hebrew, and Arabic.

9. Cf. for example, Abraham Yehoshua' Heschel, *God in Search of Man. A Philosophy of Judaism* (New York: 1955).

Distinctions Preserved

1. Henri Maret, *Essai sur le Panthéisme dans les sociétés modernes* (Paris: 1840).

2. Ibid, V.

3. Ibid, IX.

4. Ibid, XIII.

5. Vincenzo Gioberti, *Considérations sur les Doctrines Religieuses de M. Vicor Cousin*, French trans. V. Tourneur, (Reims: 1844).

6. Ibid, 19.

7. *Essai sur le Panthéisme*, 9.

8. Second edition (Paris: 1875).

9. *Essai sur le Panthéisme*, 383.

10. Jules Simon, in *La religion naturelle*, sixth ed. (Paris: 1866), XI, wrote, "Pantheism is nothing other than a scholarly form of atheism."

11. "Spinoza et la Kabbale," *L'Univers Israélite* 19 (1864).

12. *Bibliothèque de l'hebraïsme*, 10.

13. Cf. *Spinoza et la Philosophie des Juifs*, in Emile Saisset, *Précurseurs et disciples de Descartes* (Paris: 1862), 185–352.

14. "Spinoza et la Kabbale," 11. See also the memory Benamozegh recalled in *Vessillo Israelitico* XXVIII (1880): 366. "I read the *Tractatus Theologico-Politicus* 35 years ago [i.e. in 1845, at the age of twenty-two] amidst the factory bales."

15. *Essai*, 383.

16. German philosopher Salomon Maimon (1753–1800) noted in his autobiography and in the comments on the *Guide of the Perplexed* by Maimonides, that Kabbala was an expanded version of Spinoza's philosophy. See Henri Atlan, *Les Etincelles du hasard. Tome 1: connaissance spermatique* (Paris: 1999), 335–46.

17. See Moses Maimonides, *The Guide of the Perplexed*, 1.68.

18. "Spinoza et la Kabbale," 10. On the letter "yod" and what its shape suggests, see the *Zohar*, III, 10b.

19. The interpretation of *malkhut* also lies at the heart of Leibniz's critique of Spinozist monism. In this context, however, this *sefirah* was understood not as "res extensa" but as the power of God as it is manifested in the world, and the question is that of necessity in human events. See Georges Friedmann, *Leibniz et Spinoza*, second ed. (Paris: 1975), 224.

20. "Spinoza et la Kabbale," 38. On the concept of "intelligible" or "ideal matter," cf. Alain de Libéra, *La Philosophie médiévale* (Paris: 1993), 199–205, the chapter devoted to Ibn Gabirol.

21. "Il confronto con il 'moderno.' Il mondo culturale ebraico italiano e la 'questione Spinoza,' " *Bailamme* 9 (1991). Recent work on Spinoza's Jewish sources and his personality, as the descendant of Marranos, clearly show a search for a secular Jewish frame of reference to which he could relate. Along with the pioneering work of I. S. Revah in this area (*Des Marranes à Spinoza*, ed. H. Méchoulan, P.-F. Moreau, C. L. Wilke [Paris: 1995]), see also Zeev Levy, *Baruch or Benedict. On some Jewish Aspects of Spinoza's Philosophy* (New York: 1989) and Yirmiahu Yovel *Spinoza and Other Heretics* (Princeton: 1989).

22. On the problem of the antiquity of the *Zohar* and Ibn Gabirol's relationship to it, cf. Salomon Munk, *Mélanges de philosophie juive et arabe* (Paris: 1859). On this subject, see also Perrine Simon Nahum's interesting *La cité investie. La science du "judaïsme" français et la république* (Paris: 1991), especially 121–37.

23. Vienna: 1847. Curiously, Spinoza's impeccable behavior in the personal arena was explained by Luzzatto as being due to his knowledge of Hebrew, a language that conveyed the essential values of Judaism, mercy in particular. See, in contrast, Benamozegh's opinion, expressed in *Em la-Miqra*, Ex. 17b: "The fact that Spinoza moved away from the community did not stop him saying a lot that was true."

24. Scholars such as Zeev Levy persist in describing Luzzatto as "a great Jewish thinker"; but his greatness lay elsewhere—in his erudition, the precision of his methods, and the great clarity of his writing. For an overview of S. D. Luzzatto's work, see Yosef Klausner, *History of Modern Hebrew Literature* (in Hebrew), vol. 2 (Jerusalem: 1937), 40; "Nel primo centenario della morte di Samuel David Luzzatto," miscellany, *Rassegna Mensile di Israel* XXIII (1966); *Samuel David Luzzatto; The Bicentennial of His Birth*, ed. R. Bonfil, I. Gottlieb, H. Kasher (Jersualem: 2004). On the "modernity" of Luzzatto and his milieu, see Lois C. Dubin, "Trieste and Berlin: The Italian Role in the Cultural Politics of the Haskalah," in *Towards Modernity. The European Jewish Model*, ed. Jacob Katz (New Brunswick and Oxford: 1987), 189–224; Id., "The Rise and Fall of the Italian Jewish Model in Germany: from Haskalah to Reform, 1780–1820," in *Jewish History and Jewish Memory*, ed. E. Carlebach, John M. Efron, David N. Myers (Hanover and London: 1998), 271–95.

25. S. D. Luzzatto, *Hebraïsche Briefe* (Padua: 1890), letter 1134, quoted in Israel Ginzberg, *History of Hebrew Literature* (in Hebrew), Vol. VI (Tel Aviv: 1960), 92. Luzzatto expounded his thinking systematically in the lessons he wrote for the students at the Padua Rabbinical College, *Lezioni di Teologia Morale Israelitica* (Padua: 1862) and in *Lezioni di teologia dogmatica israelitica* (Trieste: 1863). The most interesting developments concerned the origins of moral feelings, and they were largely inspired by English eighteenth-century philosophy. For Luzzatto, religion had a gregarious role in relationship to ethics.

26. *Ha-Mishtaddel*, Ex. 12b, commentary on Ex. XX: 5; ibid., 15b. Cf. also *Lezioni di Teologia Morale Israelitica*, 23: "Without Religion, all social order is turned upside down, thrones are shaken and human society falls into the dreadful abyss of anarchie."

27. Chamla, in "Il confronto con il moderno," 123, writes of "apparently inverted conclusions: irrationality for S. D. Luzzatto and rationalism for Benamozegh."

28. Avraham Berliner, "Rabbi Eliah Benamozegh z.l." *Jüdische Presse* XXXI (1900): 85.

29. *L'origine des dogmes chrétiens* (unpublished). See also the Italian translation by Marco Morselli, *L'origine dei dogmi cristiani* (Genoa: 2002).

30. Ibid.

31. David Friedrich Strauss, *Das Leben Jesu* (Tübingen: 1835–1836) (Engl. trans. David F. Strauss, *The Life of Jesus Critically Examined* [London, New York: 1898]; Joseph Salvador, *Jésus Christ et sa doctrine; histoire de la naissance de l'Eglise et de ses progrès pendant le Ier siècle* (Paris: 1864–1865), *Histoire des Institutions de Moïse, et du peuple hébreu* (Paris: 1828). On Joseph Salvador, see Michael Graetz, *Les Juifs en France au XIXe siècle. De la Révolution française à l'Alliance Israélite Universelle* (Paris: 1989), esp. 220–58.

32. In his Pentateuch commentary *Em la-Miqra*, Benamozegh's attitude to Christianity is much harsher. He defines it flatly as muddled or corrupted Kabbalah (cf. Genesis 167a and Deuteronomy 155b). The same relationship existed between Christian doctrine and Kabbalah as between the monkey and man—i.e., muddled, risible imitation. See Exodus 10b and Numbers 11a for the same comparison applied to Egyptian rites. The phrase comes from the *Talmud Bavli*, tractate Baba Batra 58a, where it is used to define the hierarchy of Sarah, Eve, Adam, and the *Shekhinah* (Divine Presence). Cf. also Maimonides, *Epistle to Yemen*, ed. Y. Sheilat (Jerusalem: 1995), vol. I, 123. Vincenzo Gioberti used the same expressions ("a bad, exaggerated, witless imitation") to describe the attitude of the Stylites, Jesuits, and Trappists compared to that of true Christianity. Cf. V. Gioberti, *Della Filosofia della rivelazione* (Turin-Paris: 1856), 325.

33. *L'origine*, 24 and 32.

34. Benamozegh's attitude to Christianity is clearly ambivalent. Aimé Pallière, in his introduction to *Israel and Humanity*, depicts him as a universal character who, on rising in the morning and putting on his *tefillin*, rejoiced to hear the sound of church bells. But alongside his sincere admiration for a doctrine that furthered monotheistic belief and insisted on the importance of *tradition*, Benamozegh evinces radical criticism of Christianity, and expresses this with sternness. The harshest criticism is leveled in his Hebrew writings, *Em la-Miqra* in particular. This includes accusations of textual falsification in the Vulgate (*Em la-Miqra*, Deut.: 148b), and ironic comments on the dogma of the Immaculate Conception (ibid.: 59a).

35. Benamozegh saw the most modern heresy, Sabbatianism, as a sort of laboratory of ideas in which the modern scholar could find all the original elements of Christianity. Cf. *L'origines des dogmes chrétien*. On this subject see also, Gerschom G. Scholem, *The Messianic Idea in Judaism and Other Essays on Jewish Spirituality* (New York: Schocken, 1971), 123.

36. *L'origine*, 129. See also pages 110, 112, and 185.

37. Ibid., 128–29.

38. *Morale juive et morale chrétienne: examen comparatif suivi de quelques réflexions sur les principes de l'Islamisme* (Paris: 1867), 39 and 97.

39. *L'origine*, 91–92.

40. The book was quite successful. It won the Alliance Israélite Universelle prize, which paid for its publication, and was reprinted and translated into several languages. See the *Bibliography* at the end of this book.

41. *Morale*, 37–38.

42. Ibid., 19.

43. Ibid., 21.

44. Ibid., 164–71 and 194–99.

45. Ibid., 166.

46. Ibid., 92.

47. On this question, see the correspondence between Benamozegh and Aimé Pallière in *Le Sanctuaire inconnu*, Aimé Pallière, 118 and A. Guetta, "Due lettere di A. Pallière a E. Benamozegh," in *Gli ebrei in Toscana dal Medioevo al Risorgimento. Fatti e momenti,* ed. B. Di Porto et al. (Florence: 1980), 49–63. The Incarnation is the element of Christianity that the Italian rabbi excluded from the monotheism he proposed as a universal religion.

48. On the notion of *zivug*, see, among others, the *Zohar*, III, 72a: "When the Holy King (*tiferet*) couples with the Matriarch (*malkhut*), benedictions flow over all the worlds, those above as well as those below."

49. *L'origine*, 106, 135. In the light of such assertions, it is easy to understand why the Alliance Israélite Universelle confined itself to publishing *Morale juive et morale chrétienne* and rejected *L'origine des dogmes chrétiens*, although it had been conceived by the author as the second part of a single work. Another of Benamozegh's grievances against Christianity was its precipitous dissemination of difficult and secret doctrines without preparation. See *L'origine*, 137–38.

50. *L'origine*, 145.

51. Ibid., 141. This passage could answer the questions raised by Ya'aqov Fleischmann at the end of his chapter on Benamozegh in his work, *The Problem of Christianity in Jewish Thought* (in Hebrew) (Jerusalem: 1964), 119–30. The Israeli scholar evinces astonishment at the difference in the treatment of Christianity between *Morale juive* (highly critical) and *Israel and Humanity* (positive), ascribing it to the latter's reworking by the Christian Pallière when he edited it after the author's death.

52. J. Salvador, *Jésus Christ et sa doctrine* (Paris: 1838), second ed. 1864.

53. Cf. the works of K. F. Bahrdt and K. H. Venturini, described in Albert Schweitzer, *Geschichte der Leben-Jesu-Forschung*, in *Gesammelte Werke* (Munich: undated), Vol. 3, 95 and 105.

54. Cf. David Flusser, *Jesus*, trans. Ronald Walls (New York: 1969).

Reconciliation: Immanentist Monotheism

1. Tzvetan Todorov, *Nous et les autres. La réflexion française sur la diversité humaine* (Paris: 1989).

2. Maurice Olender, *The Languages of Paradise: Race, Religion, and Philology in the Nineteenth Century*, trans. Arthur Goldhammer (Cambridge: 1992); Id., "L'Europe ou comment échapper à Babel," *L'infini* 44 (1993): 106–23. For a "militant" analysis of the issues, see Edward Said, *Orientalism* (New York: 1978).

3. Paris: 1855. Vol. III of *Œuvres complètes* (Paris: 1996).

4. Ibid., 187.

5. *Nous et les autres*, 133–34.

6. *Œuvres complètes*, vol. VIII, 156.

7. *The Spirit of Hebrew Poetry*, trans. James Marsh (Burlington, VT: 1833), 30.

8. Ibid., 32.

9. On James Darmesteter and his elder brother Arsène, see Yakov Malkiel's recent contribution: "Les frères Darmesteter et l'aube de la philologie française," *Revue des Etudes Juives* CLIII, fascicule 3–4 (July–October 1994).

10. James Darmesteter, *La légende divine* (Paris: 1890), 112.

11. Darmesteter's passionate commitment to the new French nation is amply demonstrated in *Lectures patriotiques sur l'histoire de France à l'usage de l'école primaire* (Paris: 1881), under the nom de plume J. D. Lefrançais.

12. James Darmesteter, "Race and tradition," in *Selected essays of James Darmesteter*, trans. Helen B. Jastrow (Boston, New York: 1895), 155.

13. Ibid., 165.

14. Praising mixing as a driving force of civilization, as done by Claude Lévi-Strauss in *Race and history* (Paris: Unesco, 1958), is directly in keeping with this position. For praise of mixture in Benamozegh, see his article "Federigo Secondo e le dottrine rabbiniche," *Rivista Bolognese* 1 (1876), reproduced in E. Benamozegh, *Scritti scelti* (Rome, 1955): 273–82, which examines "free exchange between Jewish and Christian scholars." Cf. A. Guetta, "Elyjah Benamozegh, sofer mizrahi-ma'aravi" ("E. B., an Oriental-Occidental writer"), in *Zion and Zionism among Sephardi and Oriental Jews*, ed. W. Z. Harvey, G. Hasan-Rokem, G. Saadoun, A. Shiloah (Jerusalem: 2002), 217–26.

15. Cf. Vincenzo Gioberti, *Del primato morale e civile degli italiani* (Brussels: 1843). Some of Gioberti's distinctions, such as the division of mankind into priests—the guarantors of the absolute—and laity—the instruments of progress—were retained by Benamozegh. The Catholic author attributed the role of "religious nation" to Italy, the seat of the papacy; the Jewish one assigned it to the children of Israel.

16. A. Franck, *Etudes Orientales* (Paris: 1861), IX.

17. For a more detailed analysis of this poem see this volume, the chapter "Philology and Philosophy."

18. Cf. Yitzhaq Heinemann, *La Loi dans la pensée juive*, French adaptation by Charles Touati, 157.

19. The same idea of alternation or oscillation was taken up by the French philosopher Vladimir Jankélévitch, who described it a hundred years later as the Jewish tendency toward an endless cycle of *resemblance* and *dissemblance*: "I do not know how to synthesize in myself that which is contradictory, and Hegelian reconciliation has little appeal for us." "Le judaïsme, problème intérieur," *L'Arche* (May 1957). Reprinted in *Sources* (Paris: 1984), 50.

20. Benamozegh's manuscript was two thousand pages long while Pallière's edition was a "mere" 735 pages. The entire last part of the printed work consists of reworked notes, letters written to Pallière and Benamozegh's printed work *Cinq Conférences sur la Pentecôte* (1886). In 1961 Emile Touati undertook the production of a new, and further abridged, edition which systematically omitted passages of anti-Christian polemic and references to the idea of "race."

21. *Israël et Humanité, Introduction* (Livorno: 1885), Italian transl., *Israele e Umanità / Il mio Credo*, ed. Leonardo Amoroso (Pisa: 2002). Cf. Ghitit Holzman, "Universalismo e Nazionalismo in 'Israel e l'Umanità,' " *Rassegna Mensile d'Israel*

LXIII, no. 3 (1997): 89–100 and id., "Universaliut u-leumiut ba-haguto shel ha-rav Eliyahu Ben Amozegh" ("Universality and nationality in the thinking of E. B."), *Pe'amim* 74 (1998): 104–30.

22. Eduard von Hartmann, *L'autodestruction du christianisme et la religion de l'avenir* (Berlin: 1874), French trans. Jean-Marie Paul (Nancy: 1989), 151.

23. *Israel and Humanity*, 43–44.

24. On the idea of the "nation" cf. Hayden White, *Metahistory. The Historical Imagination in Nineteenth Century Europe* (Baltimore/London: 1973), 172.

25. *Israel and Humanity*, French version, 216. Gioberti, in *Protologia*, 25: "I call true those opinions in which the truth predominates. . . . The element of truth found in false opinions is like the semi-orthodoxy of heterodox opinions." In his *Scienza Nuova* (first ed. 1725, 152; *The new science of Giambattista Vico*, trans. Thomas Goddard Bergin and Max Harold Fisch [Ithaca: 1968]), Giambattista Vico had already written: "Just as there can be no wholly false ideas, there can be no tradition, even built up of fables, that contains no element of truth."

26. *Israel and Humanity*, French version, 121, 190. For this definition, see the second part of this work, on the themes of tradition and writing. Benamozegh roundly attacked Samuel David Luzzatto's theological ideas at this point, which did indeed claimed to represent what he called "pure Mosaism." It is not far-fetched to see the Luzzatto-Benamozegh polemic as a modern manifestation of two ancient Jewish "souls": orthodox rabbinism and the doctrine, similar to Gnosticism, professed by the Essenes and—much later—the Kabbalists.

27. Ibid., French version, 97. Cf. 255, on the *Shekhinah*.

28. Ibid., 72. Cf. 121: "It is now accepted that humanity's first monotheism was that of Hebraic theosophy."

29. Ibid., 80, note 5, interpretation of Gen. XIV: 19–20.

30. Ibid., 72.

31. *L'autodestruction du christianisme*, 154.

32. Ibid., 159 and 169.

33. On plurality within God, see *Em la-Miqra*, Numbers 25b and 37b.

34. See the letter by Meir ben Shim'on of Narbonne, reproduced by G. Scholem, "A New Document for the History of the Origins of the Kabbalah" (Hebrew), in *Sefer Bialik*, ed. J. Fichman (Tel Aviv: 1934), 148 (quoted in Y. Tishby, *Mishnat ha-Zohar* I [Jerusalem, 1949], 104). Cf. *Israel and Humanity*, French version, 196.

35. Ibid., 180–183. See also *Em la-Miqra*, Lev. 44b and 59b, Deut. 41b.

36. *Israel and Humanity*, French version, 184.

37. Ibid., 157–61. On this, see also Philo of Alexandria, *De specialibus Legibus*, 1. 53 (*Philo* [Cambridge, MA/London], Vol. VII, 128–29) and Flavius Josephus, *Jewish Antiquities* (Cambridge: 1998), IV, 207.

38. Gikatilla's text in fact instances strict connections (*aduquim*) between peoples and the different names of God, even those whose great holiness makes them "ineffaceable." Israel, however, is accorded a position of absolute privilege, being connected with the Tetragrammaton which enfolds all the divine names, and having a union with God that is denied to other nations. Cf. Yosef ben Avraham Gikatilla, *Sha'arei orah* (Gates of Light), ed. Yosef ben Shlomo, second ed. (Jerusalem: 1981), Vol. I, 189–219.

39. *Israel and Humanity*, French version, 269.

40. Ibid., 97.

41. Aimé Pallière was certainly instrumental in achieving this.

42. See Nathan Rotenstreich, "Volksgeist," in *Dictionary of Ideas* (New York: 1973). One example among others of the theological use of the idea of "Volksgeist" occurs in M. E. Quinet, *Génie des Religions* (Paris: 1842), which refers to the "theological principle of every people." See also the account of the work by A. Lebre in *Revue des deux Mondes* 2 (1842): 201.

43. According to some *midrashim* of the *Amoraim* period, God takes care of Israel personally when it behaves itself correctly; otherwise he places it in the care of a minister (*sar*, which is sometimes a god, *eloha*) like all the other peoples. Cf. Efraim E. Urbach, *The Sages, Their Concepts and Beliefs*, trans. Israel Abrahams (Jerusalem: 1975), 137–38. Cf. *Zohar*, III, 14a, 15a (*Midrash ha-ne'elam*): "God scattered the peoples and appointed a minister for each of them, personally taking care of the community of Israel." Benamozegh is careful not to draw attention to the passage that immediately follows this one: "The world was created for Israel alone." The Biblical sources for the idea are Daniel X: 13; X: 21; XII: 1.

44. *Israel and Humanity*, French version, 164, 256.

45. Ibid., 260.

46. Ibid., 261.

47. Ibid., 237.

48. Cf. *Teologia*, 181 and 200–202.

49. *Kitvei Rabbi Nahman Krohmal* (*The Writings of Rabbi Nahman Krochmal*), ed. Sh. Rawidowicz (Berlin: 1924). The passage quoted is from *Moreh nevukhei ha-zeman* (*The Guide of the Perplexed of Our Time*), ch. 7, 37. Cf. Rivka Hurvitz, "Goyyim ve-elohaiv le-rabbi Nahman Krochmal u-meqorotaiv ha-yehudiyym" ("The Nations and Their Gods According to Nahman Krochmal and his Jewish Sources"), *Mehqarei Yerushalaym be-mahasheveth Israel (Sefer Yovel li-Shlomo Pines)* 7, part 1 (1988): 165–287. See also Julius Guttmann, *Philosophies of Judaism. The History of Jewish Philosophy from Biblical Times to Franz Rosenzweig* (New York: 1964), 320–44.

50. *Kitvei Rabbi Nahman Krohmal*, 38.

51. Ibid.

52. Ibid., ch. 6.

53. On Benamozegh's attitude to positivism, see the many passages on the subject in *Teologia* and Y. Colombo, "Che cosa leggeva Elia Benamozegh," *Rassegna Mensile di Israel* XXXVI/2 (1970): 73.

54. *Israel and Humanity*, French version, 162–63. On the concept of *berur*, cf. Avraham Ha-Levi Horowitz, *Shnei Luhot Ha-Brit* (Two Tablets of the Covenant) (Jerusalem: 1963), 189a.

55. *Israel and Humanity*, French version, 321, 354.

56. Ibid., 321.

57. Ibid., 274. Did Benamozegh see himself as that individual? This might be concluded from his relationship with Pallière, whom he considered a true apostle of humanity's new religion. On Aimé Pallière see Catherine Poujol, *Aimé Pallière (1868–1949). Itinéraire d'un chrétien dans le judaïsme* (Paris: 2003).

58. It is interesting to note that Pallière was very interested in the philosophy of Henri Bergson, especially *Deux sources de la morale et da la religion* (1932). Imma-

nentism, the spirit of unity released by multiplicity and energy are all elements in Bergson's thought, though evidently devoid of any theological or finalist character. In these basic Bergsonian ideas we may nonetheless see the development of certain key concepts in later nineteenth-century philosophy. In Bergson, "progress" becomes "movement," a condition inherent in existence, but with no specific direction; the oneness of nature with its optimistic corollories becomes oneness without attributes, a vague, intuited tendency. The broadening of these ideas was matched by the loss of their rational meaning: an example is Dilthey's "vital experience," a sort of energy underlying history, but devoid of sense. Vladimir Jankélévitch may be considered the last representative of a school of thought that allied energy and optimism. In his essay "Bergson et le judaïsme" (*Mélanges de philosophie et littérature juives*, Vols. I and II [Paris: 1956–1957]) he identifies Judaism with prophetism and compares it to Bergson's optimistic immanentism.

59. *Ta'am le-Shad* (Livorno: 1863), 147.

Hidden Anthropomorphism: Feuerbach's Reasons

1. *Teologia*, 59.
2. *Israel and Humanity*, Eng. transl., 201–202. *L'origines des dogmes chrétiens*, 136–37.
3. *Eimat mafgia'* (Livorno: 1855), 22b. Scholem's comment on symbols is not dissimilar. Cf. *Major Trends in Jewish Mysticism* (Jerusalem: 1941), 27: "The mystical symbol is the expression of something which is outside the realm of expression and communication, something that comes from a realm whose face is, so to speak, turned inward, and outside of us." In *Sha'arei orah*, Yosef Gikatilla refers to anthropomorphic allusions in the Bible as *symanim*—signs—which allude to a reality unreachable by understanding other than through allusive evocation (*dimiyon zikhron*). He uses the example of a person's given name, which is only a sign that evokes the person without affecting the person's form or essence. Cf. *Sha'arei orah*, Vol. 1, 49.
4. *Teologia*, 30.
5. Ibid., 32.
6. Ibid.
7. Ibid.
8. The recontextualization of Feuerbach's philosophy in the tradition of Christian criticism, and its removal from the Marxist groove, where it had always been regarded as an "incomplete precedent" for dialectical materialism, changes nothing from this perspective. Even if we consider—as has recently been done—that Feuerbach's intention and aspiration derived from Christ's humanity, as evidenced in Lutheran Christology, his analysis is no less materialistic for all that. When Feuerbach wrote of "exalt[ing] anthropology into theology" (*The Essence of Christianity* [New York: 1957], xxxvii), the former term is surely given the greater weight. See J. P. Osier's preface to the French translation, 78, and Elisabeth de Fontenay, *Figures juives de Marx: Marx dans l'idéologie allemande* (Paris: 1973).
9. *Teologia*, 32.
10. *Essence of Christianity*, French trans. J.-P. Osier (Paris: 1977), 382.

From Lamentations of Exile to a Sense of Mission

1. Adolphe Franck, *Le Panthéisme oriental et le monothéisme hébreu*, lecture to the Société des Etudes Juives, January 19, 1889, Paris, 8. Cf. A. Guetta, "Politics and Culture in Jewish Studies in Nineteenth-Century France," *Shofar, an Interdisciplinary Journal of Jewish Studies* 14, no. 3 (1996): 16–31.

2. *Le Panthéisme oriental*, 9.

3. A. Franck, *La Kabbale, ou la philosophie religieuse des Hébreux*, third ed. (Paris: 1892), 101. Also 193, on which Franck offers an ethical and political interpretation of Kabbalistic symbolism: "Passing off all the facts and words of the Scriptures as symbols, it teaches man to have self-confidence: it replaces authority with reason; it gives birth to philosophy within, and under the protection of religion." Benamozegh's eye witness account claims that one of Franck's aims was to "show that the Jews too deserve a place in the sun." Cf. *Vessillo Israelitico* XLI (1893): 416.

4. *Discorso pronunciato nel Tempio Israelitico di Livorno il dì 8 settembre 1847 nel rendimento di grazie per la conceduta Guardia cittadina* (Livorno: 1847). Benamozegh was barred from teaching by the authorities of the Grand Duchy of Tuscany because of his over-strong Italian sentiments. Cf. *Scritti scelti* (Rome 1955), 329.

5. *Nelle solenni esequie a S.M. Vittorio Emanuele II, celebrate il 7 febbraio 1878 nel Tempio Maggiore Israelitico di Livorno* (Livorno: 1878). The comments on monarchy and the dangers of despotism in *Em la-Miqra* (Deut.: 71b and 73a) are of the same liberal tenor. Cf. also *Lettres à S. D. L.*, 69, in which the Jews—as a minority—are assigned the task of championing the values of reason, liberty, and progress.

6. Benamozegh was also a corresponding member of the Académie de France. Cf. *Archives Israélites*, 1900, 84.

7. *Maor va-shemesh* (Livorno: 1839): "Oh Lord, turn your attention on the desolation of your people, who, persecuted and abused, cry out from their exile."

8. *Nir le-David*, commentary on Psalms XIII and XXXVI.

9. On Livorno's economic status during the nineteenth century, see Fulvio Conti, *Infrastructure urbane e politica municipale fra otto e Novecento: il caso di Livorno*, "Passato e Presente," no. 25 (1991). On its cultural life, see Pietro Vigo et al., *Livorno nell'Ottocento* (Livorno: 1900).

10. On Livorno's Jewish community during the nineteenth century, see Michele Luzzati, ed., *Ebrei di Livorno tra due censimenti (1841–1938). Memoria familiare e identità* (Livorno: 1990); Bruno Di Porto, "La stampa periodica ebraica a Livorno," *Nuovi Studi Livornesi*, I (1993): 173–98.

11. *Nir le-David*, Ps. CVI.

12. Ibid., Ps. LXXXIX.

13. The seventeenth-century Moroccan rabbi, Hayyim Ben Attar, stayed for more than a year in Livorno while he raised the money he needed to publish his major *Torah* commentary, *Or ha-hayyim*, and for the *yeshiva* he was going to found in Jerusalem. See H. Ben Attar, *Or ha-hayyim* (Venice: 1741), introduction. In "Kabbalah in Elijah Benamozegh's Thought" (the preface to the English translation of *Israel and Humanity*), Moshe Idel identifies "Italian" sources for Benamozegh, or that confirm his "Italianization" after "Moroccan" beginnings. Recent contributions by Idel in Italian and Hebrew develop this argument further, showing the philosophical nature of the

Italian Kabbalah Benamozegh was attached to. Cf. Moshe Idel, "Elia Benamozegh e la Qabbalà," *Rassegna Mensile di Israel* LXIII, no. 3 (1997): 29–41; id., " 'Al ha-qabbalah etzel ha-rav Eliyahu Ben Amozegh," *Pe'amim* 74 (1998): 97–103.

14. *Em la-Miqra*, Gen. 81b.

15. *Israel and Humanity*, French version, 263.

16. Ibid., 66.

17. Ibid., 272.

18. *Nir le-David*, Ps. CXXII.

Philology and Philosophy

1. *Genesis Rabbah* XVIII: 6 and XXXI: 8; *Pirkei de-Rabbi Eli'ezer*, XXVI.

2. See Umberto Eco, "Forma locutionis," in *Filosofia '91*, ed. Gianni Vattimo (Bari: 1992), 162.

3. Provenzali's book is mentioned in Azariah de' Rossi *Meor 'einayim*. See the English edition by Joanna Weinberg, *The Light of the Eyes* (Yale/London: 2001), 677. On the subject of Hebrew as the perfect language, see William Chomsky, *Hebrew: The Eternal Language* (Philadelphia: 1964), 17–19.

4. Umberto Eco, in *The Search for the Perfect Language*, trans. James Fentress (Oxford and Cambridge, MA: 1995), 85. Ibid., 121, refers to Athanasius Kircher who in 1679 (in *Turris Babel*) was a late supporter of the notion of Hebrew as a universal, primordial language. "The crisis of the Hebrew language as a holy language had already begun during the Renaissance" (106). For the last pockets of resistance, see Ibid., 136. One recent contribution was made by Sophie Kessler-Mesguich, "L'hébreu chez les hébraïsants chrétiens des XVIe et XVIIe siècles," *Histoire, epistomologie, langage* XVIII, fascicle 1 (1996): 87–108. The entire fascicle is devoted to the linguistics of Hebrew and Jewish languages.

5. On Reggio, or YaSHaR (the acrostic of his name) see Vittorio Castiglioni, *The History of Rabbi Avraham Hay Reggio and His Son, Rabbi Yitzhaq* (in Hebrew) (Krakow: 1889); Israel Zinberg, *History of Hebrew Literature* (in Hebrew) (Tel Aviv: 1960), Vol. VI, 88; Giuliano Tamani, "I.S. Reggio e l'illuminismo ebraico," in *Gli ebrei a Gorizia e a Trieste tra "Ancien Régime" ed emancipazione* (Udine: 1984), 29–41; Maddalena Del Bianco Cotrozzi, *Il Collegio Rabbinico di Padova*, passim. To date there is still no specific monograph on Reggio, but significant if partial contributions include the David Malkiel articles: "New Light on the Career of Isaac Samuel Reggio," in *The Jews of Italy. Memory and Identity*, ed. Barbara Garvin and Bernard D. Cooperman (University Press of Maryland, 2000), 276–303; "The Reggios of Gorizia: Modernization in Micro," in *The Mediterranean and the Jews. Society, Culture, and Economy in Early Modern Times*, ed. Elliott Horowitz and Moises Orfali (Ramat Gan: 2002), 67–84. See also Marco Grusovin, "Isacco Samuele Reggio, rabbino e filosofo," *Quaderni Giuliani di Storia* 17, no. 2 (1996): 7–29; id., "Isacco Samuele Reggio versus Aaron Chorin," *Transylvanian Review* XIII, no. 4 (2004): 117–29.

6. *Torat ha-Elohim*, Pentateuch with Italian translation and commentary (Vienna: 1818).

7. See *Behinat ha-qabbalah (Examen Traditionis: Duo inedita et paene incognita Leonis Mutensis)* (Gorizia: 1852). On Reggio's anti-dogmatic position on the Talmud

with regard to western European Judaism, cf. *Ha-Torah ve-ha-pilosofiyah* (*Torah and Philosophy*) (Vienna: 1827), 108–30.

8. Preface to *Torath ha-Elohim*, 14 and 17. See also id., *Scriptum Probitatis, lettres à S. D. Luzzatto*, ed. Vittorio Castiglioni (Krakow: 1902), 4: "God . . . gave men the ability to invent words in every language except Hebrew, whose elements were given *in toto* to the first man."

9. Moses Mendelssohn, *Sefer Netivoth ha-Shalom* (*Commentary on the Pentateuch*) (Berlin: 1783; second ed. Vienna: 1808), Introduction. The Italian rabbi Vittorio Castiglioni (1840–1911) expressed agreement with this idea, as well as noting that "nowadays it would be impossible to affirm a different idea explicitly" (*Scriptum Probitatis*, 23, note). Written in Hebrew, this note evinces a certain concession to the spirit of the age not entirely felt by the author. For similar self-censorship by Benamozegh, cf. *Em la-Miqra* (Livorno: 1862), Lv., 71a.

10. Cf. Anna Morpurgo Davies, *Linguistica dell'Ottocento*, in *Storia della Linguistica*, ed. Giulio Cesare Lepschy (Bologna: 1994), Vol. III, 84; O. Ducrot, T. Todorov, *Encyclopedic Dictionary of the Sciences of Language*, trans. by Catherine Porter (Johns Hopkins University Press, 1979).

11. *Linguistica dell'Ottocento*, 87.

12. Cf. among others George Gusdorf, *Le romantisme* (Paris: 1993), Vol. I, 303–14.

13. The statutes of the Society of Linguistics for 1865–1866 actually forbade any discussion on the origins of languages.

14. S. D. Luzzatto, *Prolegomeni ad una grammatica* (Padua: 1836). On Luzzatto's linguistic empiricism, see his *Sefer ha-riqmah, Grammaire hébraïque de Jona ben Gannah*, ed. Beer Goldberg (Frankfurt: 1853), "Remarks" at the start of the book, unnumbered pages. Luzzatto's thesis was that the definition of the individual precedes that of the universal, contrary to the logical order of philosophy (which, for him, was synonymous with idealism). He took as a proof the fact that the words used to define individuals are simpler, and elements are added to them to define universals (prefixes or suffixes): ḤaKHaM (wise) is simpler that ḤoKHMaH (wisdom), suggesting that the former came before the latter.

15. For a historical analysis of this issue, see Mireille Hadas-Lebel, *Histoire de la langue hébraïque* (Paris: 1981), third ed., 81–83.

16. In the introduction to *Studi Orientali e linguistici* (dans *Studi critici* I [Milan: Il Politecnico, 1861]), Ascoli wrote that "linguistics can uphold the principles of tolerance and fraternity between the Nations."

17. On the debate between Luzzatto and Ascoli on "the Aryan-Semitic connection" see Isacco Garti, "Il carteggio Ascoli-Luzzatto conservato nelle Biblioteca dell'Accademia dei Lincei," *Italia* I, no. 1 (Jerusalem: 1976), 79–91. On Luzzatto's idea of alternation between Semitic and Aryan civilizations in history, see Yitzhaq Heinemann, *La loi dans la pensée juive*, 156–59 and S. D. Luzzatto, *Derekh Eretz, o Attitzismus* (*Morality, or Atticism*), in *Zion* I, 81, reproduced in id., *Writings* (Hebrew), ed. M. E. Artom (Jerusalem: 1976), Vol. 2, 41–73.

18. *Prolegomeni*, 84–85.

19. This latter poem, by Avraham Shalom (Avshalom) is in Hayyim Schirmann, *Mivhar ha-shirah ha-'ivrith be-Ytaliyah* (*Anthology of Hebrew Poetry in Italy*) (Berlin:

1934), 498. For an attempt at critical analysis of Italian Hebrew poetry, cf. Alessandro Guetta, ed., *Poesia ebraica italiana. Mille anni di creazione sacra e profana*, special volume of *La Rassegna Mensile d'Israel* IX, no. 1–2 (1994).

20. S. D. Luzzatto, *Kinnor na'im (Pleasant Lyre)*, ed. Isaia Luzzatto (Padua: 1879), Introduction.

21. S. D. Luzzatto, *Ha-Mishtaddel* (Vienna: 1847), Introduction.

22. Cf. Judah ha-Levi, *The Kuzari (Kitab al Khazari); An Argument for the Faith of Israel*, trans. Hartwig Hirschfeld) (New York: 1964), 124–27. Lelio Hillel Della Torre taught theology, Talmud, and oratory in Padua. An erudite polemicist, he excelled at exegesis, preaching and poetry. His works included *Poésies Hébraïques* (Padua 1868); *Pensieri sulle lezioni sabbatiche del Pentateuco* (Padua: 1872). An anthology of his writing was published in two volumes under the title *Scritti sparsi* (Padua: 1908). See Riccardo di Segni's entry on him in *Dizionario biografico degli italiani* XXXVII (Rome: 1989), 587–89.

23. "The behavior of some young people of our times," in *Poésies Hébraïques*, 195.

24. In a series of extremely interesting articles on a partial Hebrew translation of Dante's *Divine Comedy*, Della Torre explored the themes of Hebrew's grammatical and semantic specificity, of which scholars, writers, and translators should be aware if the language was not to be weakened by overfaithful imitation of European languages. Cf. Lelio Della Torre, *Scritti sparsi*, Vol. 1, 271.

25. If an overall interpretative schema of the history of Hebrew literature were to be assayed, one might note that literary creativity was—after six centuries—in decline in Italy at exactly the time when it began to flourish in Russia, Lithuania, and Poland.

26. The term comes from Gérard Genette, *Mimologics = Mimologiques: voyage en Cratylie*, trans. Thaïs E. Morgan (Lincoln: 1995).

27. Cf. Giambattista Vico, *On the Most Ancient Wisdom of the Italians*, 45, 64.

28. *Em la-Miqra*, Deut. 120a. Michelet's partial translation of *Scienza Nuova* (Paris: 1827) had contributed powerfully to the renewal of interest in the Italian philosopher.

29. In "The Splitting of the Logos. Some Parallels in Vico and Rabbinic Tradition," in *Salvacion en le Palabra. En memoria del profesor Alejandro Diez Macho*, ed. D. Munar Leon (Madrid: 1986), 717–33, José Faur sketches a broader parallel between Vico and the rabbis, in the light of the opposition between philosophy (Greeks) and rhetoric (Jews). Benamozegh's reference to Vico ("By far the most lucid Jewish thinker in modern times," 718) is quoted.

30. *Em la-Miqra*, Nm. 3b: "A land through which no man had yet traveled."

31. *Teologia*, 152, *Lettres à S. D. L.*, 91: "Don't you know that every rule of grammar has its own metaphysics?"

32. Ibid., 97. At this point Benamozegh quotes Vico, through Terenzio Mamiani, thereby binding himself to an entirely Italian tradition.

33. E. Benamozegh, *Storia degli Esseni*, 7. For an examination of Romantic linguistics, see G. Mounin, *Histoire de la linguistique des origines au XXe siècle* (Paris: 1967; Bertil Malmberg, *Histoire de la linguistique* (Paris: 1991), 248 and ff.

34. *Teologia*, 97. "These two languages could not express their genius more effectively: one (Greek), as a language of nature; the other (Hebrew), as a language of the absolute."

35. "L'inverno ebraico," in *L'Israelita*, no. 1 (1866), 12. The theory of opposite meanings of single words was proposed by the Egyptian specialist Carl Abel (1827–1906), in *Über den Gegensinn der Urworte* (Leipzig: 1884). It is interesting to note that Freud found confirmation in this text for the idea that in dreams a thing may be expressed by its opposite. See Giulio C. Lepschy, "Freud, Abel e gli opposti," in *Sulla linguistica moderna* (Bologna: 1989), 349–78. I owe my awareness of this article to its author, to whom I am indebted.

36. *Teologia*, 97. "L'inverno ebraico," 12. Cf. *Sefer Yetzirah (The Book of Creation): In Theory and Practice*, trans. Aryeh Kaplan (York Beach, ME: 1991), 1–4.

37. *Israel and Humanity*, English trans. 114–15; *Talmud Bavli*, Tractate Kiddushin, f. 71a.

38. *Teologia*, 116. Gershom Scholem, "The Name of God and the Linguistic of Kabbala," *Diogenes* 79 (1972): 59–80; 80, 164–94.

39. *Teologia*, 27; G. Vico, *On the Most Ancient Wisdom of the Italians*, 69. Cf. *Zohar* I, 16b on the identification of the letter *yod* as "a primordial point . . . the beginning of another word: light."

40. The *Zohar* emphasizes the principle of the immutability of the text: "The man to whom all the secrets of the *Torah* are revealed will realize that the text must stay as it is; it must not be increased or amputated by so much as a single letter." Commentary on the *Mishpatim* section.

41. On Abulafia, see Moshe Idel's monograph, *The Mystical Experience in Abraham Abulafia*, trans. Jonathan Chipman (Albany: 1988).

42. Authors such as Moshe Cordovero were particularly sensitive to the relationship between the written and the spoken word, to which should be added the thought word. Cf. *Pardes rimmonim (The Pomegranate Garden)* (Cracow: 1592), ch. XXVII, 2. On this relationship in the *Zohar*, see Charles Mopsik, "Pensée, Voix et Parole dans le Zohar," *Revue de l'Histoire des Religions* 213, fascicle 4 (Oct.–Dec. 1996): 385–414.

43. David Castelli, review of *Teologia*, in *Rivista Europea* VIII (1877): 169–81. A former pupil of Benamozegh's at the Livorno rabbinical college, Castelli was professor of Hebrew at the Regio Istituto di Studi Superiori in Florence. His works included critical translations with introductions to *Ecclesiastes* (Pisa: 1866); *The Song of Songs* (Florence: 1892); and *Job* (*Il poema semitico del pessimismo*) (Florence: 1897); *Il Messia secondo gli Ebrei* (Florence: 1874); publication of an edition of Sabbatai Donnolo's commentary on the *Sefer Yetzirah* (in *Istituto di Studi Superiori e pratici di Firenze, sezione di filologia e filosofia, accademia orientale*, n. 7 [Florence: 1880]). See Fausto Parente's article in the *Dizionario biografico degli italiani*, Vol. 21 (Rome: 1978); Cristiana Facchini, *David Castelli. Ebraismo e scienze delle religioni tra Otto e Novecento* (Brescia: 2005).

44. For the Orientalist Fausto Lasinio (1831–1914), "De Benedetti and Castelli had to do the work themselves. Castelli's teacher, Rabbi Piperno of Livorno, possessed a good command of the Hebrew language, but he was not a philologist, and neither was De Benedetti or Castelli, or any of the other rabbis of Livorno, or anyone else

from that school. Let it be understood that I am not denying their merit; however, Hebrew philology does not count them among its disciples or experts." Lasinio's letter to Angelo De Gubernatis, July 4, 1876, Biblioteca Nazionale Centrale, Florence, cass. 74, 1. Quoted in L. E. Funaro, " 'Cose d'Oriente.' Studi ebraici e orientalismo nella Firenze del secondo Ottocento. Inediti da un epistolario," forthcoming. Lasinio's master, Angelo Paggi, spoke in even harsher terms: "Not only does Rabbi Benamuseg [sic] lack the fundamental rules of Hebrew language and of theology, but now, coming out of left field, he presumes to give us some lessons in theology." Letter to S. D. Luzzatto of the year 1865, quoted in L. E. Funaro, " 'Lettere sacre e profane.' Angelo Paggi, un maestro di cultura ebraica nella Toscana del primo Ottocento," Zakhor IX (2006): 136.

45. *Una Critica criticabile* (Livorno: 1878). The dispute between Castelli and Benamozegh is analyzed by Cristiana Facchini in her monography about David Castelli (see note 43), 112–15.

46. Ibid., 12.

47. Ibid., 13.

48. Antoine Fabre d'Olivet, who had also supported the notion of a connection between elementary ideas and written signs (*La langue hébraïque restituée, et le véritable sens des mots hébreux rétabli et prouvé par leur analyse radicale*, Part I [Paris: 1815], 30 and ff.) was (alas!), in his analysis of specific cases, often in total opposition to Benamozegh. For him, the sign *sh*, for instance, represented not rest but "relative length, and the associated movement." Ibid., Part II, 225.

49. Cf. *Bahir*, trans., intro., and commentary Aryeh Kaplan (York Beach, ME: 1989), § 30.

50. Max Jacob, *L'echelle de Jacob* (Paris: 1994), 17.

51. *Em la-Miqra*, Gen., 129a.

52. Ibid., 125a and 128b.

The Inevitable Choices of Nineteenth-Century Biblical Commentary

1. Alan Richardson, "The Criticism and the Theological use of the Bible," in *The Cambridge History of the Bible* (Cambridge: 1963), Vol. III, 294.

2. We have already seen the extent to which Benamozegh developed the evolutionist angle. The frequent occurrence in his writings of the Talmudic phrase "as the monkey is to man" is probably an echo—albeit in another form—of the scientific and ideological debate surrounding the origins of man. Another reaction to the debate in the Italian Jewish community is discernable in the Hebrew poem by S. H. Zelman, dedicated to M. Y. Ashkenazy (Tedeschi) (see note 11), published by way of introduction to the latter's biblical commentary. It includes the line, "All may now do exactly as they please/ like our fathers' fathers, the chimpanzees." The position is an amusing one, though meant as an entirely serious objection to moral subjectivism and theoretical skepticism.

The truth of the following anecdote cannot be proven. A chronicler related that the divisionary commander in Livorno lived in the villa next to the home of Benamozegh, "a famous orientalist and theologian, a very scholarly man, but very neglectful of his person." The general, less than delighted by his neighbor, tried in vain to get him to move. He finally hit on the idea of building two large cages atop the separating wall, into which he introduced a pair of monkeys, who could look down onto the "illustrious linguist" (*sic*) below. Exasperated by their intrusive presence, Benamozegh was finally driven from the premises (Antonio Silvio Scarlatti, "Sul rione dell'Origine"). Did the unbearable gaze of the primates have a bearing on his repeated use of the Talmudic metaphor? For an initial hint of Benamozegh's attitude to Darwinian evolutionism, cf. José Faur, "The Hebrew Species Concept and the Origin of Evolution: R. Benamozegh's Response to Darwin," *Rassegna Mensile di Israel* LXIII, no. 3: 43–60.

3. École Pratique des Hautes Études, *Problèmes et méthodes d'histoire des religions* (Paris: 1968), preface.

4. The expression comes from the *Lettre Evangélique de S.S. le Pape Léon XIII aux archevêques, evêques et au clergé de France*, 8 September 1899. Quoted in C. Savart and J.-N. Aletti, eds., *Le monde contemporain et la Bible* (Paris: 1985).

5. Ibid., 450.

6. *Em la-miqra* is a technical term used in the *Talmud Bavli* for justifying a *halachah*—a ritual instruction—with a biblical text. It could be translated as "*reading* matrix," signifying that the text must be considered in terms of its traditional reading. The parallel to this is *Em la-massoreth*, which could be translated as "[traditional] textual matrix." See Rashi on Sukkah 6b: "What Moses wrote and passed down (*masar*) to Israel in the Torah, that, and not what we read, is the matrix and foundation." For instance, the word in Exodus XII containing the letters *yod aleph khaf lamed*, would, according to *Em la-miqra* be read as *yeakhel* (will be eaten: the subject is the paschal sacrifice); according to the *Em la-massoreth* principle the same word would be read without recourse to tradition, in a manner far closer to an ordinary reading, as *yokhal* (he will eat). See *Talmud Bavli*, Pessahim 86b. Benamozegh inverted the terms, using the phrase referring to the reading tradition for his Pentateuch commentary, and that referring to a purely textual reading for his *midrash* commentary, corresponding to oral teaching. It was certainly the immediate rather than the strict meaning of the terms that led to this choice: *Miqra* meaning "Biblical text" and *Massoreth* meaning "Translation."

7. "Limmudei ha-Shem" (Scholars of God, or Studies of God) *Ha-Levanon* 40 (1881): 313–14 and 41: 321–72.

8. Ibid., 327.

9. An Italian translation of this passage with notes (and facing-page Hebrew text), done by myself, may be found in appendix to Alessandro Guetta, ed., *Per Elia Benamozegh. Atti del Convegno di Livorno, settembre 2000* (Milan: 2000), 301–308.

10. See *infra*, the chapter entitled *L'insuffisance des interprétations littérales*.

11. Isaac Samuel Reggio, *Torath Elohim*; Samuel David Luzzatto, *Ha-Mishtaddel* (Vienna: 1847); Moshe Yitzhaq Tedeschi (Ashkenazy)'s *Hoyil Moshe* (Livorno: 1841).

12. On this subject, see *Kerem Hemed* (1856), 1, and Reggio's proposed textual reworkings, ibid. (1854), 78.

13. Samuel David Luzzatto, *Oheb Ger (Philoxenus, sive de Onkelosi chaldaica entateuchi versione, Dissertatio hermeneutico-critica)*, in Hebrew (Vienna: 1830; expanded second ed., Cracow: 1895).

14. *Ger Tzedek*, notes on the Pentateuch, *Torat Elohim* (Livorno: 1854). It comprises short philological and linguistic notes on the *Targum*, the Onkelos Aramaic paraphrase. Nahmanides' influence is considerable.

15. Samuel David Luzzatto, *Commentary on the Book of Isaiah*, in Hebrew (Tel Aviv: 1970), preface, 12. Cf. Irene Kajon, "Dalla metafisica alla scienza all'etica: S. D. Luzzatto, U. Cassuto, D. Lattes come interpreti del Pentateuco," *Rassegna Mensile di Israel*, no. 1 (1999): 1–28.

16. It was not until 1944 that the Italian Moshe David Cassuto published a major work in Hebrew on biblical sources in the form of an introduction and explanations of passages taken separately. *Commentary on Genesis* (Jerusalem: 1944–1949).

17. Reggio published a sort of presentation to his work separately, with the declared intention of boosting sales; Luzzatto owed the publication of his major work on Isaiah to a benefactor in Paris who was a friend of his son Filosseno.

18. For a positive reception of *Em la-Miqra* in some of the orthodox Jewish circles of Salonika, see Yitzhaq R. Molkho, *Nequdot hen min ha'olam ha sefarady ba-dorot ha-aharonim (Treasures of the Sephardic World in Recent Generations)* (Jerusalem: 1958), 16–17.

19. For an accurate detailed account of this episode, see Yaron Harel, "Ha'alath Em la-Miqra 'al ha-moqed—Halab 1865" ("The Edict to Destroy 'Em la-Miqra'—Aleppo 1865"), in *Hebrew Union College Annual* LXIV (1993), 27–36. It has also been the subject of an (unpublished) MA thesis on Em la-Miqra by Mordechai Agmon, in Jerusalem in 1971. For historical contextualization of the position of the Aleppo rabbis, cf. Tzvi Zohar, "Shamranut Iohemeth" ("Conservatism at War") in *Pe'amin* 55 (1993): 57–78. The rejoinder by the Jerusalem rabbi Moshe Pardo to Benamozegh's response, entitled "Teshuvah me-ahavah" ("Response Inspired by Love"), appeared in the same journal, *Levanon*, in the following issues: Ninth year, no. 1: 2–3; no. 3: 12–13; no. 4: 19–20; no. 5: 23–24; no. 7: 31–32; no. 8: 34–35; no. 9: 41–42; no. 18: 48–49.

20. For echoes of this polemic, see Benamozegh's introduction to Eliyahu Hazan's *Zikhron Yerushalayim (Remembrance of Jerusalem)* (Livorno: 1874).

21. "Tzory Guil'ad," *Kevod ha-Levanon*, year 8, no. 17.

22. Ibid.

23. On the work of Israel Moshe Hazan, see José Faur, *Ha-rav Yisrael Moshe Hazan. Ha-ish ve-mishnato (Rabbi Israel Moshe Hazan. The Man and his Work)* (Jerusalem: 1977); Robert Bonfil, "Temuroth ba-minhagim ha-datiyym shel yehudei Roma bi-tqufath kehunato shel rabbi Yisrael Moshe Hazan" (1847–1852) ("Changes in the Religious Mores of the Jews of Rome During the Rabbinic Ministry of Israel Moshe Hazan"), in *Scritti in memoria di Enzo Sereni. Saggi sull'ebraismo italiano*, ed. D. Carpi, A. Milano, U. Nahon (Milan-Jerusalem: 1970), Hebrew part, 228–51; id., "Il memoriale dell'Università Israelitica di Roma sopra il soggiorno romano di Rabbi Israel Moshe Hazan (1847–1852)," in X *Annuario di Studi Ebraici* (Rome: 1984), 29–64.

24. *Perorazione e Salmi ebraici dell'eccellso e reverito Sig. Rabbino Israel Moshe Hazan, letti il giorno della sua installazione nella cattedra di rabbino Maggiore in Alessandria d'Egitto* (Livorno: 1858), 3–5; Introduction to *Iyyei ha-yam* (The Islands of the Sea) (Livorno: 1869). In his (French) preface to the Hebrew work *Zikron Yerushalayim* (cit.), Benamozegh dwells on "the immense erudition, the method, style, great and

beautiful thoughts" contained in Israel Moshe Hazan's final work. Marc D. Angel connects Benamozegh and Hazan as "enlightened Sephardic intellectuals" in *Voices in Exile, A Study in Sephardic Intellectual History* (New York: 1991), 155.

25. *Sheerit ha-nahalah* (*The Remaining Possession*) (Alexandria [Egypt]: 1862), 35. This book, which accounted for the published section of the great work *Netzah Yisrael* (*The Eternity of Israel*), includes a dialogue, conducted in Livorno, between a naïve local tradesman and two rabbis from Jerusalem. Covering a multitude of subjects from law to grammar, the book is written in a very lively, brilliant style, comparable to that of Luzzatto's *Dialogues on the Kabbalah*.

26. Ibid., 12.

27. Cf. *Successione per Israele. Voto dell'eccellentissimo signore Israel Moshe Hazan* (Alexandria [Egypt]: 1851).

28. Ibid., 55. Quoted in Bonfil, "Changements dans les mœurs religieux des Juifs de Rome," 249.

29. This is the contention of Yitzhaq R. Molkho, in the chapter on Benamozegh in his book *Nequdot hen me-ha-'olam ha-sefarady ba-dorot ha-aharonim* (*Treasures of the Sephardic World in the Most Recent Generations*), 18–19, and of Menahem Dayan in *Universal Elements in the Jewish Thought of Elia Benamozegh*, unpublished PhD thesis, JTS New York 1986, 6.

30. I Samuel I: 2

31. Cf. *Talmud Bavli*, tractate Baba Kama 60b.

32. Cf. ibid., tractate Sanhedrin 39a, and Rashi's *in loco* commentary on the words *hormiz* and *ahormiz*.

33. Amos VII: 14.

34. *Kevod ha-Levanon*, no. 43: 352. The same image recurs, in a different context, in "Del Congresso rabbinico proposto dal Rev. Rabbino Mortarta," *L'Israelita* (Livorno: 1866). For an overview of *Responsa* literature in modern Italy, see David Malkiel, "Yetzirah ve-sugiyah be-sifrut ha-halakhah be-Italiyah be'et ha-hadashah," in *Pe'amim* 86–87 (2002): 258–95. On the issue of cremation, see Id., "Technologiyah ve-tarbut be'iniyan serefat ha-metim. Nittuah history v-fenomenology" ("Technology and Culture in the Question of Cremation. A Historical and Phenomenological Analysis"), *Italia* 10 (1993): 37 ff.

35. Aesop, *Fables*, French ed. by E. Chambry (Paris: 1927), 26.

36. These were *'Anaf 'Etz Avot* (A branch of the paternal tree), on the admissibility of eating in a house of prayer, published as an appendix to Avraham Coriat, *Berith Avoth* (The Alliance of the Fathers) (Livorno: 1862); *Le fonti del diritto ebraico e il testamento Samama* (Livorno: 1882); *Ya'aneh ba-esh* (He will respond with fire, or on the subject of fire) on cremation; and, finally, an interesting opinion on the introduction of the organ in liturgical services. Benamozegh accepted its use even on holy days, on condition that it was played by a "noachide," proof of philosophical and ritual consistency. See E. Toaff, "Storia di un organo," in *Rassegna Mensile di Israel* no. 4 (1949): 173–81.

37. *Em la-Miqra*, commentary on Lv. XXIII.

38. Ibid., 5a and 41b.

39. Ibid., 62a.

40. The phrase comes from Henri Cazelles in *Le monde contemporain et la Bible*, cit., p. 443.

41. *La verità sulle due Tipografie Tubiana e Benamozegh*, 64.

42. *Em la-Miqra*, Gen. 157b.

43. Yosef ben Avraham Gikatilla, *Sha'arey orah* (Gates of Light), ed. Yosef ben Shlomo. Vol. 1, 45–51.

44. See, inter alia, the lovely passages of *Ha-Mishtaddel* on Genesis, 10a and 11a.

45. See the essays by B. J. Diebner and T. Römer in *Le livre de traverse. De l'exégèse biblique à l'anthropologie* (Paris: 1992).

46. *Em la-Miqra*, Lv. 72b.

47. Ibid., Gen. 94b.

48. Ibid., Ex. 34a.

49. Ibid., Num. 12a and Deut. 172b.

50. *Una critica criticabile*, 15.

51. Tractate Yoma, ch. 5.

52. Malbim, *Ha-Torah ve-ha-mitzvah* (Bucharest: 1860), Introduction, 227. On this subject, see Charles Touati, *L'exégèse biblique au XIXe siècle: MALBIM*, in the Annuaire EPHE, Section des sciences religieuses XCV, 1986–1987, 22. Touati characterizes Malbim as "an encyclopaedic mind of dizzying subtlety" who was perfectly aware of the development of the exact sciences but utterly indifferent to the new biblical science.

53. See "Criticism of the traditional use by scientists," in *The Cambridge History of the Bible*, 25.

54. He did not renounce this approach entirely. He saw in the word *tekhelet* (blue), which shares a root with *takhlit* (purpose, end), a confirmation of the Newtonian theory of colors. Cf. *Em la-Miqra*, Numbers 41a, and the same remark in Reggio's commentary, Introduction, 16b.

55. Praise for literal meaning ("Good, right, and pleasant") may already be discerned in *Gher tzedeq* (Ex. 47a). It goes without saying that other Italian interpreters took the same position. Throughout his work Reggio expressed a preference for what he called "the dry bread of the literal word" over philosophical interpretations unsupported by philology.

56. On this, see *Teologia*, 276. In *Storia degli Esseni*, 184, Benamozegh described the *midrash aggada* as "Theosophy in mythological garb."

57. Avi'ad Sar Shalom Basilea, *Emunat Hakhamim* (*The Faith of the Wise*) (Mantua: 1730). On this author, see David Ruderman, *Jewish Thought and Scientific Discovery in Early Modern Europe*, New Haven, London 243–28; Alessandro Guetta, "Cabale et rationalisme en Italie à l'époque baroque," in *Réceptions de la cabale*, ed. Pierre Gisel, Lucie Kaennel, Paris-Tel Aviv, 103–26.

58. See also *Em la-Miqra*, Gen. 27a, 30b, and 37a.

59. Ibid., Gen. 14a, Num. 74a, and Gen. 23a respectively.

60. *EPHE, Section des sciences religieuses* (Paris: 1907), 1–28. On Israel Lévi, see Israel Lévi, *Le ravissement du Messie à sa naissance et autres essais*, ed. Evelyne Patlagean (Paris-Louvain: 1994); Charles Touati, "Israel Lévi et la recherche sur

la littérature talmudique," *Revue des Etudes Juives*, 155 (Jul.–Dec. 1996): fasc. 3–4, 479–83.

The Notes on the Zohar

1. *Zohar*, ed. Belforte (Livorno: 1851). See Guido Sonnino, *Storia della tipografia ebraica in Livorno*, on Jewish typography in Livorno. Five editions of the *Zohar* were published there, three in the eighteenth and two in the nineteenth century.

2. Moshe ben Menahem Kunitzer, *Ben Yohai* (*The Son of Yohai*) (Vienna: 1815). One of the things Kunitzer, a pioneer of *Haskalah* (the Jewish Enlightenment), did in the book was attempt to prove the authenticity of the *Zohar*.

3. Introduction to the *Zohar*, signed by the three Livorno rabbis Yitzhaq Hayyim Nunes Alvarenga, Avraham ben Moshe Coriat, and Avraham Barukh Piperno.

4. With a pride scarcely hidden under the stereotypical religious discourse, Benamozegh wrote by way of presentation, "That this holy book be cleansed of any imperfection—insofar as God has been willing to grant that to me—has been my real consolation for nights of exhaustion, and all the hard work I have put in, both in revising the text and writing the reference notes."

5. Gershon Shaked, *Ein maqom aher* (There Is Nowhere Else: An Essay on Literature and Society in the Modern Jewish World) (Tel Aviv: 1983), 22.

6. Hayyim Nahman Bialik and Yosef Hayyim Rawnitzky, *Sefer ha-aggadah* (*The Book of Legends*) (Jerusalem: 1930); Hayyim Schirmann, *Mivhar ha-shirah ha-'ivrit be-Ytaliyah* (*Anthology of Hebrew Poetry in Italy*) (Berlin: 1934); Yeshayahu Tishby, *Mishnat ha-Zohar* (*The Wisdom of the Zohar*) (Jerusalem: 1949).

PART TWO: TRADITION, ORALITY, AND TEXT

Issues in Play

1. Gershom Scholem, *On the possibility of Jewish Mysticism in our Time and other Essays*, ed. A. Shapira, trans. Jonathan Chipman (Philadelphia and Jerusalem: 1997), 51–71.

Tradition and Text: Between Enlightenment and Romanticism

1. Hans Georg Gadamer, *Truth and Method*, ed. and trans. Garrett Barden and John Cumming (New York: Seabury, 1975), 244.

2. Ibid., 242. This is what Gadamer called "a prejudice against prejudice."

3. Ibid., 241. See also *Encyclopaedia of Religion and Ethics* (New York), under "Criticism."

4. Gadamer, *Truth and Method*, 244.

5. See Bernard M. G. Reardon, *Religion in the Age of Romanticism* (Cambridge: 1985), 23–24.

6. Ibid., and 181.

7. Friedrich D. E. Schleiermacher, *Hermeneutics and Criticism and Other Writings*, ed. and trans. Andrew Bowie (Cambridge and New York: 1998), 227.

8. Ibid., 235. See also 240.

9. In Gianni Vattimo, *Schleiermacher filosofo dell'interpretazione* (Milan: 1968), 53.

Tradition and Texts for a Science of Judaism

1. On Wissenschaft des Judentums, see Salo W. Baron, *History and Jewish Historians, Essays and Addresses* (Philadelphia: 1964) and Michael Meyer, *Ideas of Jewish Modern History* (New York: 1974).

2. Immanuel Wolf, "Über den Begriff einer Wissenschaft des Judentums," *Zeitschrift für die Wissenschaft des Judentums* I (1822): 1–24.

3. Ibid., 12.

4. Ibid., 13.

5. Ibid., 16; My italics.

6. Ibid., 18.

7. Leon Wieseltier, "Etwas über jüdische Historik. Leopold Zunz and the Inception of Modern Jewish Historiography," in *Philologie et herméneutique au 19ème siècle*, ed. Mayotte Bollack and Heinz Wismann and compiled by Theodor Lindken (Göttingen: 1983), 217.

8. Ibid., 224.

9. Ibid., 227. On the polemic surrounding this statement and a similar one by Moritz Steinschneider, cf. G. Scholem, "Réflexions sur les études juives. Préface pour un discours d'anniversaire qui n'a pas été prononcé," *Pardès* 5 (1987): 105–22, and David Biale, *Gershom Scholem, Kabbalah and Counter-History* (Cambridge, MA and London: 1979), 227, note 1. Moritz Steinschneider's statement was quoted after his death by Gotthold Wiel in *Jüdische Rundschau* in 1907. It was subsequently quoted by Scholem, which brought it to the attention of a wider audience. David Biale's book, especially chapter 1 ("The Nineteenth-Century Legacy") includes much interesting information and comment on the role of Kabbalah in modern Jewish studies.

10. Ibid. On this, see also Nathan Glazer, "The Beginning of Modern Jewish Studies," in *Studies in XIXth Century Jewish Intellectual History* (Cambridge: 1984).

11. Literary critic Emilio Cecchi sees in the Jewish protagonists of English novelist Israel Zangwill "the product of a race that does not have traditions anymore." "Alcuni ebrei," *Tribuna*, January 22, 1914. I would like to thank Marie-Brunette Spire for this insight.

In Defense of Tradition

1. The essay was published in several issues of the paper, in Paris, between 1866 and 1868. See bibliography.

2. *L'Univers Israélite* published this long article by Benamozegh, with extensive interruptions, between 1868 and 1889.

3. See above, in the chapter on Philology and Philosophy.

4. "La tradition," *L'Univers Israélite* (December 1868): 165. Moses Mendelssohn, whom Benamozegh criticized in his letters to S. D. Luzzatto for having relegated the Torah to the rank of national law, was fundamentally saying exactly that when he wrote in his *Jerusalem* that the oral tradition had to "enlighten, enlarge, delimit, and state more precisely" what was undetermined in written law.

5. Ibid., 169. Benamozegh seems to have been very attached to this definition. He even proposed the same passage, in Italian, in a short note that appeared in *Vessillo Israelitico* VI: 181–83. It was accompanied by a recommendation that it be inserted into Jewish "catechism" books in Italian Jewish schools.

6. Manuscript of "La tradition," 3. Page references are to the typescript held in the Livorno Jewish community archives. The text was reworked for publication, as we shall see. The references are Maimonides' introduction to the *Mishneh Torah* and the *Introduction to the Mishnah Commentary*, by the same author, which repeat the explanations given to *Leviticus* 24, 26; by *Sifra*, Behukkotai and by *Talmud Bavli*, tractate Berakhot 5a. The Jewish "reformer" Marco Mortara, who was a contemporary of Benamozegh's, uses this text verbatim to describe traditional Law. He refers to "revealed hermeneutics." Cf. *Corriere Israelitico*, 1867, 301.

7. "La tradition," *L'Univers Israélite*, 169.

8. "Introduction générale," *Ha-Levanon* III (1866): 75.

9. "La tradition," manuscript, 96.

10. Ibid., 87.

11. *Em la-Miqra*, Gen., 163a, "Introduction générale," Deut. 146a.

12. *Ha-Levanon* III (1866): 312.

13. *Em la-Miqra*, Gen., 82a.

14. On the concept of *asmakhta*, see Moses Maimonides, *The Guide of the Perplexed*, trans. with intro. and notes by Shlomo Pines, with an introductory essay by Leo Strauss) (Chicago: University of Chicago Press, 1963), III, 43, and. Judah, ha-Levi, *The Kuzari* (*Kitab al Khazari*) III, 73. It is interesting to note that Benamozegh's position is utterly opposed to that of Maimonides: he categorically refutes the text as the repository of all the ritual tradition given weight within it, whereas Maimonides accepts this idea at least in part (cf. *Maimonides' Introduction to His Commentary on the Mishnah*, trans. and annotated by Fred Rosner [Northvale, NJ: 1995], 3). Conversely, the Maimonidean principle of the arbitrariness of textual support for the purposes of *Aggadah* (*Guide* III, 43) is systematically rejected in the exegesis of Benamozegh, who takes rabbinical *Aggadot* seriously—and literally—and tries to understand them from a philological and philosophical viewpoint.

15. Moshe Cordovero, *Pardes rimmonim* (*The Pomegranate Garden*), XXVII, 2.

16. "La tradition," manuscript, 87.

17. "La tradition," *L'Univers Israélite* (Dec. 1868): 169. The reference is to the discussion in *Talmud Bavli*, tractate Sukkah, 35a, and Maimonides, *Introduction to the Mishnah Commentary*, 3. Isaac Samuel Reggio offers an interpretation similar to Benamozegh's, though with slightly more emphasis on linguistics. For him too, rabbinical debate on the meaning of the word *hadar* only exists in order to find textual support (*asmakhta*) for accepted tradition. See *Biqqurei ha-'ittim* 11 (1830): 10–13.

18. See the article by Benamozegh's pupil, Arrigo Lattes in *Lux*, August 1904, "Immutabilité et progrès," which was based on notes taken at an 1896 lecture held by Benamozegh.

19. *Em la-Miqra*, Gen. 163b.

20. "La tradition," *L'Univers Israélite* IX (October 1869): 85.

21. "La tradition," manuscript, 84. On this issue, see Maimonides, *Maimonides' Introduction to His Commentary on the Mishnah*, 4 and id., *Mishneh Torah*, Hilkhoth Mamrim, 1.

The Written and the Spoken Word

1. Johann Jakob Rambach, *Institutiones Hermeneuticae Sacrae* (Jena: 1723).

2. *Kuzari*, II, 72–74.

3. Quotations are taken from the new edition of *Ha-Ketav ve-ha-Kabbalah* (Jerusalem: 1961). The first edition was printed in Leipzig, 1839.

4. *Ha-Ketav ve-ha-Kabbalah*, Introduction, IX–X.

5. Ibid., 15.

6. Ibid., 14.

7. Benamozegh was familiar with Mecklenburg's work, citing it in *Teologia*, 164, when discussing "philosophical" etymology.

8. "La tradition," *L'Univers Israélite* (March 1885), 378. Gestures can also be considered from a historical perspective. The Italian philosopher Giorgio Agamben has come up with a very interesting thesis on the "loss of gesture" among the late-nineteenth-century bourgeoisie (see "Pour une éthique du cinéma," *Trafic*, no. 1 [1991]). Agamben's argument takes Balzac's *Anatomie d'une démarche* as its starting point and views cinema as an externalized, artificial substitute for this loss. In the context that interests us, this thesis would place Benamozegh, like Mecklenburg, as being consciously on the "antimodernist" side because he remains attached to meaningful gesture that has not been delegated to outside agencies.

Polemical context

1. See *Teologia*, passim.

2. Giuseppe Laras, "Quattro lettere di Benamozegh a Terenzio Mamiani," *Rassegna Mensile di Israel* XXXIV (1968): 155–62.

3. Ya'aqov Abihatzira, *Elef binah* (Livorno: 1890), Introduction.

4. "La tradition," *L'Univers Israélite* (November 1869): 117.

5. Cf. Eugenio Garin, *Storia della filosofia italiana* (Turin: 1978), vol. III, 1153.

6. "La tradition," *L'Univers Israélite* (October 1869): 117.

7. Ibid. (September 1869), 21.

8. *Ha-Levanon*, 312.

9. "La tradition," manuscript, 58. See also *Israël et l'Humanité*, 74–75: "Better science than an attempt to compromise between science and religion."

10. Walter Benjamin, *Correspondence, The Correspondence of Walter Benjamin, 1910–1940*; ed. and annotated by Gershom Scholem and Theodor W. Adorno, trans. Manfred R. Jacobson and Evelyn M. Jacobson (Chicago: 1994), *passim*.

11. Samuel David Luzzatto, *Epistolario italiano francese latino* (Padua 1892), 1030.

12. Letter, dated December 26, 1836, in *Vessillo Israelitico* XXIV (1876): 325–27.

13. *Derekh Eretz, o Attitzimus*, Italian translation, *Il falso progresso. Capitoli tre di Samuel David Luzzatto al suo secolo*, intro. and trans. Esdra Pontremoli (Padua: 1979).

14. Balzac himself—to give an example of just one of Luzzatto's despised fashionable, superficial "novelists"—denounced the present-day dominance of money and egotism of morals.

15. Lelio Della Torre, *Poésies Hébraïques*, 179–96.

16. Ernest Renan, *L'avenir de la Science* (Paris: 1890), Preface. See also in E. Renan, *Histoire et parole, Œuvres diverses*, ed. L. Rétat (Paris: 1984), 813.

17. Felicité-Robert de Lammenais, *Essai sur l'indifférence en matière de religion* (Paris: 1817), IV. 313.

18. "La tradition," *Univers Israélite* (November 1869): 147. The negation of the importance of philology in understanding the Bible engendered in the Romantics an individualistic attitude with a mystical background. On this subject, see Novalis's position in *Werke, Tagebücher, und Briefe* (Munich: 1978), Vol. 2, 737, Munich 1978. Benamozegh's polemic attacked exactly this kind of consequence.

19. Cf. Piero Pieri, *La differenza ebraica. Ebraismo e grecità in Michelstaedter* (Bologna: 1984), 97–102.

20. Malbim, *Ha-Torah ve-ha-mitzvah (The Law and the Commandment)*, in *Treasury of Biblical Commentaries* (in Hebrew), first series (Jerusalem: 1957), Introduction, 227.

21. See *The Jewish Encyclopaedia* (New York—London: 1901–1906), under the entry "Reform Judaism."

22. Malbim, *Ha-Torah*, 227.

23. Ibid.: "All the words of the oral tradition are understood at a literal, as well as a deeper, level of language."

24. Michael Meyer, *Response to Modernity: A History of the Reform Movement in Judaism* (Oxford: 1987). Meyer defines Italian Judaism as "classical in its impermeability to change, esteemed and venerated by nearly everyone but rarely observed in entirety." Telling testimony to this attitude comes from Israel Costa, Chief Rabbi of Livorno, and a friend of Benamozegh's, who summarized thus the negative response of the Tuscan rabbis to the proposed reforms: "Sustained Reform is impossible in Italy. There is no religious feeling here . . . no reformer would be able to convince the nonreligious, and would also estrange the religious who keep the faith alive." Letter dated May 26, 1865, in *Corriere Israelitico* (1867), 207. On the same subject, see also Menahem E. Artom, "On the Reform Movement in Italy," in *Scritti in memoria di Sally Meyer* (Jerusalem: 1956), 110–14; Id., "Tentativi di riforma in Italia nel secolo scorso e analisi del fenomeno nel presente," *Rassegna Mensile di Israel* XLII (1976): 355–66; Gadi Luzzatto Voghera, *Il prezzo dell'eguaglianza. Il dibattito sull'emancipazione degli ebrei in Italia (1781–1848)* (Bologna: 1998). For the French situation, see Roger Berg, *Histoire du Rabbinat français* (Paris: 1992).

25. In 1873, an educated Jew talks about the community in Livorno in the following terms: "No one can call into question the spirit of nation which still exists in the souls of the Jews of Livorno . . . but as far as religion is concerned, it has completely disappeared. The families that are still religious are quite few." Letter of Raffaello Ascoli to Sabato Morais, May 29, 1879, University of Pennsylvania, Center for Judaic Studies Library, Sabato Morais Collection, Box 8 File Folder 1. Quoted in Liana Elda Funaro, "Il ruolo degli ebrei livornesi: due percorsi individuali su uno sfondo mediterraneo," in *I laboratori toscani della democrazia e del Risorgimento*, ed. L. Dinelli, L. Bernardini (Livorno: 2004). It is to be noted that the environment of the painter Amedeo Modigliani, a Livornese Jew born in 1884, was already completely secular.

26. Mosè Soave, *L'Israelitismo moderno* (Venice: 1865), 5.

27. Ibid.

28. Ibid., 20. For Benamozegh's (negative) opinion of Soave, cf. Elijah Benamozegh, *Lettres à S. D. L.* (Livorno: 1890), 56.

29. For a Mortara bibliography, see *Vessillo Israelitico* XXXIV (1886): 188–90.

30. Marco Mortara, "Della Convenienza e Competenza di un Congresso Rabbinico," *Corriere Israelitico* (Trieste) IV (1865): 371–75; V (1866): 13–16; 41–44, 71–75; VI (1867): 202–11, 266–73, 299–303, 330–31. Mortara never went into the details of his propositions to avoid premature polemic. His suggestion that a rabbinic conference be held gave rise to violent controversy, and eventually came to nothing.

31. Ibid., V (1866): 72.

32. The notable exception on this subject was S. D. Luzzatto, for whom any notion of a mission relativized, and thus weakened, what he called "pure Mosaism." See Yitzhaq Heinemann, *La Loi dans la pensée juive*, 156.

33. The rabbinical authority in Livorno had lobbied to keep this reformist congress from taking place. Cf. the letter dated June 12, 1867, of rabbi Marco Mortara to rabbi Israel Costa of Livorno, in the Archives of the Jewish Community of Florence, D.8.2–18, quoted in Liana Elda Funaro, " 'Vita e legge.' Note per una storia della comunità ebraica livornese nel secondo Ottocento," *Rassegna storica toscana* XLVIII, no. 1 (2002): 154. Lois C. Dubin analyzed in an important article the short period during which Italian Judaism worked as a model for Germany: "The Rise and Fall of the Italian Jewish Model in Germany: From Haskalah to Reform, 1780–1820," in *Jewish History and Jewish Memory. Essays in Honor of Yosef Hayim Yerushalmi*, ed. E. Carlebach, J. M. Efron, D. N. Myers (Hannover and London: 1998), 271–95.

34. "Del Congresso Rabbinico proposto dal Rev. Rabbino Mortara," *L'Israelita* (Livorno: 1866): 290 and 356. Mortara did not deign to respond to Benamozegh's polemical contribution. He refers to it—but without mentioning it specifically—in comments on a slanderous article by a "famous author" who had attacked an "Adamitic religion" that did not exist in his proposal. Benamozegh's severity was indeed unfair: Mortara had at no point alluded to the faintest possibility of radical reform—or abolition—of ritual.

35. Ibid., 357.

36. *Ta'am le-Shad*, 46. In his anthology of the *Zohar* (*Mishnat ha-Zohar*, 59), Tishby quotes extensively from a passage in *Ta'am le-Shad* in which Benamozegh established the political nature of Judaism, and he defines the entire work as "the only scientific contribution made to the debate following Luzzatto's *Dialogues on the Kabbalah.*" Here, as with the relationship between the written and the spoken word, Benamozegh followed the *Kuzari* of Judah ha-Levi closely.

37. "General Introduction to the Monuments of the Oral Tradition," *Ha-Levanon* III (1864): 73. On this subject, see also various passages in the commentary *Em la-Miqra*, especially Numbers 97b, on the occasions that gave rise to the writing down of oral teachings.

38. On the image of the tree as symbolic of the hierarchy of knowledge in Porphyrus, see the article by Umberto Eco in *Il pensiero debole* (Milan: 1987). It is almost unnecessary to state that the relative positions of the *sefirot* create a "tree" structure. The same tree image was picked up by the Romantics, who used it to represent an epistemology founded on the model of biology rather than physics. See George Gusdorf, *Les origines de l'herméneutique* (Paris: 1988), 365.

39. "Del Congresso Rabbinico," 296.

40. On the polemic surrounding Kabbalah during the Renaissance, see primarily Robert Bonfil, *Rabbis and Jewish Communities in Renaissance Italy* (London-Washington, DC: 1993), 280–98. For Leone Modena, see Yehuda Ariyeh mi-Modena, *Ari nohem* (*A Lion Roars*), ed. I. Fürst (Leipzig: 1840; new ed. N. S. Libavitch, Jerusalem: 1929). For Simone Luzzatto, see Simone Luzzatto, *Discorso circa il stato de gl'hebrei et in particolar dimoranti nell'inclita città di Venetia* (Venice: 1638; new facsimile ed. Bologna: 1976), 80–85.

41. The use of Italian in the nineteenth century represents the culmination of a trend begun in the seventeenth century by the Venetian rabbi Simone Luzzatto, who used that language to compose the apologia *Discorso circa il stato de gl'hebrei* and *Socrate, ovvero dell'humano sapere* (Venice: 1651). On the gradual changes to the written language, see R. Bonfil, "Changing Mentalities of Italian Jews between the Periods of the Renaissance and the Baroque," *Italia* XI (1994): 61–79.

42. On E. Luzzatto see David Mirsky, *The Life and Work of Efraim Luzzatto* (Hebrew) (Jerusalem: 1987; new ed. 1994); Laura Bonifacio, "I sonetti di Efraim Luzzatto nella poesia ebraico-italiana del Settecento," *Italia* 1–2 (1990): 97–113. On Romanelli, see Hayyim Schirmann, *Shemuel Romanelli. Ha-meshorer ve-ha-noded* (*S. R., Poet and Traveler*) (Jerusalem: 1969) (taken from *Peraqim* 2, Schocken Institute of Jewish Studies directory); Samuele Romanelli, *Massa' ba-'arav-Visioni d'Oriente. Itinerari di un ebreo italiano nel Marocco del Settecento*, ed. Asher Salah (Florence: 2006).

43. Cf. Giulio Busi, *Anania Coen, Editore e letterato ebreo tra Sette e Ottocento* (Bologna: 1992).

44. Opposition to Kabbalah during this period can be generalized if it is seen more as a rejection of the later doctrines of Yitzhaq Luria and his disciples rather than of mediaeval Kabbalah. In this respect, the attitude of the German scholar Isaac Bernays approaches Benamozegh's: he defines sixteenth-century Kabbalah as "mere ascetic subtleties." See Rivka Hurwitz, "On Kabbalah and Myth in 19th Century Germany: Isaac Bernays," *Proceedings of the American Academy for Jewish Research* LIX (1993): 137–83.

45. Cf. Roland Goetschel, "Samuel David Luzzatto et David H. Joel: deux regards sur la Kabbale," in *Samuel David Luzzatto. The Bi-Centennial of His Birth, Italia*, ed. R. Bonfil, I. Gottlieb, H. Kasher, Conference Supplement Series 2 (2004): 35–54.

46. For a review of the various positions on the problem of the authenticity of the *Zohar*, see Y. Tishby, *Mishnat ha-Zohar*, Introduction.

47. *Yalqut Yashar (Collectanea Dissertationum)*, Vol. 1 (Gorizia: 1854), cap. V, 101–102 entitled "Is There an Opposition between Research and Kabbalah?"

48. Ibid., 103. Benamozegh devotes several interesting pages to the issue in *Eimat mafgia'*, 22b.

49. An attraction to mystery, positive in itself, should not encourage a boundless imagination, which can lead to dangerous excesses. On this subject, Reggio refers to the Shabbetai Tzevi episode. Cf. *Yalqut Yashar*, 111–12.

50. Ibid., 117.

51. *Ta'am le-Shad*, 33.

52. "Sulle dottrine cabbalistiche," in *Strenna Israelitica per l'anno della creazione del mondo 5615 . . . elaborata de Isaaco Reggio* (Gorizia: 1854), 27–30.

53. Hebrew title: *Wikkuah 'al khohmat ha-qabbalah* (Gorizia: 1852). His position on Kabbalah had already been summarized in the 1818 Hebrew poem "To the Kabbalists." Cf. S. D. Luzzatto, *Kinnor na'im*, part 2, 94–97, republished in Id., *Kinnor na'im* (Warsaw: 1913), Vol. 2, 258–61.

54. *Autobiografia de S. D. Luzzatto, preceduta da alcune notizie storico letterarie sulla famiglia Luzzatto* (Padua: 1882), 38.

55. Ibid., 57. In 1817 Luzzatto's cousin Rachel Morpurgo asked him for a copy of the *Zohar*, and once she had it, asked him what he would like in return. He replied, "That you don't believe the doctrines it contains." Rachel's answer was, "You ask something very hard of me." Cf. Rachel Morpurgo, *'Ugav Rahel (Rachel's Flute)*, ed. Vittorio Castiglioni (Trieste-Cracow: 1890), 21–22.

56. The letter, written in 1820, can be found in *Devar Shemuel (Samuelis Verbum)*, the letters of Samuel Vita Lolli, published by Vittorio Castiglioni (Cracow: 1895), 40–58.

57. See *supra*, "The New Challenges of Apologia."

58. *Dialogues*, 46.

59. Reggio shared this opinion of things, as is demonstrated in the long commentary that accompanies the publication of the writings of Elia del Medigo. Cf. *Sefer Behinat ha-dat (Examen Religionis, insignis Philosophi et Theologi R. Elias del Medigo Librum, Commentarius et notis illustravit Isaacus Reggio)* (Vienna: 1833), 38–49 and 67–102. Cf. Maurice-Ruben Hayoun's recent French translation, *L'examen de la religion* (Paris: 1992).

60. S. D. Luzzatto, *Epistolario italiano francese latino di Samuele Luzzatto*, ed. Giuseppe Luzzatto (Padua: 1890), 9.

61. As regards attribution, Luzzatto oscillates between Avraham Abulafia and Moshe de Leon. Luzzatto's friend the Paduan bibliographer Yosef Almanzi added a few lines to the copy he made of *Sheqel ha-Qodesh* (the Holy Sheqel), a major Kabbalistic text. In these lines, he alludes ironically to the difficulty of comprehending Kabbalistic texts ("the burden we find so heavy is light for the Kabbalist") and has no problem identifying Moshe de Leon as the author of the *Zohar* ("the author

takes Plato for his king; the *Zohar* of Shim'on bar Yohai was written by him"). See A. Guetta, "The Last Debate on Kabbalah in Italian Judaism: I. S. Reggio, S. D. Luzzatto, E. Benamozegh," in *The Jews of Italy. Memory and Identity*, ed. Bernard D. Cooperman, Barbara Garvin (Bethesda, MD: 2000), 256–75. I am indebted to Charles Mopsik, the author of the critical edition of *Sheqel ha-Qodesh*, for passing this short text on to me. Almanzi's copy is indicated in the *Catalogue de la Bibliothèque de Littérature Hébraïque et Orientale de feu Mr Joseph Almanzi (Yad Yosef)*, ed. S. D. Luzzatto (Padua: 1864), n. 150.

62. *Dialogues*, preface.

63. This was *Ta'am le-Shad*.

64. See *infra*, par. *Cabbale et philologie*.

65. *Ta'am le-Shad*, 147.

66. *Lettres à S. D. L.*, 14. The same metaphor is used by the secular Zionist writer Berl Katzenelson around 1920 to describe the new creativity of the Jewish people, who had freely shaped the themes of tradition: "The revival generation . . . discovers forgotten things and cleans the rust off them" (in G. Shaked, *Ein Maqom Aher*, 22). The ends of the revival sought by Benamozegh were doubtless quite different, but the use of the same phrase nonetheless betrays a shared desire to see Jewish studies "modernized."

67. *Ta'am le-Shad*, Introduction, VI.

68. "Il sig. Reynach e la Cabbalà," *Vessillo Israelitico* XL (1892): 324.

69. *Del Congresso rabbinico*, 295.

70. *Lettres à S. D. L.*, 59. Deism, for instance, was grafted to the edifice of the commandments like the head of a dwarf on the body of a giant.

71. *Eimat mafgia'* (Fear of the small animal, quotation from the *Talmud Bavli*, tractate Shabbat, f. 77b) (Livorno: 1855), part 1, 7a.

72. *Ta'am le-Shad*, 169–70. Another response to the *Dialogues* by Luzzatto is Yedidiyah Nissim's *'Anah kesil* (Livorno: 1834).

73. *Em la-Miqra*, Gen. 82a. See also *Introduction générale*, 234.

74. *Em la-Miqra*, Gen. 104a. The similarity between the ideas expressed by Benamozegh and those found in the introduction to the Moroccan rabbi Habib Toledano's book *Derekh emunah* (*The Path of Faith*) (Livorno: 1838) is clear, right down to the choice of phrase. Toledano stated that "he who inclines too much toward research ends up falling into a crevice" and that the literal meaning of a text was only "a surface that hides delights." Cf. Dan Manor, *Qabbalah ve-musar be-Maroqo. Darko shel Rabbi Ya'aqov Abihatzira (Kabbalah and Ethics in Morocco. The Path of Rabbi Jacob Abihatzira)* (Jerusalem: 1982), 79–80.

75. *Eimat mafgia'*, I, 1b.

76. Ibid., 16a.

77. Ibid., 21b.

78. S. D. Luzzatto, *Dialogues*, preface.

79. *Eimat mafgia'*, I, 18a. S. D. Luzzatto tried to reconcile faithfulness to a literal interpretation of the text with adherence to religious orthodoxy—which was largely based on the oral tradition—by separating theory and practice. To him, sticking to the letter did not mean being a "Karaite," as it was action, and not theory,

that mattered. This action is conditioned by the decisions of the authorities of the past, who took them in the best interest of the Jewish people. Cf. the Pentateuch commentary *Ha-Mishtaddel*, Introduction, and *Ha-Levanon* (1866), 107.

80. S. D. Luzzatto, *Epistolario italiano francese latino*, 1029, n. DCLXXXII (index no. 1186). Letter dated September 8, 1863.

81. *Lettres à S. D. L.*, 91.

82. Ibid., 66: "I can admit that the *Zohar* is completely false: and so what? Kabbalah existed long before . . ." Cf. *Storia degli Esseni*, 162.: "The *Zohar* is the bazaar [*emporio*] of kabbalistic ideas, a warehouse of the deepest and most secret traditions."

83. *Ta'am le-Shad*, 41. See also 49.

84. *Eimat mafgia'*, I, 5a, 7a, 22a; II, 26b.

85. Moshe Hayyim Luzzatto, *Hoqer u-mequbbal (Maamar ha-vikkuah)*, in *Sha'arey Ramhal* (Bnei Brak: 1989), 36–37.

86. I. Zinberg, *A History of Jewish Literature*, Vol. 2, section 2; G. Scholem, *Major Trends in Jewish Mysticism*, 35; M. Idel, *Kabbalah—New Perspectives* (New Haven: 1988), *passim*. See also the same author's *Maimonides et la mystique juive*, French trans. (Paris: 1981), 3. Charles Mopsik, *Les grands textes de la cabale. Les rites qui font Dieu* (Paris: 1993), 33–65.

87. Georges Vajda, *Introduction à la pensée juive du Moyen Age* (Paris: 1947), 197.

88. Charles Mopsik, "Philosophie et souci philosophique: les deux grands courants de la pensée juive," in *La storia della filosofia ebraica*, ed. Irene Kajon (Rome: 1993), 247–54. Mopsik's position is entirely justified. After all, authors such as Spinoza and Heidegger, some of whose preoccupations recall those of the Kabbalists, are seen as part of Western philosophical history.

89. *Dialogues on the Kabbalah*, 51.

90. Ibid, 62.

91. See G. Vajda, "Joseph Avraham Ibn Waqar et sa tentative de conciliation de la philosophie et de la religion," in *Recherches sur la philosophie et la kabbale dans la pensée juive* (Paris and The Hague: 1962).

92. Ibid, 143.

93. Moshe Cordovero, *Elima Rabbati* (Lvov: 1881), VI, 7. See also Shemuel Horodetzky's anthology, *Torath ha-kabbalah shel Moshe Cordovero (The Kabbalah of Moshe Cordovero)* (Jerusalem: 1951), 227.

94. M. H. Luzzatto, *Hoqer u-mequbbal (Maamar ha-vikkuah) (The Philosopher and the Kabbalist)*, cot.

95. Ibid, 79.

96. See Dan Manor, *Kabbale et éthique au Maroc*, 15. The *Zohar*, which occupies an important place in Benamozegh's thinking, was considered by Moroccan Jews as a sacred text almost on the same level as the Talmud. The gap between Benamozegh's original background and the "Western" development of his thinking can be evaluated by the fact that, during the years of idealism and positivism (and the skepticism or religious agnosticism that derive from it), in Morocco, it was still commonplace to comment on Luria's Kabbalistic writings. See Moshe Halamish,

"Al sugey ha-yetzirah ha-qabbalyth be-Maroqo," 38. On Kabbalah in Morocco, see also Haim Zafrani, *Kabbale, vie mystique et magie* (Paris: 1986), and issue 43 of the journal *Pe'amim*, Jerusalem (Spring 1990).

97. Yehudah Coriat, *Maor va-shemesh* (*The Lamp and the Sun*) (Livorno: 1839), Introduction, 6a.

98. *Kabbale et éthique au Maroc*, 77. In this book Dan Manor posits that Benamozegh was born in Fez and studied under Abihatzira. He deduces this from a few sentences Benamozegh, in his position as editor, added to one of the Moroccan's books. The hypothesis is not true, but the very fact that a serious scholar could have come up with it shows the degree to which Benamozegh's personality was rooted in such different worlds.

99. *Nir le-David*, Introduction. Benamozegh is to some extent parodying the standard *hitnatzlut* (justification) in which the author confesses his youthful transgressions and asks forgiveness (*teshuvah*) for them.

100. *Eimat mafgia'*, 9a.

101. Ibid., 6a.

102. Ibid., 6b.

103. *Ta'am le-Shad*, 141 and 155.

104. *Eimat mafgia'*, 9a.

105. *Ta'am le-Shad*, 140, and *Em la-Miqra*, Deut. 174b.

106. *Israel and Humanity*, 188–89.

107. *Bibliothèque de l'hébraïsme*, "Theosophie," 6.

108. *L'origine des dogmes chrétiens*, 41.

109. *Teologia*, 277.

110. *Lettere dirette a S. D. Luzzatto* (Livorno: 1890), 74.

111. On the efficacy of religious action, see Yoseph Colombo, "Che cosa leggeva Elia Benamozegh," *Rassegna Mensile di Israel* XXXVI/2 (1970): 73. Glossing an assertion by the Italian philosopher Terenzio Mamiani, Benamozegh wrote that prayer could be seen as "an extended act of will." Since, he mused, "if we recognize that a metaphysical power such as free will indubitably influences the course of physical causes, why might we not admit that its extension might affect the unknown—and unknowable—side of nature, which is so huge?" Here Benamozegh connects the Kabbalistic notion of the efficacy of human action in the world and on God with the idea of "unknowableness" as defined by the positivists (Spencer, Ardigò).

112. *Israel and Humanity*, passim.

113. This relationship is the subject of the massive manuscript *Les origines des dogmes chrétiens*, the first part of *Morale juive et morale chrétienne*. See *supra*, chapter on "Christianity's error."

114. Taking a line rather similar to Benamozegh's, in *Kabbalah. New Perspectives*, Idel evokes a historical approach that admits of the possibility of a slow-maturing Jewish esoteric tradition. The fairly abrupt appearance of Spanish Kabbalistic literature "reflects earlier stages of development that have eluded historical documentation" (21) and hides "a silent growth of Jewish esotericism" (32). Idel's opinion appears to be shared by Charles Mopsik: see "Une querelle à Jérusalem: la femininité de la Chekhina dans la cabale," *Pardès* XII (1990). The historian of Hebrew literature Y. Lachover stresses this very aspect of Benamozegh's work: the notion of a subterranean

culture alongside the "official" one, and the frequent exchanges between the two. Lachover sees Benamozegh as the only author of his generation to defend tradition effectively. Cf. Y. Lachover, *Toedot ha-sifrut ha-'ivrit ha-hadashah* (*History of Modern Hebrew Literature*) (Tel-Aviv: 1947–1948), Vol. 2, 190–91.

115. *Em la-Miqra*, Deuteronomy 147a.

116. Ibid., 149a. See also "General Introduction to the Monuments of the Oral Tradition," *Ha-Levanon* III: 75, 76, 188.

117. Benamozegh expresses this idea in his debate with positivist D. Castelli. Cf. C. Facchini, *David Castelli*, 113 and 159. In his criticism of anti-Kabbalistic Leone Modena, articulated in *Eimath mafgia'*, Benamozegh claims that Modena did not "grasp" Kabbala because he did not possess the right mind-set, the same way some people may lack the understanding of law or mathematics.

118. *Eimat mafgia'*, 15a. It is interesting to compare this attitude with the one expressed by Georges Vajda on the antiquity of Kabbalah. "The philosopher is better served than the historian or the philologist: it seems . . . that there is something ancient in Kabbalah, but what that might be is infinitely hard to grasp, as it is no more than a set of tendencies . . ." See *Introduction à la pensée juive du Moyen Age*, 199.

119. Cf. Aristotle, *The Metaphysics: books I–IX*, trans. Hugh Tredennick (Cambridge, London: 1980), book III, 2.

120. *Revue des Etudes Juives* 13 (1914): 121.

121. S. D. Luzzatto, *Epistolario italiano francese latino*, letter dated August 1863, Index no. 1185.

122. *Lettere dirette a S. D. Luzzatto*, 66. In *Ta'am le-Shad*, 32 and 50 Benamozegh calmly accepts the possibility of the *Zohar* being a concocted work.

123. *Eimat mafgia'*, 4b.

124. Ibid., 2b, and passim.

125. I. S. Reggio, *Yalquth Yashar*, Vol. 1, 101.

126. S. D. Luzzatto, *Dialogues*, 46.

127. Ibid., preface. In Italy, the "dangers" of Hassidism were abstract indeed. Luzzatto wrote to Reggio (who lived in Gorizia, and thus far closer to the heart of the Austro-Hungarian Empire than Padua was), "On Italian soil, there is not so much as a speck or a whiff of this Hassidic sect that inhabits your country." *Lettres hébraïques*, no. 323. See also Immanuel Etkes, "Magic and Miracle Workers in the Literature of the Haskalah," in *New Perspectives in the Haskalah*, ed. Shmuel Feiner, David Sorkin (Oxford and Portland: 2001), 113–37, who quotes a letter written in 1835 by Luzzatto about Ba'al Shem Tov, published in *Kerem Hemed* (1836): 149–51.

128. "Il sig. Reynach e la cabbalà," in *Il Vessillo Israelitico* (1892): 323; "Sulla Cabbala" (a polemic with rabbi E. Lolli), ibid. (1894): 218; *Israel and Humanity*, introduction, 78.

129. See Avraham Ha-Levy Horowitz, *Shnei luhot ha-brit* (*Two Tablets of the Covenant*), part 2, 1. On the theme of the written and oral *Torah*, see *Sefer ha-Bahir*, ch. 196, and *Zohar*, II, f. 200a.

130. "La tradition" in *Univers Israélite*, 168. On Benamozegh's stylistic individuality in the various languages (French, Italian, and Hebrew) he uses, cf. Cyril Azlanov, "Elia Benamozegh scrittore trilingue: il fattore della lingua nelle sue opere," in *Rassegna Mensile di Israel* LXIII, no. 3 (1997), 29–41.

131. *Les origines des dogmes chrétiens*, 52.

132. Cf. Pier Cesare Bori, *La Madonna di San Sisto di Raffaello. Studi sulla cultura russa* (Bologna: 1990).

133. Ibid., 100. *Bibliothèque de l'hébraïsme*, section on "Theosophie," 2; Franz-Joseph Molitor, *Philosophie de l'histoire*, 197: "Catholic liturgy contains a wealth of things that are clearly based on ancient Jewish mysticism, for instance, the image of the Blessed Virgin crowned with twelve stars and a serpent at her feet." On the feminine side of God in the Kabbalah see the brilliant synthesis of Charles Mopsik, *Le Zohar. Lamentations* (Paris: 2000), 13–31.

134. Pier Cesare Bori, *L'interpretation infinie*, French trans. (Paris: 1991), 158.

135. *Morale juive et morale chrétienne* (Paris: 2000), 15. Benamozegh's "disciple," Aimé Pallière spoke of his mother as "a visible angel God has given the little children," who turned the pages of a large Bible for him (*Le sanctuaire inconnu* [Paris: 1950], 17). In her book on Aimé Pallière (*Aimé Pallière (1868–1949). Itinéraire d'un chrétien dans le judaïsme*), Catherine Poujol suggests that the nineteenth century was one of feminine piety: the dogma of the Immaculate Conception and the cult of Lourdes both date from then. See also Gérard Haddad, "Aimé Pallière et la vraie religion," *Histoire* 3 (November 1979): 244; Jean Delumeau, *La religion de ma mère. Le rôle des femmes dans la transmission de la foi*, Paris 1992.

136. E. Benamozegh, *Discorso pronunciato nel tempio Israelitico di Livorno il dì 8 settembre 1847 nel rendimento di grazie per la conceduta Guardia Cittadina*, 7. Also published in *Il Corriere Livornese* I, no. 2 (September 28, 1847).

137. "Discorso del signor Elia Benamusich," *Il Corriere Livornese* II, no. 70 (February 22, 1848). Quoted in Carlotta Ferrara degli Uberti, *La "nazione ebrea" di Livorno dai privilegi all'emancipazione*, MA thesis prepared at the University of Pisa, 2000–2001, 258. Pages 257–80 of the thesis are devoted to Benamozegh.

PART THREE: STYLE AS WITNESS

1. The "Bulletin de la Société des amis de la paix," no. 2 (February 1872) referred to Benamozegh's *Le crime de la guerre dénoncé à l'humanité*, which had won the Ligue de la Paix [Peace League] medal, as a "remarkable literary achievement, with a verve and sonorousness that must be the envy of many a Frenchman. This verve is however too scarcely contained, and above all too sustained; the oratory style leads the author to employ to excess all the colors of a seemingly inexhaustible palette. Chapter VII . . . written in more measured style, shows how his argument might have benefited from less brilliance and greater concision."

2. Cf. Cyril Aslanov, "Elia Benamozegh scrittore trilingue: il fattore della lingua nelle sue opere." The article's author correctly points out that Aimé Pallière's linguistic work on *Israel and Humanity* rendered the text more fluid, but in so doing betrayed the style of its author, and thus, to a considerable extent, his thinking.

3. *La verità svelata ai miei giudici intorno le tre lettere prodotte dalla querela Tubiana davanti l'Ill.mo Sig. Pretore del Terziere di San Leopoldo in Livorno per Elia Benamozegh* (Livorno: 1861), 16.

4. Ibid., 4.

5. Ibid., 10.

6. S. Reggio, *Introduction to* Eliyah del Medigo, *Behynath ha-dat*, 1.

7. This was the case with *Credo*, published at the end of *Teologia*, and intended as a summary of the preceding text. Benamozegh feared—correctly—that he would be unable to publish it.

8. *Lettres à S. D. L.*, 92. "I regret that you season your thoughts with a bitter, acidic sauce." Luzzatto had said of Benamozegh, "Let him bray!" A certain amount of protestation aside, Benamozegh continued to maintain that he was Luzzatto's friend and admirer.

9. Cf. *Ta'am le-Shad*, 222; *Teologia*, 152; *Em la-Miqra*, Deut. 127a.

10. S. D. Luzzatto, *Ha-Mishtaddel*, 12a, Id., *Introduction to the Commentary on the Book of Isaiah* (Tel Aviv: 1970), 11.

11. S. Morais, *Italian Hebrew Literature* (New York: 1926), 213. In *Em la-Miqra*, Deut. 94a, Benamozegh discusses the importance of "familiarity with the text as a major part of understanding it": memory is thus crucial. He goes on to write that an interpretative "sensibility" is needed to pick up the smallest linguistic subtleties.

12. *Storia degli Esseni*, 34. In *L'Origine des dogmes chrétiens*, 87, Benamozegh claimed that Joseph Salvador was mistaken in seeing ancient Judaism as a living protest against the Oriental spirit and as a precursor of the modern West.

13. *Storia degli Esseni*, 18.

14. Ibid. Cf. Benamozegh's statement in his preface to Eliyahu Hazan, *Zikhron Yerushalayim*, 1, on the subject of the author's family. "Enlightened religion, that which takes into account the state of science, which attempts to persuade rather than simply having adherents, is all the more agreeable for coming from the country whence everything has come to us, which is to say from Palestine, from our holy and beloved Jerusalem. Voltaire said of Catherine of Russia, 'now the light comes from the North.' We in turn may say with greater truth, 'it is from the East.'"

15. As the publisher of Ya'aqov Abihatzira's *Elef binah*, Benamozegh interjected at the end of the author's entreaty to have complete faith in *sod*, the hidden meaning of the Torah to say, "Nowadays denial of Kabbalah is far too widespread. But I, like the author of this work, have contributed to reaffirming it."

16. *Spinoza et la kabbale*, 38. Benamozegh's interest in the Orient could naturally be interpreted in the light of fin-de-siècle Orientalist fashion. Cf. Paul Mendes-Flohr, "L'orientalisme fin-de-siècle, les Ostjuden et l'esthétique de l'affirmation juive de soi," *Pardès* 5 (1987): 49–74. In any case, even if Benamozegh shared with European Orientalism a certain reserve regarding the rationalist mindset and the "soulless" materialism of the West, he remained an opponent of all occultism and mysticism, which he construed as none other than esotericism. In one of his rare allusions to the popular culture of the North African Jews, he relates a "miraculous" healing worked through an amulet and ironically attributes it to some kind of "placebo" effect. Cf. *Eimat mafgia'* II, 16b.

17. *Em la-Miqra*, Deuteronomy, 120b.

18. Gérard Genette, *Paratexts: Thresholds of Interpretation*, trans. Jane E. Lewin (Cambridge and New York: 1997), 319ff.

19. A very flattering obituary in the *Gazzetta Livornese* (February 6–7, 1900) described him as a person "of quick and profound intelligence bordering on genius."

20. *Lettres à S. D. L.*, 2.

21. Ibid., 6.

22. Ibid., 108.

23. Letter from Benamozegh to De Gubernatis, June 19, 1867, Biblioteca Nazionale di Firenze, De Gubernatis, cass, 10, 100, quoted in Liana Elda Funaro, " 'Speculiamo, amiamo, combattiamo'; Lettere inedite di Elia Benamozegh," *Nuovi Studi Livornesi* X (2002–2003): 133.

24. *Israel and Humanity*, French version, 2.

25. *Nir le-David*, 3. See also *Ta'am le-Shad*, 118 ("May God give me the time to finish my project"); *Introduction to the Monuments of the Oral Tradition*, 188, 235, and 312 ("I am only saying a small part of what should be said if there were enough time . . ."); *Spinoza et la cabbale*, 15 and 18 ("This work cannot encompass all of Spinoza's philosophy, as was our privilege, let us begin by stating . . ."); *Em la-Miqra*, Lev. 72b, Deut. 8b ("I have many more examples . . ."), 126a ("Compared to how I would like to treat the subject, the allusions I have just made are as the water licked by a dog is compared to the sea"), 150a, 151a.

26. *Ta'am le-Shad*, V.

27. Ibid., 56 and 123; *Em la-Miqra*, Deut., 12a and 160b, where he adds that the work is already available.

28. *Teologia*, 47.

29. Ibid., 49.

30. *Ta'am le-Shad*, 118.

31. *Em la-Miqra*, Deut., 94a.

32. Ibid., Num., 37a. In a letter to Luzzatto (*Lettres à S. D. L.*, 87), he mentioned a second part to *Ta'am le-Shad* which he would write "se piace a Dio."

33. "Le mie letture," *Vessillo Israelitico* (1889): 306.

34. Elémire Zolla, "Il marocchino Elia maestro di Cabala. Un 'eccezionale figura de pensatore ebreo," in *Corriere della Sera*, Milan, January 10, 1991, 5. Reprinted Id,. *Uscite del mondo* (Milan: 1992): 519–22.

35. Cf. for instance the Bialik poem *Ha-matmid* (in *Shirim* [Tel Aviv: 1966] 301), in which the author describes a *yeshivah* student who has lost all contact with nature. Unlike Benamozegh, for Bialik the renewal of Judaism inevitably meant the supersession of orthodox religiosity.

36. An allusion to the famous novel *Le ultime lettere di Jacopo Ortis* (1802) by the Italian poet-novelist Ugo Foscolo, a protagonist of literary Romanticism in Italy.

37. *Storia degli Esseni*, 171–72.

Index

225